The Barling Darling

Hal tags out Milwaukee's Bill Bruton trying to score after a single by Hank Aaron. Ken Boyer relayed the ball to Hal just in time to catch the speedy centerfielder in this June 14, 1958, game at Busch Stadium.

The Barling Darling:
Hal Smith in American Baseball

Billy D. Higgins with Hal Smith

BUTLER
CENTER
BOOKS

Little Rock, Arkansas

BUTLER
CENTER

BOOKS

The Butler Center for Arkansas Studies
Central Arkansas Library System
100 Rock Street
Little Rock, Arkansas 72201

ISBN (paperback) 978-1-935106-09-8
10-digit ISBN (paperback) 1-935106-09-0

10 9 8 7 6 5 4 3 2

Acquired for Butler Center Books by David Stricklin
Project manager: Ted Parkhurst
Book design and cover design: H. K. Stewart
Project editor: Rod Lorenzen

Photographs used in this book are the property of the author or were secured for use in this book by the author.

Front cover: St. Louis Cardinals vs. Brooklyn Dodgers at Ebbets Field, June 20, 1956: Hal Smith has just tagged out Gil Hodges, the Dodgers' first baseman, trying to score from first base on a Carl Furillo double off the right field wall. The relay from Wally Moon to second baseman Bobby Morgan to Hal kept the score at 0-0, but the Dodgers won 4-2 behind Roger Craig, the winning pitcher. The plate umpire is Dusty Boggess.

Library of Congress Control Number: 2008942763

Printed in the United States of America

This book is printed on archival-quality paper that meets requirements of the American National Standard for Information Sciences, Permanence of Paper, Printed Library Materials, ANSI Z39.48-1984.

This book is dedicated
to the once and present members
of the Fort Smith Boys & Girls Club

Contents

Acknowledgments

Iapproached Hal Smith in 2004 about the possibility of a book on his life in baseball. In his generous and good-humored way, and with the hearty approval of his wife Carolyn, he agreed to become an interviewee. I had known Hal for a long time and, of course, was aware that his professional career had resulted in, among many other things, his selection to the Arkansas Sports Hall of Fame. I was eager to get started and when we did, my eyes were opened wider with each interview. As Hal and Carolyn shared memories of their life on and off the field with me, I began to realize their accomplishments in fuller measure. I respectfully thank Hal for taking the time for us to explore his life and my wish for this book is that it conveys the same excitement and amazement that the author felt in hearing Hal's stories firsthand.

Hal's teammates gladly provided details of his career and explained how they all lived and played the game. Especially forthcoming were Alex Grammas, Ernie Broglio, Wally Moon, John Romonosky, and Joe Cunningham, whose memories mark the book. Alongside Hal, each had his own wonderful career. Hall of Famer Red Schoendienst shared some of his memories of Hal. The friendliness and responses of these teammates to the good of the book are much appreciated by this still awestruck author.

The author thanks David Stricklin and the Butler Center for Arkansas Studies for agreeing to publish this book and for being delightful partners in the enterprise. Ted Parkhurst, manager of Butler Center Books, took the project under his wing and guided it steadily through the designing and publication processes. For his faith and professionalism, the author is profoundly grateful.

I would like to thank the following gentlemen who assisted in all phases of the preparation of the book. Rod Lorenzen became convinced of the worthiness of the original manuscript for publication by the Butler Center and then gave it the precision and polish it needed through his careful editing. Brad Kidder, a historian, read the manuscript and supplied the author with valuable suggestions for its betterment. Larry Malley provided the author with constructive comments on the manuscript and supplied a fitting story that tied together one section. Ed Brooke, Jerry Glidewell (Director of the Fort Smith Boys & Girls Club), and Madison McEntire (president/founder of the SABR Brooks Robinson-George Kell Chapter), gave welcomed assistance in providing the author with materials used to illustrate the book and Hal's career. Daniel Maher, Ed Levy, Tim Higgins, my son, the brothers Karber, Phil and Greg, plied me with friendly, but continual and probing questions about baseball, society, and my manuscript—the effect of which caused further reflection on and perhaps improvement in the organization of the book.

Baseball is a game of percentages and many statistics are used to describe player performances in the frankest manner. Box scores list batting, fielding, and pitching performances for players, show attendance, the length of each game, the umpires, and count everything except the number of ballpark franks sold. Keeping and making available such baseball statistics, and the interpretations derived there from, is a significant industry in the United States. One organization in particular, the Society for American Baseball Research (SABR), affords researchers, writers, and lifelong fans a wealth of data, compilations, and interpretive studies. My heartfelt gratitude extends certainly to Retrosheet, an independent research group founded in 1989 by David Smith, that puts play-by-play accounts of major-league baseball games on line.

The Sporting News is digitized and accessible because Paper of Record built and maintains a searchable archive of historical newspapers. For this remarkable contribution to the study of American culture and history, the author hails Bob Huggins and Paper of Record with a big "Hats Off!"

The assistance of Carolyn Smith and Peggy Higgins in all the small, medium, and large ways that spouses contribute to their life mates helped us see this project through to completion. Thank you, ladies, and thank you to all who have asked about this project and who have encouraged Hal and me to pursue it. We are ever grateful to you and hope that you enjoy the book.

1

The Desire

Hal Smith, a few days away from his 25th birthday, drove toward his new home in Florissant, a suburb northwest of St. Louis. Hal's wife, Carolyn, normally his greatest fan, would be a bit disappointed with his day's work. He wasn't exactly happy either with how he had just spent this late October afternoon. Hal had been in the office of general manager Frank Lane, where he had negotiated without much zeal his contract with the St. Louis Cardinals for the 1957 season. Lane, a hard man and a crafty bargainer, loved multi-player trades. Shortly after arriving in St. Louis, Lane dealt Cardinal hero and Stan Musial's best friend, Albert "Red" Schoendienst, to the New York Giants. Lane packaged Bill Sarni, the Cardinals' starting catcher, into the Schoendienst deal. Thus, one of Frank Lane's most notorious actions as Cardinal general manager opened the door for Hal, Sarni's backup, to become THE catcher on the club's roster. In the Schoendienst-Sarni trade, Lane threw in Jackie Brandt, a promising outfielder in his second big league year, who had batted .298 with 12 home runs in his rookie season.

While Frank Lane lived to make deals, Hal Smith lived for baseball. He enjoyed almost every aspect of it. He had been a Cardinal fan since the 1946 World Series, which he had heard via KFPW radio from Fort Smith, Arkansas. Stan Musial, now his teammate, had emerged in that dramatic series as young Hal's idol. The only thing about baseball that Hal roundly detested was what he had just been through—working out his next year's contract with the front office. Quiet, self-effacing men like Hal were designed for action, not words. This was a huge disadvantage when sparring verbally with men like Frank Lane. Lane was a true power-hitter in his business and knew the insecurities of the players with whom he negotiated.

Since baseball was his career, Hal was delighted to sign for another year. In a way, however, he felt slighted, particularly after a very good rookie year in 1956. Carolyn wondered if the money would be enough to support a growing family. She and Hal both knew that his services as starting Cardinal catcher were worth more than the $1,000 raise that the front office had offered and he had accepted. Still, he was mindful about the competition. Someone else could easily take his place and he couldn't go too far in arguing for a decent raise. So, Hal had settled for a salary that fell short of fully supporting his family. Once again, he would have to find work in the off-season. Hal and 5,440 other major- and minor-league players were ruled by baseball's "reserve contract clause," which was vigorously defended by major-league owners because it kept players completely under their control. The players could do nothing about their contracts except argue with the general manager or quit. In the late 1940's, some players even joined the Mexican League. This was baseball "as we knew it!"

In accepting these facts, Hal knew that he was locked into the one-sided bargaining position of professional baseball. Baseball great Lou Gehrig could not bring himself to hold out or argue for more money at contract time, even at the insistence of his wife, Eleanor. Gehrig and his no-fuss attitude pleased Yankee owner and Knickerbocker beer baron Jacob Ruppert, who nevertheless only paid his Iron Horse $8,000 to Babe Ruth's $80,000 in 1927, the year Ruth hit sixty home runs. Batting fourth in the lineup behind Ruth, Gehrig hit forty-seven homers, batted .373 and drove in a record 175 runs. Gehrig's batting average and RBI totals exceeded Ruth's in 1927 and made him the league's MVP. Ten years later, after Ruth's retirement in 1937, Ruppert boosted Gehrig's yearly contract to $39,000. That made him baseball's highest paid player in 1938, his last full year as a starter. In offering this contract, Ruppert told Gehrig of his pleasure in seeing him do his work without a murmur—running out every batted ball and hustling every minute of a game. Nobody, including Lou, knew that he had the disease that would come to bear his name and end his playing days the next year. Gehrig's presence dominated a baseball field. He was a certain Hall of Famer.

Viewed with the perspective of history, Gehrig represents much more than just his reputation for being a great player. He set the standards for "player-speak" and "player-face." A man with comparable influence in setting standards for his profession was X-1 test pilot Chuck Yeager. With his soft, West Virginia drawl, Yeager's manner of speech and coolness under pressure became a model for pilots everywhere. Similarly, Gehrig was the uncomplaining, hustling, reliable, and modest professional baseball player. He never showed up another player on the field nor promoted himself to listeners. The Yankees named Gehrig as captain, their first ever, in 1937. Rupert told Gehrig in one contract session, "you have never given us a moment of worry." He was the kind of ball player that made owners drool—high production with little upkeep and *no* embarrassment! While Yeager's influence yet pervades aviation, especially among military flyers, Gehrig's soft-spoken modesty appears less and less around the league.

In 1956, when Hal broke into the majors, the Gehrig standards of on-field performance and off-field expectations by the ownership ruled baseball. While Cardinals' owner Gussie Busch never had the revenues the Bronx Bombers generated, he still paid Stan Musial $100,000 in 1957. It was the highest contract for a Cardinal and ranked in the top five for a professional baseball player in that day.[1] What about the rest of the St. Louis boys of summer? They garnered far, far less money than did Musial. No one complained in public or held out or even argued too much in the contract sessions. Players signed for what was written by the general manager on their contract. Newspaper reporters didn't question the process either. The Cardinals gave Curt Flood a contract for $5,000 in 1958 and he signed it without discussion.

Thus, there is no question that Hal played professional baseball for the love of the game and that his wife, son, and daughters supported him because they loved him and the game, too. Athletes have a built-in desire to reach the top of their sport and play against and with the best. Material benefits followed, of course, even in the years before multi-million dollar contracts and jerseys with player names on the back. Players had local star status, supplementary incomes, ready-made friendships, and the ease of meeting new business associates. To have the ability to earn a living as a professional athlete in the major leagues is a claim few can ever make.

Imagine the immense satisfaction of coming through in a clutch situation or of making a play that turns an important game. Major leaguers face the daily pressure of performing at the top and beating the competition. Large numbers of paying customers demand to see the best every play, every day. Players train themselves to respond to that pressure through excellent conditioning and sound mental preparation. Even so, there is the agony of the loss of a crucial game and the blown chance to turn it, but that is the other side of the coin. Players and fans both know that much was sacrificed just to get into position for that play or for that chance. Teammates help each other in victory and defeat. In Hal's day, men bonded in a way that helped them perform at high levels. They depended on each other to win games and this was a huge part of the makeup of the professional athlete. Ted Williams, Bobby Doerr, Johnny Pesky, and Dom DiMaggio never won a pennant for the Boston Red Sox after 1946. But, the men remained close friends and stayed in touch with each other for sixty years, despite Williams' claim that he had never been able to teach "that Bobby Doerr a single thing about hitting."[2] Hal, Alex Grammas, Joe Cunningham, and John Romonosky have had the same carryover from their own playing days—a sixty-year friendship. Such long-term relationships are typical for teammates who have been through the grind of long seasons. The money lagged for Hal in his playing days, especially in the minors, and also when compared to the two decades that followed his retirement. Hal's highest major-league salary was $22,000 but the excitement and the superb, gritty and gifted men in his clubhouse and in the other dugout made it one of the country's best occupations. The seven years Hal spent in the minor leagues were worth his struggle to make it to the big leagues! Besides, his baseball career brought him good opportunities for jobs in the winter months. Bob Gibson, Cardinal pitching great, played basketball for the Harlem Globetrotters to boost his income in the off-season. Hal spun country songs for radio station KMOX while hosting his own early-morning show. In the summer months, Hal turned over that time slot, along with his audience, to Clyde Lovellette, a center for the St. Louis Hawks' basketball team. Lovellette's need for an off-season job is ironical in light of the fantastic salaries paid these days by the National Basketball Association. As low as they were, salaries for major-league baseball players were better than other professional athletes of Hal's day.

2

Barling

A career in baseball was worth the ride for Harold Raymond Smith. But, how did a stocky guy from tiny Barling, Arkansas, and the son of a storekeeper make it to the major leagues? Hal was born on June 1, 1931, in the back of his family's grocery store during the first years of America's Great Depression. He was the third child of Ronald and Katherine Smith, who would bring three more children into the world. For this large family, a mere curtain separated the living quarters from the shelves, counter, and stock of groceries that formed the business end of the rock building that served as a home and means of livelihood. A pot-bellied stove, fueled by coal, provided warmth and a kettle of water could be heated on top of it. Mrs. Smith poured the hot water from the kettle into a galvanized No. 3 wash tub when the children's bath time came.

Mr. Smith, a former school teacher who did not get beyond the eighth grade, had the spirit of an entrepreneur but, as Hal recalled, "there wasn't a lot of money going around." Mr. Smith often used empty boxes to make the shelves appear full and well-stocked. Still, steady cash came from the sale of gasoline from a pump that fronted the store. The customer hand-pumped the gas into the glass bowl at the top and gravity carried the fuel down the hose and into his automobile tank at a rate of seventeen cents a gallon. At the center of a community of farmers, the store became a familiar stop. Ronald Smith, full of humor and conversation, had a ready line of credit for those in need. He became a favorite with the farmers and it was no surprise to anyone that he eventually was elected mayor of Barling. The store became the court house, where he ruled on traffic tickets and other offenses while kibitzers sat in chairs around the pot-bellied stove. State Highway 22, which connected Fort Smith and Dardanelle, passed right in front of Smith's Grocery. During Governor Henry Martineau's administration, the state highway department paved the road. This cut down on the dust but increased the number of speeders roaring through the quiet farming community.

The fortunes of the Smith family took an upturn in the late 1930's when threats from abroad roused the federal government to build more army posts in the middle of the country. The War Department set out to acquire a huge tract of land east of Barling. It stretched along the south side of Highway 22 and encompassed some 240 square miles. On this land, some if it purchased by "forced sale," sat productive farms that were tied to a thriving community called Center Hill. The rules of society held that even private property could be confiscated in the case of a higher need. The U.S. Army decided this was such a case. The Army post was named Camp Chaffee after General Edwin Chaffee, a respected tank commander and tank designer. The Nazi *blitzkrieg* had demonstrated how important speedier and more mobile tanks were to modern military strategy and fast attacks. The brand-new Camp Chaffee would be designated as a tank division training center, headquarters of the Fifth Armored Division.

Perched on the edge of the western edge of the development, Barling escaped the Army land grabs. Hal's grandfather, a little closer in, lost property in the confiscations. Ever the entrepreneur, Ronald Smith saw opportunity in all the commotion. He borrowed money to buy a decent piece of property and built a new store at a cost of $3,000. It was a heady sum in those days and an indication that bankers knew a solid risk when they saw one. Surveyors, truck drivers, construction workers, and land levelers now flocked to the site of America's newest and largest fortification. They also gathered at the store for lunch and Katherine's sandwiches began to generate much of the monthly payment money. Today, a visitor to the mostly abandoned fort still can marvel at the vastness of the project, which was completed in only two years. A city was built from scratch—including water, electricity, sewage infrastructure, barracks, paved streets, training facilities, warehouses, service facilities—and was large enough for 10,000 people. At the time, that made it the fifth largest city in the whole state of Arkansas.

Hal was ten years old when Camp Chaffee was under construction. The surveyors who came to the store for sandwiches were baseball players at heart. Before returning to work, they liked to play catch near the store. Harold watched them intently, itching to show off his own baseball skills. But, he found that he would have to earn his way into sharing their recreational time. One day, a surveyor who was clearing a path through the reeds at Vache Grass Creek accidentally slung his machete into the murky water. The man waded in and groped to find it but came up empty. After a lunch break at the Smith store, Hal returned with the men to the creek. He splashed around in the water while they worked and somehow managed to snag the machete. After that, the surveying crew allowed him to join their game of catch. Hal still believes that these hard-throwing men taught him a lot about how to handle a glove. He honed his skills and caught everything they threw at him. The experience provided an ironic twist.

Years later, one of the surveyors heard Hal's name on the public address system during a game at Busch Stadium in St. Louis. This was in the 1980's and Hal was long retired but still returned occasionally to see a game. The surveyor made his way through the stands to see his former young pal. Hal said that he indeed recognized the man. They greeted each other warmly and talked awhile about those days when life then was so different from today.

On the side of the Smith store, the bottling company in Fort Smith had painted a giant Dr. Pepper sign, which looked like the face of a clock. For hours at a time, Hal kept himself occupied by throwing the baseball against the sign, trying to nail the 10 o'clock, 2 o'clock and 4 o'clock marks consistently.[3] When he got to the majors, Hal Smith wowed spectators with the power of his arm and often showed it off when the team took pre-game infield practice. He believed that the many hours of banging that sign on the side of the grocery had a lot to do with it.

With his childhood companions, Lawrence Smith and next-door neighbor Marion Boatright, Harold played "one-eyed-cat" or "work-up" in the vacant lot across the highway. Marion might have looked longingly at the convoys with their trucks full of soldiers. His family had moved to Barling only because the Army had taken their place near Center Hill. Sometimes, the boys would hike over to the railroad siding near the camp entrance, where rolling stock like trucks and tanks were unloaded to join the growing fleet. As a training facility, Camp Chaffee had the advantage of occupying land on both sides of the Arkansas River. Soldiers had to undergo strenuous river crossings with pontoon bridges and practice amphibious landings. All of this training later became vital to the area's civilians when the flood of 1942 struck the area. The Fifth Armored Division set up emergency crossings of the river between Fort Smith and Van Buren and between Fort Smith and Oklahoma.

As the Army dug in at Chaffee, the Smith store climbed into the black and new excitement came to the Smith household. Once, a soldier who was a regular customer at the store brought a home movie to show. Hal got to see it and thought it was a marvel. Getting to see any kind of movie was a rare event for Barling boys. Another sign of the new success was the arrival of electricity at the store. This allowed the gasoline pumps to be fitted with motors. Customers still served themselves out front but, at least, they no longer had to pump the gas into their cars by hand.

As World War II ended and Hal turned fifteen years old, a new bus line connected the Chaffee gate and downtown Fort Smith. Usually, the bus was filled with soldiers. Either they were headed out on "passes" for an adventure in the city or on their way back, exhausted from their recreational labors. Garrison Avenue, the main street of Fort Smith, extends from the bridge across the Arkansas River into Oklahoma to the magnificent Immaculate Conception Church at its eastern end. Garrison Avenue was named during the early days of the town's existence. It was used for parades by military regiments that were stationed near the historic Belle Point site, where the first fort was built in 1818.

With their meager, monthly wages in tow, the young, robust soldiers of Chaffee headed to Garrison Avenue where dozens of business establishments catered to them. "Walk-up" dance halls—one flight of stairs above the street—and penny arcades made good use of the brand-new art of neon signage. The two-mile stretch of main street boasted four movie houses, twenty eateries and restaurants, two pool halls, three multi-story hotels with inviting lobbies and coffee houses, plenty of bars and taprooms and an upstairs bowling alley. On side streets, a few blocks over and in the shadows, were several brothels. Considering its long history—much of it spent as a frontier town—Fort Smith had passed through several eras of notoriety. The immense Camp Chaffee, just the other side of Barling, created yet another one. Fort Smith became a garish army town and was recognized by *Look* magazine as one of the nation's top ten "sin cities." No doubt, that was an overstatement. There existed alongside the cheap-thrill peddlers a lot of other enterprises of higher merit. These included a hundred or more churches, a splendid new high school and junior college, a thriving USO club, a busy Kansas City Southern Railroad central station, the Carnegie Library, museums, an annual regional rodeo and a two-state fair. Of course, there was also a minor-league baseball team that played its night games under the lights at Andrews Field.

A few blocks from Subby Valenti's tattoo parlor on Garrison Avenue, the Fort Smith Boys Club occupied a splendid rock building at 215 Wheeler Avenue. Courtesy of the New Deal and its Works Progress Administration, the Boys Club opened in 1941 and was a state-of-the-art facility. It had an indoor swimming pool (the first in the city) and a full-sized, hardwood-floored gymnasium. When Hal rode the bus into Fort Smith from Barling, he headed for the Boys Club and a ball game. He had developed his love of sports on the vacant fields of Barling and shagged balls for the semi-pro team on which his brother played. He got serious about baseball, however, when he "tried out" for the American Legion team in Fort Smith. Clarence Higgins, director of the Boys Club, served as head coach for the team.

In 1945, Higgins had arrived in Fort Smith to succeed Bob Kuykendall as the executive director of the Boys Club. Kuykendall had resigned to go into the furniture business. "Hig" found out that his duties included coaching the American Legion team—the Fort Smith Randall Victors.

Hig took an instant liking to Hal, who was always smiling. After seeing Hal's arm in the tryouts, Hig placed him at third base. As Hal gained playing experience over the next two years, the Victors won a lot of games. By the summer of 1948, they were set to challenge the Little Rock Doughboys, Arkansas's perennial champion, for the state crown. Hig had persuaded Frank "Smokey" Smith to help him coach the team. Smokey Smith had been a teammate of Hig's in northeastern Arkansas semi-pro leagues. Smokey was a native of Monette and had moved to Fort Smith when Arkansans began a post-war migration from rural places into towns and onto college campuses.[4] Fortunately for the Legion team, Smokey brought his son, Jimmy, a phenomenal athlete. The only problem was that Jimmy's natural position, considering his good arm and quick reflexes, was at third base where Hig already had a good player. Smokey made a suggestion to Hig and the coach listened to his old friend. Then, he asked Hal if he would be willing to move behind the plate. Hal responded with "whatever you say, coach!" It was a fateful switch. In just this way, Harold Raymond Smith discovered the position that would take him all the way to the major leagues. Jimmy Smith, no relation, did well enough at the hot corner but later was moved to first base. Jimmy Smith's hitting attracted the attention of scouts. After his Legion days, he signed a professional baseball contract and played three years in the minors. Eventually, he became the head baseball coach of the LSU Tigers.

The 1948 state legion championship tournament was played in Little Rock at Traveler's Field, which was built in 1932 and maintained by the city as home to the minor-league Little Rock Travelers. In 1966, the city changed the name to Ray Winder Field in honor of the gruff, Damon Runyon-type character who long served the team as its general manager. In 2006, the taxpayers of North Little Rock approved a bond issue for construction of a new minor league stadium and named it after the great Yankees' catcher, Bill Dickey, and Little Rock financier, Jack Stephens. Dickey-Stephens is home to the Class AA Arkansas Travelers of the Texas League.

Despite its heritage as one of the country's oldest, Ray Winder Field is no longer used as a ball park. But in 1948, Travelers Field had a terraced outfield and a tunnel that led from each dugout into the two dressing rooms, which boasted hot showers. Built-in bat racks and telephones in the dugout added luster to this minor league jewel. Caretakers carefully groomed the infield, cutting the grass diagonally with reel mowers. Limed foul lines and batter's box lines grandly marked the field when it was ready for play. Flood lights brightened all but the left and right field corners of the park. Traveler's Field represented real excitement to American Legion clubs that were more familiar with town ball on sand lots where weeds and Ford pickup trucks full of horn-honking spectators marked the foul lines. Despite being awed by this great field and by the swagger and formidable record of the Doughboys—they had advanced to the national American Legion baseball tournament *championship game* the previous year[5]—Hig thought his Randall Victors might just remember how to play. If they did, he thought they had a chance to win. The Victors opened the tourney by defeating Pine Bluff, always a tough team to beat. Against Little Rock in the next game, however, the Doughboys rallied for five runs in the ninth to win a game that the Victors had controlled throughout. The teams were evenly matched, but in that ninth inning the Randall Victors' pitchers simply could not get anybody out. The Doughboys sent so many batters to the plate that finally a guy in the stands passed a note down to the coach. The note said, "It's an emergency. Call this number!" From the dugout, Hig dialed the four-digit telephone number that was used in those days. The victim of a practical joke from a Doughboy fan, Hig had reached the Little Rock Fire Department. Relieved that it was not a real emergency call, he said to the firemen, "Well, you probably can't get them out, either!"

The next day, the Fort Smith hitters swamped West Memphis to get to the Sunday championship game with the Doughboys. The Smith boys played and hit well throughout the double-elimination tournament. In the game with West Memphis, Hal picked off the same guy three times with rifle shot throws—the third time at third base. The player lay there glaring at the umpire. Finally, he jumped up with dust flying off his back, glanced back at Hal, and stomped off the field saying "***, I just quit!" A trip to the regional was in sight for Hal Smith and his teammates. All they had to do was beat the Doughboys twice on Sunday. But, no sooner had the game gotten under way than rain forced a delay until Monday, August 15.

In the first game, Hal went three for five, knocked in two runs and scored two while Jimmy Smith was two for four. The Victors scored seven times in the second inning on their way to a resounding 13-0 win over the Doughboys.

Box Score of First Game

FT. SMITH

		ab.	r.	h.	o.	a.
Charles Coleman	cf	6	1	1	0	0
J. Coleman	2b	3	2	1	3	1
Ray Leroy	3b	6	0	1	1	1
Jim Smith	1b	4	2	2	6	1
Harold Smith	c	5	2	3	7	1
Dub Perkins	p	4	1	2	1	1
Ears McGinnis	lf	3	1	1	3	0
Sullivan	rf	5	2	2	1	1
Rogers	ss	3	2	2	1	3
x White		1	0	0	0	0
Perkinson	p	0	0	0	1	1
Totals		40	13	15	27	10

LITTLE ROCK

		ab.	r.	h.	o.	a.
Richard M'Murry	cf	2	0	0	4	0
Gale Harris	p-lf	3	0	0	0	1
Bobby Spann	3b	3	0	2	2	2
Drexel Rowland	lf	1	0	0	0	0
Skippy Churchwell	rf	2	0	0	1	0
Frank Lucas	c	1	0	1	0	0
Kenneth Mosley	ss	3	0	0	1	6
Donald Richards	1b	3	0	0	10	2
Hal Norwood	2b	2	0	1	5	0
Jerry Kennedy	c	3	0	0	3	3
Billy Lynch	p	2	0	0	0	1
Judd Williams	cf	1	0	0	0	0
James Cauthron	lf	2	0	0	0	0
Totals		28	0	4	27	15

x—Batted for Perkins in 8th

Ft. Smith	0	7	0	1	1	2	1	0	0	– 13
Little Rock	0	0	0	0	0	0	0	0	0	– 0

Errors—Lucas, Spann 2, Mosely, J. Coleman, C. Coleman. Runs batted in—Perkins 3, McGentis 2, Hal Smith 2, Leroy, J. Smith. Two-base hits—J. Smith, McGentis, Perkins. Stolen bases—Perkins, McGentis, Coleman. Double plays—Norwood to Kennedy to Richards. Sullivan to Leroy to Rogers to H. Smith. Leroy to J. Coleman. Left on base—Ft. Smith 9, Little Rock 15. Base on balls—Off Perkins 13, Perkinson 1, Lynch 2. Hits—Off Harris in 2 innings 7; off Perkins in 7 innings 2. Hit by pitcher—By Lynch (J. Coleman). Wild pitch—Lynch. Passed ball—Kennedy. Umpires—Graves and Larry. Time—2:10.

In the second game for the championship, however, a misplayed ball in centerfield let in two runs and sealed the defeat for Fort Smith, 3-1. The Doughboys, not the Randall Victors, would go on to Austin, Texas to play in the regional Legion tourney.

Box Score of Second Game

FT. SMITH

		ab.	r.	h.	o.	a.
Charles Coleman	cf	3	0	0	0	0
J. Coleman	2b	3	0	0	5	3
Ray Leroy	3b	3	0	0	1	2
Jim Smith	1b	2	1	1	6	0
Harold Smith	c	3	0	1	3	3
Dub Perkins	rf	3	0	0	0	0
Ears McGinnis	lf	3	0	0	3	0
Rogers	ss	2	0	1	0	0
Bill Stanley	p	1	0	1	0	3
Bill Pitcock	p	1	0	0	0	0
x Sullivan		1	0	0	0	0
Totals		25	1	4	18	11

LITTLE ROCK

		ab.	r.	h.	o.	a.
Richard M'Murry	cf	2	1	1	3	0
Gale Harris	p-lf	3	0	1	2	0
Bobby Spann	3b	3	0	1	0	1
Drexel Rowland	lf	3	0	1	0	0
Frank Lucas	p	1	0	0	0	4
Donald Richards	1b	3	0	0	8	0
Kenneth Mosley	ss	3	1	0	1	6
Jerry Kennedy	c	2	0	0	4	1
Hal Norwood	2b	1	1	1	4	1
Totals		19	3	5	21	7

x—Batted for Pitcock in 7th

Ft. Smith	0	0	0	0	0	1	0	–	1
Little Rock	0	0	0	3	0	0	–	3	

Errors—McMurry, J. Coleman. Runs batted in—Norwood, Hal Smith. Two-base hits—H. Smith. Stolen bases—Mosley. Sacrifice—Stanley. Double plays—Stanley to Leroy to J. Coleman, Stanley to J. Coleman to J. Smith. Leroy to J. Coleman to J. Smith. Left on base—Ft. Smith 5, Little Rock 3. Base on balls—Off Stanley 1, Pitcock 1. Struck out—By Lucas 4, by Stanley 3. Umpires—Graves and Larry. Time—1:15

Since the two Smith boys were in their final year of eligibility for American Legion baseball, this had been their last chance. Charles Allbright, the sports writer who covered the tournament for the *Arkansas Democrat*, wrote this summary:

No official award was made, but most of those present at all the tilts believed Harold Smith, Fort Smith catcher, to be the tourney's outstanding performer. His hustle, rifle-like arm, and field generalship fired the Victors at all times. The strapping 17-year-old backstop also mace-mauled tournament pitching at a .422 clip. His mate, James Smith, first baseman, was the leading hitter with a resounding .591 mark. His 13 hits included four doubles and a pair of triples.[6]

The story of the Legion tournament in the *Arkansas Democrat* took second place in Tuesday's sports section to a headline and feature article reporting the death of Babe Ruth. Ironically, the Doughboys and the Randall Victors had been presented baseballs autographed by Babe Ruth only a few hours before the great slugger and American icon took his last breath, at age 53, in a New York City hospital.

Scouts had attended the Legion championship game and one of them, Freddie Hawn of the St. Louis Cardinals, made it a point to visit with Hal. Seeing Hal catch convinced Hawn that he had a prospect and he asked the young catcher, "are you interested in playing professional baseball?" Hal had heard the same question from a Yankee scout. When Hawn asked it, however, Hal answered "yes sir" with total enthusiasm. After all, Hal explained, "I was a Cardinal guy." In those pre-draft days, nothing prevented Hawn from offering Smith a contract, but the 17-year-old's parents would have to sign the contract, too. Harold's mother fretted a bit until Ronald Smith assured her. Thus, in the fall of 1948, Harold Raymond Smith of Barling, Arkansas, had a contract to play professional baseball in the St. Louis Cardinal organization and was scheduled to report to spring training in 1949. Over the winter, Hal enrolled as a sophomore at Fort Smith Junior College. He played on the college basketball team, which seemed to be fairly good, but no score books survived to document the success of the 1948-49 Lions. One newspaper article, however, mentions a particular oddity. The coach was Frank Jones and his starting five all had the last name of Smith. To be exact, they were: Harold Raymond Smith, Jimmy Smith, Squeaky Smith, Jack Smith, and Donald Smith, none of whom were related to the others.

Jimmy Smith had a chance to play professional baseball, too. An article in the *Southwest-Times Record* on August 18, 1948, was headlined, "Jimmy Smith, Victors' first sacker, to Try Out with Tigers." The article, by Ken Ray, the *SWTR* sports editor, continued:

Smith left by plane for Detroit ... where he will work out with the Tigers.... Smith has had feelers from the [New York Yankees] as well as the St. Louis Cardinals.... Although earlier he expressed an intention to return this term to Fort Smith Junior College where he played on the Lions basketball team last year ... he may sign with the highest bidding major league club and not return to Fort Smith. His father, Frank "Smokey" Smith," formerly athletic director of the Boys Club here, left for Detroit several weeks ago and is operating his private business there.

Jimmy Smith led the Victors in batting during the season with an average of .410 in Legion play. He led in total hits, total bases, doubles, and home runs and was a close contender for the leadership in triples. The husky youngster weighs 170 pounds, bats right and throws right.[7]

Two former Fort Smith-Van Buren Legion players were already playing professional ball before the 1948 season ended. Marvin Blaylock, two years older than Hal, had signed with the New York Giants and was in their farm system. Shelby Breedlove, a shortstop who had played Legion baseball and semi-pro baseball with the Bohannon Spinach Kings, was picked up by the Texarkana Bears of the Class B Big State League. His high school coach, Clair Bates, accompanied Breedlove, a 1948 graduate of Van Buren High School, to Texarkana. The Bears soon departed on a road trip. Playing against the Waco Pirates, the 17-year-old Breedlove made his debut in the world of professional baseball. Years later, Breedlove was president of Fort Smith Junior College and helped guide its growth into a state-funded institution of higher education known as Westark Community College. In 2001, Westark became the University of Arkansas–Fort Smith.

Newspapers in 1948 devoted considerable space to baseball in all of its forms, from young amateur teams to semi-pro games and tournaments to minor league standings and box scores. Major league games and their stars, of course, got most of the attention on the sports pages. If that was not enough, fans could immerse themselves in *The Sporting News*. Published in St. Louis under the watchful eye of editor-owner-publisher J. G. Taylor Spink, *The Sporting News* carried reports and articles from minor and major-league teams and players.

Baseball often took a back seat, however, to world news events. The summer of 1948 saw Harry S. Truman crossing the country by rail to drum up popular support for his Square Deal programs and his candidacy for the presidency. Vaulted into the White House by the death of Franklin Delano Roosevelt, Truman, a virtual unknown before his ascension as vice-president, was trying to take the office in his own right. His opponent, Republican Thomas E. Dewey, a business-like and formidable governor of New York, garnered ringing predictions from newsmen of his coming success in the November elections. He didn't win, but in the summer of 1948 most Americans seemed to think that he would. Truman, from Independence, Missouri, was an underdog.

In 1948, the Soviet government put up gates and placed guards across the autobahns leading to Berlin in their zone of occupied Germany. Thus began the Berlin Airlift, which lasted thirteen months, and the Cold War, which lasted until 1989. Atomic bomb tests and spies in the government—the Hiss-Chambers hearings led by Congressman Richard Nixon were underway that summer—and the heated presidential campaign filled the news pages in both local and major city papers. The Arab League threatened that it might "clear the 100,000 Jews out of Jerusalem" any day. At the time of the American Legion state tournament in Little Rock, the University of Arkansas School of Medicine made the decision to admit Edith Mae Irby, a "20-year-old Negro woman from Hot Springs." Irby was one of twelve African-American students who applied for admission to the medical school. Out of that group, though, only Irby was admitted. She ranked 28th out of the top 91 who were selected on the basis of their aptitude test scores. The announcement stated that she would be enrolled "without segregation" since the medical school had no way to set up separate laboratories for Ms. Irby.[8]

In the third year after the Second World War, American society and the rest of the world verged on great change. The idealism of the immediate post-World War II years fueled anti-colonial movements in Africa and Asia. One by one, former colonies of the European powers and now emerging nation-states like India, Indonesia and Ghana— gained entry into the nascent United Nations. The time for independence, for countries as well as individuals, had arrived. At home, racial segregation was under attack. Harry Truman had desegregated the nation's military services with the stroke of his pen. He signed the executive order on the Oval Office desk that bore his reminder that "The Buck Stops Here!" The year before, Branch Rickey desegregated major-league baseball with his introduction of Jackie Robinson on the 1947 Brooklyn Dodger roster. Thus, organized baseball and the U.S. military led the American society toward desegregation and overdue social change. Southerners, however, dug in their heels. African-American baseball players had to ignore or somehow adjust to the attitudes of white teammates, fans, and sportswriters of that day. Spring training in Florida had its trials for non-white players. Future superstars like Willie Mays and Monte Irvin waited in the team bus for the trainer to bring food out from the white-only lunch counters where the New York Giants stopped to eat on their spring training road trips.[9]

3

Vinegar Bend

Fred Hawn, who lived in Fayetteville, wore his gray, bristly hair in a crew cut. Short of stature with broad shoulders and gnarly hands, Hawn smoked cigarettes like most baseball men did in those days. The Lucky Strike habit, along with years of sitting in the sun, had turned Hawn's face the texture of wrinkled, brown leather. Hawn scouted Arkansas and Missouri for the St. Louis Cardinals. Driving a 1951 model Buick over two-lane highways for thousands of miles, he slept in the houses of friends or in the occasional tourist court. Hawn subsisted on soft drinks and concession-stand hot dogs and watched thousands of innings of amateur, semi-pro, and college baseball games. With his piercing blue eyes and immense knowledge of the game, Hawn sized up young players by their abilities in three categories thought to be crucial for success in baseball—can they run, hit, and throw? Great ball players in the majors—Joe DiMaggio, Ted Williams, Stan Musial, Jackie Robinson, and Willie Mays—set the standards of the game. Selectors picked them all for Baseball's Hall of Fame in their first year of eligibility.[10] Scouts used the talents of these players as a yardstick to judge the raw prospects for which they beat the bushes. Despite having these evaluation tools to go by, scouts saw most of their recruits drop out somewhere on the way to the big leagues. In fact, the success ratio was worse back then because the eight major-league teams in each league stockpiled players in vast farm systems. Low pay, the military draft, injury, homesickness, uncertainty about the future, discouraging words, cocky umpires, leather-lunged boo birds, hopeless slumps, and immaturity riddled the ambitions of many promising minor-league players. As an 18-year-old, Ron Tabor signed a contract in 1957 with the Cubs' organization and went to play third base for the Pulaski, Virginia, Cubs in the Class D Appalachian League. His signing was the envy of his American Legion teammates in Fort Smith. A terrific low-ball hitter with a good arm, Tabor lasted one summer and batted a dismal .184 with one home run. Though professional baseball had been his dream, the reality of going to the ballpark everyday and trying to meet expectations proved to be an excruciating experience for him. Tabor said that, "I prayed for rainouts where I could go to the movies instead." He returned home and went to work on "factory row," where he stayed employed until the 21st century. He satisfied his athletic impulses on the golf course. His upper-cut swing and great power could send a golf ball a long way, enough to remind him of his American Legion days when he launched baseballs high and far out of Hunt's Park.

In his American Legion days at the same Fort Smith ballpark a few years before Tabor, Hal Smith hit well enough for Fred Hawn and, of course, had that rifle for an arm. Hawn had on-the-field experience with young minor-leaguers. In July of 1941, Cardinal general manager Branch Rickey called Hawn and assigned him to take over the Cardinals' prized Class D farm team, the Union City, Tennessee, Greyhounds, who were floundering near the bottom of the Kitty League standings. Under Hawn's guidance, the Greyhounds proceeded to win fourteen games in a row and jumped to second place in the league. In early August, the club hosted Freddie Hawn Appreciation Night, which attracted more than a thousand fans. After the presentation of gifts and a short speech by Hawn, his Greyhounds completed a sweep by beating the visiting Fulton Tigers (Detroit's farm club), 3-1. But, trouble loomed on the horizon. Unfortunately, for Union City and its fans, Hawn's magic couldn't last. The team fell into a losing skid—probably on account of lousy pitching—that reached nine games. The Greyhounds finished the year in fifth place. Soon after, Hawn abandoned his managerial career in the Cardinal organization and bought pleated slacks, short-sleeve shirts, and a straw hat—regulation attire for a professional baseball scout during the Truman and Eisenhower administrations.

Hawn's luck in signing Hal Smith was as good as having a fourteen-game winning streak. The Barling-born catcher became one of his five signees to make it to the St. Louis Cardinals. Wally Moon, Jim King, and Lindy and Von McDaniel were the others. In late February of 1949, Hawn drove his Buick from Fayetteville down to Barling on Hwy. 22, where he picked Hal up at the grocery story for a long drive to Texas. It was the first time Hal had ever ridden in an air-conditioned car. "See," Hawn explained, "You can ride with the windows up!" In spring training, Hawn worked with Houston, the Class AA club in the Cardinal organization. He invited Hal to accompany him to the camp of the Houston Buffs at Sequin (pop. 10,000), located twenty miles east of San Antonio on the Houston road. The old scout and the young prospect stopped in Hot Springs, where Hawn introduced Hal to Cardinal legend Rogers Hornsby. Hornsby ran a baseball camp near the Spa City and Hal's visit with him was brief but memorable. More thrilling experiences awaited on this trip, the next one being a stop in Austin for a visit with Coach Bibb Falk and his Texas Longhorns. Falk, a native Texan, had played twelve seasons with the Chicago White Sox in the 1920's, ringing up a .312 lifetime batting average. Falk managed the Cleveland Indians for one game—a win—in the 1933 season, giving him a 1-0 record as a major-league manager. Falk and Hawn talked baseball while watching the collegians take infield. That spring, Falk's Longhorns finished atop the Southwest Conference and stormed into Omaha for the national collegiate tournament which the Longhorns won, the first of their two straight NCAA baseball championships.

At Houston's training camp, Hal met Buff manager Del "Babe" Wilber. Wilber was a 38-year-old giant of a man who had been a part-time catcher and pinch-hitter for the Cardinals in the '47 and '48 seasons. Wilber had managed one game in the majors and that was with the Texas Rangers in 1973. That was the year the Rangers had three managers. Whitey Herzog and Billy Martin both had losing records. With his one win for the Rangers, Wilber equaled Falk in their 1-0 careers as big league managers. In 1949, Wilber liked what he saw in Hal, who credited Wilber with teaching him the footwork a catcher needed. Hal spent spring training with the Buffs and Wilber wanted to keep him in Houston to begin the Southern Association season. The front office, however, said no to the request and sent Hal to Albany, Georgia, the Cardinal minor-league training camp where the lower classifications trained. The immensity of the Albany facility startled Hal. "I never saw so many ball players in my life! There must have been 600 down there. We trained at what used to be an air base and they had twelve diamonds." The system was impersonal and so huge that one writer described the tryout as a cattle call. Each prospect wore a number pinned to his sweatshirt. "You might be 5 or 6, or 627," Hal said. Most there expected to play somewhere in the minors. But, if a number was called out over the public address system as the young players finished practice, that meant bad news. "You would hear 'number 525, please report to the main office,'" Hal recalled, "and everyone knew that he was gone!" The hopefuls fielded balls and threw across the diamond or from the outfield. They swung bats in the cages, all yearning to be kept on one of the Cardinals' farm clubs. These were the boom times for the minors in America. There were 50 to 60 leagues and about 450 teams operated by agreements with the major-league clubs. Branch Rickey, who had been the Cardinal general manager in the late 1930's, had installed perhaps the first expansive farm system. This innovation was copied by most other clubs. By 1940, the Cardinals reached their high-water mark in minor-league affiliates with 31. Today, they have six. In those days, kids had a burning desire to improve their skills in the minors and live out their baseball dreams. The expense to the Cardinal organization in maintaining such a farm system was minimal because of low player salaries. In 1942, Albert Schoendienst hitch-hiked from Germantown, Illinois, to St. Louis for a tryout with the Cardinals. The nineteen-year-old spent the night on a park bench, but succeeded in getting a minor-league contract. Overjoyed to be paid $75 per month—the going rate—Red thought that life just couldn't be any better than this. Schoendienst developed his skills and, despite an eye injury while in the army during the war years, finally made the Cardinal roster in 1945. He played eighteen years in the majors and managed the Cardinals to their back-to-back World Series appearances in 1967 and 1968. Schoendienst was elected to Baseball's Hall of Fame in 1989 and his jersey, No. 2, subsequently was retired by the Cardinals.

Players in the minor-league camp stayed in private homes. Sometimes four or five slept in one room, crowding onto double beds or making pallets on the floor. The players vied for slots on one of the twenty Cardinal farm teams. At the top of the minor-league system were the AAA clubs and the Cardinals had two—Columbus in the American Association and Rochester in the International League. The International was a venerable league—headed by Frank J. Shaughnessy—with franchises in Toronto, Montreal, and Ottawa.

The Cardinals had one AA club in Houston. Their teams in A through D leagues were scattered across the eastern half of the country. At the close of the Albany spring camp, Hal found out that he was staying put. He would play with Albany in the Class D Georgia-Florida League. While most of the other players left Georgia for their assignments, Hal stayed in the same host house with plenty of roommates. Among them were Al Bogner and Frank Marsh. The 1949 Albany Cardinals were managed by Sheldon "Chief" Bender, who pitched for the team as well. Hal split the catching duties that year with another young talent, Bill Osteen, a relative of Dodger pitcher, Claude Osteen. Osteen had been around for a couple of years, having spent the previous season in St. Joseph playing in the Western Association where he hit .308. Although Osteen was a good hitter, Hal had the advantage of being three years younger. Summer double-headers in steamy Georgia were murderous on players wearing wool uniforms. In the minor leagues, players had only one uniform. After a hot, humid Saturday night game, the uniforms were hung out on the fence. Even by game-time on Sunday afternoon they still weren't dry and seemed to weigh a ton. The smell of heavy, sweat-soaked wool is unforgettable and, when one gets used to it, somewhat intoxicating.

Around the first of June, a left-handed pitcher named Wilmer Mizell joined the Albany Cardinals and the team took off. Mizell had a blazing fastball, a high leg kick, and a slightly skewed cap. Like many young left-handers, he was a tad on the wild side. Hailing from rural Greene County, Mississippi, Mizell chewed tobacco in enormous wads. He got his colorful nickname from Vinegar Bend, Alabama, where the Mizell family picked up its mail. Their farm was just across the state line from the post office. Mizell, who was gangly and had a shock of hair on his forehead, could have been mistaken for actor Andy Griffith. Mizell's ability to spit tobacco juice with explosiveness, length, and accuracy astonished witnesses. He became an instant favorite of the Albany fans. Even today, tobacco spitting is considered a fine art in parts of the South where festivals and contests are devoted to it. Hal remembered that Mizell "didn't have to buy a meal that whole year in Albany. He'd be walking down the street and somebody'd say, 'Vinnie, I'll buy you a hamburger.' He was the talk of the town. I'm not sure that he got interviewed on the radio because I

don't believe they even had a radio station, but he made the
newspapers quite often."

Mizell's natural exploits often carried over into the letters Hal
wrote to his folks. In one, Smith testified that Mizell cleanly picked off
a bug from the dugout railing fifteen feet away with a stream of
tobacco juice. In another letter, Hal wrote that "when Vinegar Bend
was in his windup, you couldn't see anything but the bottom of his
foot!" Ed Bailey, a catcher in the Reds' organization from Strawberry
Plains, Tennessee, one day explained Mizell's delivery to Hal: "What
he does, he goes back like this and then all of a sudden he comes up
and looks down to see what kind of damage he did!" Harry Caray
remarked in a radio broadcast that his dream battery was Vinegar
Bend Mizell pitching to Strawberry Plains Bailey.

With Mizell pitching, Bender relieving, and Hal behind the plate,
the Albany Cardinals finished first in the league by a margin of ten
games. Mizell went 12-3 with an ERA of 1.98. Three years later, he
made the big leagues, where he was pitching to his favorite catcher,
Hal Smith, and trying to get St. Louis into the World Series. Mizell
had a habit of screwing his cap down on his head with his glove hand,
giving it an off-center look, with the bill over to the right side of his
head. Hal once told a batter, "I don't know if he's taking the signal
from me or the third baseman."

The Albany Cardinals' championship in the Georgia-Florida
League was the first of four high finishes that Hal's teams registered in
the minors. Hal went back to Barling for the winter, satisfied that his
baseball career was off to a great start. About 150 miles from Barling,
up in the northeastern Oklahoma coal country, another 18-year-old
came home from his first year of organized ball. After hitting .313 in
the Class D Kansas-Oklahoma-Missouri League, his career was off to
a good start, too. His name? Mickey Mantle.

4

Niagara Falls Honeymoon

Hal hurried to get back to Arkansas to see his girlfriend, Carolyn Treece, and now they began to make plans for their wedding. Hal and Carolyn had met through the matchmaking of American Legion teammate, Marvin Blaylock, who had been signed by the Philadelphia Phillies. Carolyn had a steady job as a telephone operator and often rode to work from the family home on South "V" Street with her father, Hobart Treece. Mr. Treece would drop Carolyn off and then head to his job at National Cylinder Gas Company on Wheeler Avenue. Mr. Treece and the employees of National Cylinder Gas handled pressurized, six-foot steel bottles that contained pure oxygen for use in cutting and welding metal. Fort Smith Structural Steel Company, a few blocks away, bought a lot of those bottles. The welders and steel cutters at the steel company used oxygen cylinders as they fabricated steel bridge trusses. Carolyn and Hal hit it off right away and their separation during the 1949 baseball season had fanned the flames—a sign, the poets say, of true love. Their hearts had indeed become fonder and it was evident to both that they couldn't keep their sanity while living apart for another season and married in March, 1950 after Hal hustled home on a short break from spring training.

The Cardinals cooperated with a $50 raise in salary for Hal—upping him to $250 a month—and promoted him to Lynchburg, Virginia, in the Class B Piedmont League. Before the first game, however, the Cardinal management changed the assignment and sent Hal to Hamilton, Ontario. It was Class D ball, but at least he was in the faster PONY league, so called because it had teams in Pennsylvania, Ontario and New York. Carolyn accompanied Hal and the bus route to Hamilton went right by Niagara Falls, America's most famous honeymoon location. While they held hands in the mist below the huge waterfall, Carolyn and Harold relished such a glamorous vacation before the season got underway. A life in baseball seemed perfect!

Within walking distance of the ballpark in Hamilton, the newly-weds took a one-room apartment in the home of a friendly couple named Evans, who charged the Smith's ten dollars a week in rent and provided company (and unusual local recipes) for Carolyn while Hal was on long road trips. The Canadians must have found much to delight in during the four-month stay of the effervescent couple from Arkansas. Carolyn had to be cautioned by Mrs. Evans, however, not to use the term "little booger" when playing with her young son. Back home in Arkansas, "little booger" was a term of affection. To some Canadians, however, it sounded too much like the British term, "bugger," a street-wise, slang word. Welcome to cultural diversity!

Other new experiences, such as Northern food specialties and the chatter of fans in Yankee accents, greeted Hal in western New York and towns like Bradford, Pennsylvania. For the 1950 season, the Hamilton Cardinals were stocked with good players. Hal and three other future major-leaguers—Kenny Boyer, Stu Miller, and Hal "Pidge" Browne, all pitchers—were on the 1950 Hamilton roster. Boyer, a hard-throwing right-hander was from Liberty, Missouri, where in 1867 Jesse James robbed his first bank. Boyer could also swing the bat. Hal remembered that "they used to send him up as a pinch-hitter for me sometimes!" As a pitcher and part-time position player with

Hamilton, Boyer hit .349 with nine home runs. The next year, Boyer jumped to Class A Omaha, where George Kissell managed. Upon seeing the powerful swing of Boyer, Kissell promptly converted him to an outfielder. He was so good at hitting that he later started eleven years for the Cardinals in centerfield or at third base and hit 262 home runs with a .287 lifetime batting average. His jersey number has been retired to the Cardinal Wall of Honor at Busch Stadium.

At Hamilton, a salty Canadian and former minor-league pitcher, Vedie Himsl, managed the club and filled in when needed on the mound. But, Vedie declined to drive the team bus. Instead, he paid an extra $50 a month for that job to Stu Miller, a slightly-built but crafty little pitcher. At the start of a road trip, he slid in behind the wheel of an ex-school bus decorated with the Cardinal logo on the side and headed south across the Niagara River and back into the United States. The Hamilton team's usual out-of-town series began with Lockport, which was located right on the old Erie Canal. The team traveled from place to place in a clockwise circuit, with stops at Batavia, Hornell, Wellsville, and Olean. All are tradition-rich baseball towns that developed out of the "burnt-over district" of the state. It was called that because of the "fires" of evangelicalism that swept across the area in the 1830's. Some even claim the game of baseball itself originated there. The Hamilton, Ontario, Cardinals drew 92,673 fans in 1950, the second highest attendance in the league. The Hornell Dodgers, 81-43 that season, finished first and were led by the 23 home runs of Don Zimmer. Zimmer finished the year with a batting average of .315 and 122 RBI's. As an 18-year-old rookie shortstop the previous year, Zimmer had set an Eastern Shore League record with six errors in one game. Later, with the Brooklyn Dodgers, Zimmer was known for crashing into fences. It was a reputation that stuck. As Yankee manager Joe Torre's bench coach, he is remembered for charging at Boston's Pedro Martinez in a famous 2003 brouhaha. Coach Zimmer was 72 at the time; pitching great Martinez was 32.

On June 25, 1950, Miller was driving Smith, Boyer, and their Hamilton teammates in the lumbering bus toward a series with Elroy Face's Bradford, Pennsylvania, Phillies. At a café stop, the young players heard stunning news. Eleven North Korean divisions had crossed the 38th parallel to attack the South Koreans and their American allies. Within a few days, the North Korean juggernaut overran Seoul. The invading army continued its drive, pushing American and South Korean troops rapidly southward. The roads were jammed with a million refugees fleeing the Communists. The Hamilton players felt uneasy with the news about conditions in East Asia. Their futures might be affected, just as war in the preceding decade had interrupted many other baseball careers. They were partly right. Instead of landing in the military, Miller made it to the Cardinals in 1952 and was 6-3 in his rookie season. His catcher, Hal Smith, would be directly affected by the military turn of events in the very next year.

5

Kissell

Cold War worries about a nuclear confrontation between the world's super powers—the U.S. and the U.S.S.R.—intensified with the invasion of South Korea. Faced with a land war in Korea (officially it was termed a "police action"), Congress reactivated the draft in order to build strength for the military. Back home in Fort Smith in the winter of 1950, Hal and Carolyn felt a personal necessity to act in the face of these emergencies. With his draft status A-1, Hal weighed his options for military service before deciding to volunteer for the U.S. Air Force. The rapidly growing Air Force needed manpower. It had become the newest military branch when it was split from the U.S. Army in 1946. Astounding inventions and discoveries in weapons, medicine, and technology marked World War II, particularly in the field of air power. During the fighting in Korea, jet fighter planes like the F-86 Sabre Jet were streaking over battlefields and engaging in aerial combat with MIG-15's. The new planes had made World War II heroes like the P-47 Thunderbolt and P-51 Mustang obsolete in less than five years. Huge bombers like the B-50 and B-36 and huge, new cargo planes like the C-97 and the C-124 could carry much more weight aloft than the old planes. For Hal, the

Air Force seemed an adventuresome and promising branch of the military. It was a good way of serving his country and also might serve him well as a career choice.

As soon as he was sworn in, Hal reported to Shepherd Air Force Base in Texas for basic training. The minor-league catcher learned new skills in "this man's Air Force." When his training was completed at Shepherd in the spring of 1951, Hal was transferred to George Air Force Base in Victorville, California. He was assigned to Special Services, the recreational squadron. The base commander wanted a professional player like Hal to join the George Air Force baseball team to play against teams at other bases in California and Arizona. Just as the season started, Hal began to get a steady stream of unsettling news from home. He was concerned about Carolyn's pregnancy and both of her parents also were ailing. The urgency of the situation led Hal to figure out a way to get home. One day, he walked into the orderly room and explained his situation to the clerk. "Do you think I could get a leave or something like that?" he asked. The clerk, who was from Paris, Arkansas, said, "Well, maybe we can get you out with a hardship discharge." The medical doctors for each family member wrote a letter in support of Hal's application. Two weeks later, in June, the clerk called Hal in, smiled broadly, and said, "Hello, civilian!" Hal had been in uniform only six months but was glad to get back to Fort Smith to help in restoring his family's health.

Being at home, however, didn't relieve Hal of having to earn an income. He went to work for the Dixie Cup Company, Fort Smith's first, giant "New South" factory. After a day's work in the factory, Hal often played baseball with a crack local team, the South Fort Smith Smokers. The Smokers were perennial contenders for the state semi-pro crown, which carried with it a trip to the National Baseball Congress Tournament in Wichita, Kansas. Teams from all over the country vied to advance through the double-elimination bracket to win what was considered to be the national championship of non-professional baseball.

In July, Carolyn gave birth to the Smiths' first child, daughter Sandra. Working at the cup factory and helping his wife with the new baby didn't leave much time for semi-pro baseball. Hal thought seriously about leaving the game. He hadn't hit much in Hamilton, batting only .224. Because of his arm, his defensive skill was his best feature. The war, his military experience, being a new father, and working a shift to bring in groceries seemed to change Hal's priorities.

About the time he'd decided to quit baseball, Hal got advice from two local baseball heroes, Jimmy Charles and Delmar Edwards. Charles once had slammed a long home run out of Andrews Field as a 15-year-old American Legion player. Years later, that homer was still talked about in Fort Smith. He had broken his ankle while playing football for Hendrix College in Conway and the ankle didn't mend correctly. The legendary athlete had been denied the mobility necessary for major-league players and he deeply regretted it. In 1953, Charles satisfied a little of his urge for professional baseball by signing a minor-league contract as a third baseman for the Fort Smith Twins of the Class C Western Association. For the Twins, who were playing in the last season of minor-league baseball for the city, Charles hit .321 with 16 home runs and 71 RBIs. Delmar, a lanky right-hander who had pitched in the Three I League in the Cardinal organization, went 20-13 with a 2.56 ERA for the 1953 Twins. "Those two guys," Hal recalled, "talked me into going ahead with my baseball career." They persuaded Hal to try again, so the young catcher called his old mentor, Freddie Hawn. Hawn got his protégé a roster spot on the Class A Columbus, Georgia, club for the tail-end of the 1951 season. Hal went to Columbus but didn't stay long. He had grown homesick for his wife and child and decided to return to Fort Smith. That winter, Hal went to work at the Fort Smith Boys Club.

Reluctant to let go of their strong-armed catcher, the Cardinals assigned Hal to Allentown, Pennsylvania, in the Class B Interstate League for the 1952 season. No sooner had Hal arrived in Allentown than he got a call to report to Omaha, the Cardinals' team in the Class A Western League. He was to fill in for the starting catcher, who was going on Army reserve duty for two weeks. The manager at Omaha was George Kissell, who had a lengthy career with the Cardinals and finally retired in 2007. He was a fine baseball strategist and the one primarily responsible for developing the Cardinal playbook. Kissell, according to Hal, "took a liking to me and kept me there in Omaha for the rest of that year. I went back to Omaha in 1953 for the full year." The Western League was full of solid prospects and the level of play no doubt helped Hal hone his skills. The league included the Denver Bears (Pittsburgh), the Wichita Indians (Cleveland), the Des Moines Bruins (Cubs), the Lincoln A's (Philadelphia A's), the Pueblo Dodgers (Brooklyn), the Sioux City Soos (New York Giants), and the Colorado Springs Sky Sox (Chicago White Sox). Under the tutelage of Kissell, Smith's hitting and his defense improved. Major-league manager and former player Joe Torre once confided to an interviewer that he "learned more baseball from George Kissell than from anyone else in my life."[11] Jackie Brandt recalled his playing days for Kissell in Columbus, Georgia. One time, Kissell locked the door of the clubhouse and then started a team meeting. Brandt, who was a few minutes late, couldn't get in until after the meeting. "Be on time, Jackie," Kissell growled. Brandt said that Kissell once made up a false balk play. With runners on first and third, the man on first would take a lead. While the pitcher was in his stretch, the runner would fake a break toward second and then fall down on purpose. The pitcher would, according to the plan, either balk or throw legally to first base. The man on third would time his break with his teammate's fall and score easily.

On one occasion, however, Hal's rocket arm backfired on one trick play and caused Kissell to drop a scheme that he had invented. The play was meant to trap an over-confident runner who was leading too far off first base. According to the script, the catcher attempts a pick-off that looks poorly executed because he throws wildly over the first baseman's head. The response of the runner is, of course, to get up quickly and take off for second base. A prearranged signal, however, alerts the rightfilder, who cheats over, then breaks to back up the first baseman and is in position to field the overthrow. The rightfielder then guns down the runner trying to advance to second. Scratch one decoyed runner. Sounded simple enough to work and nobody else but Omaha had it. The play was a gem, straight from the creative mind of Kissell and could be used at exactly the right time to get the pitcher out of a jam.

In a game at Denver, Kissell put the play on with Hal behind the plate. Everything was on cue, except that Hal shot the ball not only over the head of first baseman Pidge Brown, *but* over the head of rightfielder Jim King, too. King chased the ball down in the corner and relayed it to the Omaha second baseman, a feisty guy by the name of Earl Weaver, who fired it home to Hal. The throw was too late. The runner scored all the way from first. It goes unrecorded what Kissell, whose big ears could turn Cardinal red when he was agitated, might have said to Hal back in the dugout. Hal remembered that George "used to get on me something *fierce*, man, because I'd be the first one in the dugout so I was the one who caught it all! We deleted that little trick from the play book."

One night, Hal recalled, "our starting pitcher, Paul Dewey, was being knocked around at Colorado Springs, so Kissell came to the mound and yanked him. Dewey trudged to a gate out in dead centerfield, which led into the dressing room. An inning later, George was coaching third base and blew a fuse when Omaha wound up with three runners on third base at the same time. I don't know how we did it," Hal continued, "but George threw down his cap, stomped on it and shouted, 'Dammit, I'm going home,' and started walking out to the centerfield gate." He barged into the locker room just as Paul Dewey stepped out of the showers. Seeing how Kissell was slinging things around and drop-kicking his bag, Dewey tried to console him. "Hey Skip," he said, "you want me to help you pack?"

The Omaha Cardinals traveled into and out of Denver, Pueblo, and Colorado Springs by train. The hours together in the club cars with teammates and coaches provided time for cards, sightseeing, and bonding. Hal kibitzed or played gin rummy or bridge with Larry Jackson, Pidge Browne and Jim King or watched the glorious western vistas from the over-sized windows. Hal said that "across the prairie out there, you'd see buffalo and antelope and all that stuff." The big, coal-burning locomotives blew their whistles, mournful sounds on the wide-open land that once was witness to creaking covered wagons and braying mules as 19th-century pioneers traveled these same paths toward their destinations of Oregon, Colorado, or California. For the 20th-century ball players, steel wheels clacking on steel rails set up a comforting rhythm for all but the most restless. The sleeping and lounge cars had no air conditioning. To cool off, the players would pull the windows wide open. "Then," Hal remembered, "we'd go through a tunnel and the smoke would come into the car like you wouldn't believe." As they traveled, Kissell often would get the pitchers and catchers together to talk baseball. He'd go over situations and explain how to set up certain hitters. Hal picked up a lot in these sessions. A former player, John Mabry, once said of Kissell, "That man IS baseball." A spring training instructor for the Cardinals for fifty years, Kissell was bow-legged and wore his cap so that the bill pointed straight up. He was known simply as "the Game." Kissell never played an inning in the major leagues but was a good minor-league hitter. His career extended from those meager years to the present, where multi-million dollar contracts are the norm. Up until 1997, he had never earned more than $55,000 in the sport that distinctly bore his mark. Years after their first meeting in Omaha, Kissell got Hal to instruct his catchers at the Cardinal spring training camps.[12]

In the 1952 season, the Omaha Cardinals finished third in the league and Hal batted .255. He'd played with future major-leaguers Wally Moon and Jim King. Like Hal, they had both been signed by Hawn. In a letter home to Hig, his old Legion coach, Hal described how the wind caught his drive in Denver and blew it right out of the park. That was Hal's way of putting things—with modesty, understatement and quiet confidence, just like Gehrig or Boyer. During his second season at Omaha, the Cardinals went to St. Louis for an exhibition game and Hal met Stan Musial and Eddie Stanky, the Cardinal manager. Stanky, nicknamed "The Brat" during his playing days with the Dodgers, the Braves, and the Giants, had the quintessential little man's approach to the game. It was hustle, hustle, hustle and take advantage of every crack in the opponents' armor. Fight at the drop of a hat. Fire up teammates with a pat on the butt. Rain down insults on umpires and players in the other dugout. Such men are often referred to as "holler guys." Stanky was shaped, in part, by Leo Durocher, who managed him in his first two seasons of major-league ball in Brooklyn. Durocher was a furious competitor who had been a second baseman and shortstop as a player. Durocher, a bench jockey and umpire baiter, was nicknamed "The Lip." Stanky went to the World Series with each of the teams for which he started. Branch Rickey said once that Stanky had the "intangibles." With a reputation as a winner, he seemed the right choice when owner Fred Saigh sought a manager for the Cards in 1952. Once installed at the helm of the Cardinals, Stanky considered himself still capable of playing and occasionally spelled his young shortstop, Solomon Hemus. Stanky liked to demonstrate such inside techniques as deliberately slowing down his swing and hitting to right field with no outs in order to move up a runner. Hemus became a holler guy, too, eager to learn Stanky's "intangibles." Solly Hemus, so steeped, would become Hal's manager in 1959.

When asked if he had any impressions of Stanky that stand out, Hal answered, "Oh, yes!" Called "Little Napoleon" by the players,

Hal recalled that Stanky wanted to "change the Cardinals, make them toe the line." Hal said that "one time Del Rice and I happened to be sitting in the dugout [at spring training camp] going over the signs—the pitcher signs—just the two of us. Stanky came up and saw us sitting there and told one of the coaches, 'would you tell those two fellows to get back out on the field where they belong?' We got out there. He wouldn't let you sit in the shade." If the Cardinals lost even a "grapefruit" exhibition game, Stanky was known to come into the clubhouse and "start slinging the lunch meat and mustard from the sandwich buffet." Stanky was secretive about player assignments and if coaches tipped off someone before Stanky thought they should, he would absolutely chew them up one side and down the other for such indiscretions. Stanky never admitted an error or apologized if shown to be wrong.

But Hal had good memories of Stanky, too. One of those occurred after he headed south with his growing family to start another season. By this time, Hal was the father of a second daughter, Sharon. "In 1955, when I first went to spring training," he recalled, "Stanky knew that I had my wife and two girls with me. He also knew that I was going to be sent down, that I wasn't going to stay with the club. So, he called me in the office one day and said 'I just wanted you to know that you are going to be sent to Houston and you might want to make arrangements to get your family back.' They wouldn't let you drive your own family home after spring training. Someone else had to do that. But, I think I was the only one he told that to, so I figured he liked me." Later, as a Cardinal scout, Hal saw his old field boss a few times when Stanky coached the college baseball team at the University of South Alabama. "He was a good guy, he really was," Hal said. "I mean he was a family man from the word 'go.' But on that field, he was a different person!" Stanky's 1952 Cardinal team went 88-66 and finished in third place in the National League. It was his first season as a manager in the big leagues and the most successful team he had in eight years of managing. For that feat, he was named by *The Sporting News* as the "Manager of the Year." Edward Stanky died on June 6, 1999 and is buried in Mobile.

6

Dixie

On February 11, 1954, Hal was preparing to leave Fort Smith for training camp in Florida when he received a terrifying telephone call from Carolyn's mother in Tulsa. Only a few years before, Carolyn's dad, Hobart Treece, had been transferred by his company from Fort Smith to Tulsa. A huge explosion had blown apart the factory of Treece's employer, the National Cylinder Gas plant on Peoria Avenue. Two men had been killed instantly and three others were critically injured by the blast, which demolished the building. A plant manager had lost an arm, a second man lost a leg, and the other employee battling for his life was Treece. The explosion literally had thrown him out of the building and he was in a state of shock. His condition was worsened due to ammonia gas in his lungs and by the fact that he was already under treatment for heart problems. Hal and Carolyn rushed to his bedside at Hillcrest Medical Hospital. Once Hobart seemed out of immediate danger, however, the family decided that Hal should go ahead and report for spring training. Carolyn stayed in Tulsa for a month while her father slowly recovered.

In Florida, Hal kept in daily contact with Carolyn, even as he started the tough six weeks of training. Kissell, who had watched him play two seasons at Omaha and knew his worth, recommended that Hal be assigned to Triple A Columbus, Ohio. But when the final rosters were distributed, Hal found that instead he was to join the Cardinals' AA affiliate in Houston. Hal was to be the back-up to Dick Rand, who was being groomed as the "next Cardinal catcher." Rand, a 6-2 Californian the same age as Hal, had been called up to the big club at the end of the previous season and appeared in nine games. He had cracked out nine hits in his 31 at-bats with the Cardinals. For 1958, Rand was sent to Houston to get a full season under his belt and play plenty of games. Hal was destined, he said, to "fill in on doubleheaders and when they wanted to give [Rand] a rest." That plan, however, soon went awry when Rand took a foul tip off the finger in San Antonio. While their big starter sat out to wait for the broken finger to mend, Hal caught all the games. "That was my big break," Hal recalled, "I happened to get there at that right time." Pipe-smoking Fred "Dixie" Walker was the Houston Buff manager and, like previous skippers, liked what he saw in Hal. Walker knew that Hal had the ability and the attitude to take him to the majors. He worked overtime with Hal on developing his batting stroke. Coincidentally, the Buffs went on some long winning streaks and climbed into second place in the Texas League standings—good enough to earn a playoff berth. In his modest way, Hal acknowledged the team's success but took no credit for the turnaround. According to him, guys like Kenny Boyer, Don Blasingame, and Bobby Boyd broke out of slumps about the same time and all started playing great baseball. In fact, they were Houston's first version of the "Killer B's." Boyd, a 5-10, left-handed first baseman, played nine years in the majors, mostly with Baltimore. He finished his career with a hefty .293 lifetime batting average. Blasingame, a Mississippian like Boyd, got to the Cardinals in 1956. He and Hal shared the same rookie season. Blasingame was sheer hustle. A fiery competitor at second base, he made everyone around him play a little better. His twelve-

year career with four teams resulted in a lifetime batting average of
.258—exactly the same as Hal's. Branch Rickey had been impressed
in seeing Blasingame and Boyer play in Cuba. He summed up the wiry
Mississippian in unerring Rickey fashion: Blasingame was "a pest at
the plate. He should become a good base on balls man (he got 552 of
them in his major-league career) and his power is ample (he averaged
about two home runs a year)." Boyer had large hands, which further
helped his fielding skills. Rickey was impressed and noted that Boyer
was "the best ballplayer on first impression that I have seen in many
a day. Never loafs."[13]

After his injury healed, the Houston Buffs put Rand back in the
lineup as catcher. Hal watched from the bench as the team began to
slide into a losing streak. "So, they put me back in to start catching,"
Hal explained, "and we went ahead and won the Texas League
pennant and went to the Dixie Series against Atlanta." Now, the
Cardinals had decided that Hal was their catcher of the future.
Eventually, they dealt Rand to Pittsburgh, where he caught 60 games
and batted .217. He retired from baseball after that season.

But Houston had been the proving ground for Hal. Of the team's
136 regular season games, he had started in 110 of them, plus all seven
games of the Dixie Series. Hal had matured as a hitter while
continuing to work well with pitchers. His personality added to the
good will and camaraderie of the locker room, an intangible that can
morph a good bunch of players into a championship team.

The Buffs flew to Atlanta for the 1954 Dixie Series. It was a
departure from their normal modes of travel—buses to San Antonio
and Beaumont or trains bound for Shreveport, Oklahoma City, and
Tulsa. Atlanta was the champion of the Southern Association, a fast
league with a reputation for good, hard-nosed play that could trace its
origin as far back as 1902. By 1954, the Atlanta Crackers had become
the prime farm club of Milwaukee.[14] When the Braves decided to leave
Milwaukee after the 1965 season, their old AA city had reached

major-league size. Atlanta became the new home of the Braves, destined to be called by some "America's Team."

The geographic and ethnic backgrounds of organized baseball in that era encompassed the Southern Association, the Texas League, the Dixie Series and Dixie Walker. It included white players of average size from Alabama, Arkansas, Mississippi, Missouri, and teams with nicknames like the Crackers. The Negro League operated separately and drew thousands of fans in the northern and eastern cities, despite the scorn heaped on it by major-league executives like Rickey. Players, black and white, rose through the ranks of professional sports in a segregated society. It was a system that seemed entrenched and was defended by public opinion. But, most baseball people—fans, management, and players alike—knew that things were about to change. Hal's first year in organized baseball preceded that of Willie Mays by one year. In 1949, an African-American shortstop for the Oakland Oaks, Artie Wilson, led the Pacific Coast League in batting with a .349 average.[15] Hal, along with Mickey Mantle, Ken Boyer, Willie Mays, and Don Drysdale set out on their baseball careers just as the nation began to face gut-wrenching issues on civil rights. While baseball itself had been in the forefront of desegregation in America, southern-born white players often felt trapped. Their natural loyalties tilted toward home and friends, most of whom were far from wanting to see full equality for black players. Most southerners of the 1940's-1950's weren't exactly on the cutting edge of desegregation. In fact, some were reacting defensively and violently. Players from the South found that their pull toward southern traditions clashed with their feelings toward African-American teammates. Hal, along with other white players, were confused by how black players were treated and often could do little to help the situation. For instance, black players had to stay in separate quarters during spring training. They could not participate in golf tournaments that Florida cities arranged for ball players. They had to sit in the bus while teammates brought them carry-out orders from segregated diners on grapefruit league road trips.

Hal's manager and mentor at Houston, Fred "Dixie" Walker, was born in Villa Rica, Georgia. He was a popular Brooklyn Dodger outfielder from 1940 to 1947 and a consistent .300 hitter during those years. In a marvelous pennant race with the Cardinals in 1941, Walker appeared in 148 games for the Dodgers and batted .311. He emerged as a leader on the hard-driving Dodger team and became "the people's cherce," as Brooklyn fans put it. When Jackie Robinson integrated the team, Walker wrote to Branch Rickey that he wished to be traded but didn't mention why. Rickey declined to trade Walker, who stayed with Brooklyn through the 1947 season. He played in 148 games alongside Robinson. Usually, the two went about their business on the field but ignored each other the rest of the time. That year, Walker hit .306 with nine home runs, while Robinson batted .297 with twelve home runs and the Dodgers won the pennant. Apparently, the first black player in the majors and the popular white southerner got along well enough to keep the team winning. Dixie Walker, in the twilight of his playing career, was traded to Pittsburgh for the 1948 season. Later, he was quoted as saying that Robinson was "as outstanding an athlete as I ever saw."[16] He had seen a few in his life, too. Walker remembered the stories told by his father, also called Dixie, who pitched for the Washington Senators in the pre-World War I years. The elder Dixie was born in Pennsylvania but redeployed to Alabama, Georgia and Mississippi as a baseball man. He raised his future major-leaguer sons in the South, where they developed strong ties. Fred's younger brother, Harry, was a major-league player and manager who would have a great influence on young Hal Smith. Both Dixie and Harry liked Hal and saw his potential as a major-league catcher. Along with George Kissell, they convinced Cardinal execs to give him a shot in 1956.

Years later, in a documentary film on Robinson's entry into the major-leagues, Harry Walker went on camera to defend his brother, Dixie. He was responding to comments made by Pee Wee Reese, a former Dodger from Kentucky, who befriended Robinson. Harry described Dixie as, first and foremost, a baseball man who respected the abilities of any player who proved himself on the field. When his playing career ended, Dixie managed and instructed many African-American and Latino players. He once confided that he was "not the same man I was in 1947," referring to his attitudes on race at the time the National League was first integrated. Even back then, Walker declared he was "not a ringleader" in trying to stop Robinson, although some of his "friends" in Alabama would have wanted him to do so. Many southerners were of Scots-Irish descent, a heritage that has received recent attention from scholars who label them as "born fighters."[17] Undoubtedly, competitiveness between whites and blacks, as well as pride in one's self and in one's heritage, caused uneasiness and even dislike on and off the field in those days. Players of widely different backgrounds suddenly were brought together before the society at large could challenge old attitudes. The segregated world in which they had lived abounded in stereotypes that created emotional justifications for rigid separation of different cultures. Skin color, as trivial and illogical as it now seems, defined many social norms. In that world, ethnic and personal idiosyncrasies offered juicy bait for raunchy nicknames and bench jockeying often had a personal edge to it. Despite a rough beginning, integrated baseball was here to stay. On the diamond, and especially in the clubhouse, camaraderie ruled and helped demolish prejudices and skin-color boundaries. The game and the players began to adjust to the presence and the style of African-American and Latino players. Major-league baseball finally went after these new "talent pools." The 1954 Dixie Series, which Hal's team lost to the Crackers, was played in the same year the U.S. Supreme Court ruled in the *Brown v. Topeka Board of Education* case that segregation was unconstitutional. By that year, it is worth noting that all the major-league teams had African-Americans on their rosters or, at least, in their farm systems. In that same year, the exploits of Willie Mays with bat and glove became the talk of the American man on the street. Known as the "Say Hey Kid," his smile and style were transcendent qualities that helped conquer prejudice, except among the most hard-bitten, in America.

The Sporting News carried a team photograph of the Houston Buffs in its September 27th issue. The Buffs' team, with African-American star, Bob Boyd, represented the Texas League in the Dixie Series. To reach a berth in the series—one of the most popular spectator events in the South—the Buffs had rolled past Oklahoma City in the first round of the Texas League playoff, then defeated the Fort Worth Cats, the Dodger franchise, four games to one. In Game Three, the Buffs beat the Cats, 3-2, in 17 innings. One sportswriter filed a story that mentioned the losing pitcher: "Victim of the four-hour, twenty seven-minute defeat was Cats' ace Karl Spooner who weakened [italics added] after 16 innings."[18] Against Spooner, Hal went three for four. Smith had faced Spooner back in the PONY League when both were beginning their careers. In the bottom of the ninth, Fort Worth leftfielder Ray Coleman doubled and the Cats tried to move him over with a sacrifice bunt. Hal catapulted from behind the plate, bare-handed the ball in mid-air and fired a bullet to second baseman Blasingame to double-up Coleman. Fort Worth never threatened after that. The grueling, extra-inning game took the wind out of the Cats, who then lost the next two and sent Houston on to the Dixie Series.

Although Houston was only a Class AA team, the Cardinals stocked the franchise with quality prospects because it was such a great baseball town and fans attended in droves. The Buffs' 340,000 attendance figure in 1954 led the Texas League and was the third highest in all of minor-league baseball. The team outdrew AAA clubs like Los Angeles and San Diego in the Pacific Coast League and trailed only Atlanta in the Southern Association and Toronto in the International League. Obviously, major-league executives took notice because Houston later won out over rival cities to become one of the first two expansion teams in the modern National League—the

New York Mets being the other expansion team in 1962. Upon being awarded the major-league franchise, plans for the air-conditioned Harris County Domed Stadium were on the drawing board. The air conditioning was a gift for the fans in a city that often experiences suffocating heat and humidity. The Houston Colt .45's played their first two seasons in Colt Stadium, which had been hastily built and was an open-air ballpark just down the street from where the Domed Stadium was rising. Across town, wrecking balls demolished Buff's Stadium for a shopping center. Today, inside the Finger Furniture store on Cullen Boulevard, the exact spot where home plate in old Buff Stadium was positioned is marked on the floor.

The Harris County Domed Stadium, brainchild of Harris County Judge and Colts' owner Roy Hofheintz, became known as the Astrodome. After natural grass refused to grow under the dome, a synthetic grass with the trade name AstroTurf was installed. The team changed its name from the Colt .45's to the Astros. AstroTurf surfaces became the designer norm for stadiums built in the 1970's. The Astrodome, which cost $15 million, supplanted St. Peter's Basilica as the largest domed building in the world.

The Buffs did not win the 1954 Dixie Series despite going up three games to one. The Atlanta Crackers made a come-back by getting some great pitching from Dick Donovan, who had two complete-game victories, and from hard-throwing Glen Thompson. The Crackers won three straight to take the series. As a result of his great 1954 season with the Buffs, Hal gained the full confidence of Dixie Walker, his manager and friend, who started him behind the plate in all the Buffs' post-season games. Walker wanted to see that the young catcher got a chance to play major-league baseball and gave Hal special instructions on how to improve his batting eye and swing. Walker convinced Hal that he needed to play winter ball to further develop his skills as a hitter. Dixie Walker, a career .306 hitter, knew what he was talking about. As a Dodger outfielder, he hit for the cycle against the rival

New York Giants. Hitting for the cycle—that is, knocking a home run, a triple, a double, and a single in one game—was a rare feat and a hitter's dream. Musial, Mantle, and Williams all did it, but hitting for the cycle eluded most major leaguers, including Ruth and Mays. The great Joe DiMaggio and the great Lou Gehrig did it twice.

More seasoning, more baseball, and Mexico were on the 1954 horizon for Hal and Carolyn and their two daughters, Sandra and Sharon. Carolyn made the airline reservations to Guadalajara, Mexico, after Hal returned from Atlanta and the Dixie Series. With tips from wives of players who had preceded them to Guadalajara, Carolyn arranged housing for the family at a place called California Courts. "It was nice," she recalled. "You could walk around the town and it was so cheap to live there." The tropical temperature was moderated by the elevation, giving Guadalajara good baseball weather year-round. The family stayed in Mexico from the first of October until the last of February—five months of baseball and bus rides, with an occasional bullfight mixed in. Four-year-old Sharon delighted in the colorful bullfights, but Hal felt sorry for the bull: "He's already got the knives stuck into his back, then here comes the guy on the horse and the toreadors. By the time the matador makes his sword thrust for the kill, the bull can hardly stand. The fans are going crazy. The matador gets the ears and then they take those bulls right outside and butcher them. The people line up for a piece of the bull!"

Hal's personal agenda was to work on the hitting tips supplied by Walker. "I had really started to come around with the bat," Hal said, "so I went to Mexico and had a good year." The lively league combined Mexican talent with that of American players like Hal who wanted to work all winter and get the improvement they needed to advance in professional baseball. The odd assortment of pitching impressed Hal, who saw pitches from "submariners, side-armers, and over-handed curve-ball pitchers!" The league had a "salary cap" and each of the five American players earned the maximum of $450 a month. Hal, John Romonosky, Ron Plaza, Ben Downs, and Bob Burns made up a pretty good cadre of American baseball players. Just before Christmas, about halfway through the season, the Guadalajara owner fired the manager and paid Hal extra to step in as manager for the Charros. It was an indication that baseball men could see that Hal had talent for handling people and a nose for good baseball decisions. The team responded to the new skipper by winning four straight games.

The first of those wins was behind the pitching of Burns, who told Hal his nickname was "Blood." When Hal asked why, the big right-hander, an African American, replied, "when you see me pitch, you'll *know* why they call me Blood!" Blood, who went 10-5 that season, roomed with Hal when the team was on the road. The Charros had Ramiro Cuevas, who pitched a no-hitter against Navojao on October 29th. During that game, Hal concentrated on getting each batter out and didn't realize how well Ramiro was doing. Besides, it's considered bad luck to mention a possible no-hitter to a pitcher while the game is in progress, so it's generally better not to keep up with that stat. In the seventh inning, Plaza broke up a scoreless ballgame by driving in a run with a triple. Ramiro followed with a triple of his own. That was the total of the offensive output for both teams and the game ended with a Guadalajara victory. A crowd of joyous fans rushed out onto the field and put Ramiro on their shoulders. A surprised Hal thought to himself, "boy, they really go crazy here when they win a close game!" Once he reached the locker room, Hal realized that Cuevas had pitched a no-hitter. It was one of only two that Hal caught in his organized baseball career. The other was a seven-inning no-hitter in the Texas League. Following the no-hitter, Hal caught the second game. Future Cardinal pitcher, John Romonosky, threw pretty well until the game was called in the 10th inning because of darkness.

Carolyn and the girls stayed at home in Guadalajara when the team departed for road games in the Pacific Coast League of Mexico. The other five teams were the Mazatlan Deer, Obregon, Culiacan,

Navojoa, and Hermosillo. Trips were long, the roads were narrow and curvy, and the team bus was a bit rickety. The driver hired to transport the team had competed in the wild and wooly Pan American stock car races. "We'd take a trip, the longest being the one from Guadalajara to Hermosillo, which is about 1,500 miles," Hal recounted. "This guy would drive the whole way. He wouldn't sleep and when he started the weaving with no guard rails and deep drop-offs, it just scared the fire out of us!'

When they got to Hermosillo, Hal's pitchers were in for another scary sight—huge Luke Easter, wearing an Orange Pickers uniform, was digging in at the plate. Hal made out lineups and, as he said, "came up with signals from the dugout and all that stuff." He was 23 years old but was losing hair around the crown of his head. The strap that held on his mask, he thought, was cutting down on the blood circulation to the roots of his hair. The Mexican players noticed and began to call him "Cura." Baseball players everywhere love nicknames, especially ones that are subtle and humorous in regard to a player's idiosyncrasies. "Cura?" Hal asked. "Why?" The Mexican players laughed delightedly and patted their likeable manager on his shiny circle. "Cura!" one explained, "Esta Padre!" The round, bald spot reminded them of a priest's tonsure. Their nickname stuck with Hal throughout his career.

Winter baseball gave Hal a chance to work daily on Walker's hitting tips. For Hal, the extra season in Mexico served him well. The advice by Harry and Dixie Walker came with a southern twang that resonated among professional ball players. Jim Bouton wrote in his book, Ball Four, that Harry, "the Hat," would show up for Old Timer games. Bouton said it never failed. The Hat would take two strikes and then line a single up the middle.

Back home and in spring training, however, Hal wilted a bit. Instead of going north to St. Louis or even to a Triple A club, the Cardinals reassigned him to Houston. He responded by having an even better year than the last, raising his batting average 50 points. Hal hit .299 with 67 RBI's in the 1955 Texas League season and showed a little punch, too. Hal banged out eight homers, equaling his combined home run total for the previous five seasons. At Tulsa, Hal hit a shot off Bobby Locke that soared high into the Oklahoma night sky. Locke, a right-hander, was good enough to pitch for Cleveland, Philadelphia, and assorted other teams for nine years. He won 16 games in his big-league career while losing 15. Flustered because Hal took him deep, Locke came up to bat and had some choice words for the Houston catcher. He looked down and said "You'll never hit another one off of me!" "Just like that," Hal said, "and I was the first one in the park to believe him because to hit one off that guy surprised me, too. So, I'll be doggone, the next time I came up, I hit another home run. And again, I was the most surprised guy in the ball park." It was that kind of a year for Hal. Though remaining as modest and congenial as ever, he had become a much better hitter in winter baseball. Houston lost to Shreveport in the playoffs and did not return to the Dixie Series, but Hal knew that he was ready for the big leagues and looked forward to spring training in 1956. More importantly, the St. Louis brass was beginning to see it that way, too.

Hal didn't figure to play another season of winter ball and went home to work as the athletic director at the Fort Smith Boys Club and coach a junior high-age basketball team.

7

A Rookie in St. Louis

Mike Reba, who had played with the Boston Red Sox, managed the Houston Buffs in 1955. Reba was the man in the 1946 Cardinal-Red Sox World Series that so impressed Hal when he was growing up in Barling. Now, he had become a fan of Hal's and wanted assistant general manager Bing Devine and Harry Walker, the Cards' interim manager, to come and watch Hal play. Hal thought this was THE defining moment for his baseball future and said he "tried to put on a show for them, but I was scared to death!"

The "show" must have been pretty good. In spite of all the endorsements—Hal had them from the Walker brothers, from George Kissell, and now Reba—he still had to convince the brass that he deserved a spot on the forty-man Cardinal roster.

Hal had already caught the same pitchers the Cardinals were counting on as their mainstays in 1956—Mizell, Larry Jackson, and Lindy McDaniel. Mizell would be trying to pick up where he left off in 1953, when he went 13-11 with a 3.59 ERA. After that season, Uncle Sam had drafted Mizell and he spent two years at Fort McPherson, Georgia. Even though fighting had stopped in Korea because of an armistice, the Cold War kept the military nervous enough to draft all young men who couldn't arrange to be deferred. The normal tour of duty for draftees was two years. They entered the service by going through basic training at Army installations like Camp Chaffee. Since the draft only supplied men to the U.S. Army, you could choose one of the other branches if the draft board was breathing down your neck. Usually, these branches wanted commitments for longer than two years.

These young Cardinal pitchers of the '56 season liked throwing to Hal. They appreciated his ability to "read" hitters and handle different situations, not to mention his gift for calling the right pitches. He had a sense of humor that could break the tension and lessen the pressure for pitchers. They certainly liked his ability to throw out runners because that always helped take the pressure off of them.

A refreshed Hal signed in at the Cardinal spring training camp at St. Petersburg. His skills had grown and he was more determined than ever. When asked later if he thought 1956 was the year he would move to the big leagues, Hal said he "had a fairly good idea [that he would stick with the Cardinals] because I was out of options. They had just so many options where they could send you back down to the minor leagues. I felt like I had a pretty good chance to stay, but even then I started out as a back-up for Bill Sarni." Hal got the good news via a letter from the Cardinal front office in the off-season that he had been added to the forty-man roster. Even then, it was unusual for a player to jump from Class AA to the majors without having played an inning in Triple-A ball.

"When I got to spring training in 1956 and saw Musial for the first time as a teammate, he came up and it was like you had known him all your life. When he shook hands with me then, it was my greatest thrill in baseball. I kept thinking, 'is this real?' I just can't describe that feeling because it's something that you'd dreamed about. All of a sudden, here you are! Musial was my idol and he was just a good guy. Schoendienst was the same way."

Coaches like Walker Cooper and Gus Mancuso instructed Hal and other catchers in the daily spring training sessions and in the exhibition games of the grapefruit league. The manager and coaches watched for weaknesses in all the players before deciding on the final cuts. One of the things the Cardinal brass witnessed was Hal picking off four base runners. In one exhibition game, Phillies' outfielder Del Ennis—a huge, likeable man known more for his home run shots than his speed—tried to steal a base. Hal threw him out "from here to there." The old pros doubled up with laughter and catcalls issued from the Cardinal dugout. New Cardinal manager Fred Hutchinson, a big guy with a hot temper, thought his club might have the makings for a good season. (In 1955, the Cardinals won only 68 games under Stanky and interim manager, Harry Walker, who replaced Stanky midway through the season.) The front office constantly pruned the Cardinal farm system in these days of remodeled baseball recruiting and signing strategies. Still, the farm clubs had yielded the kind of players that could make a big difference in the '56 pennant chase. Hal and Boyer and Blasingame had put together good offensive statistics in their minor-league stints with Houston. Mizell returned to the '56 Cardinal staff from his two-year hitch in This Man's Army. Two more of Hawn's signees were there—Lindy McDaniel and Wallace Wade Moon. Moon had been the National League Rookie of the Year in 1954, when he batted .304 with 12 home runs. Hal's old coach in Fort Smith, Clarence Higgins, was following baseball closely in the 50's as his former player steadily worked up the ladder of professional baseball. Higgins won a straw hat after Moon's remarkable rookie season. He had bet Phillies' scout Ray Baker, a former player for the Fort Smith Giants, that Moon would hit .300 as a rookie. "Hig" had made his bet out of sentiment, since Moon was from his old stomping grounds of eastern Arkansas. Baker bet on the percentages of professional baseball, which he had been around for twenty years. Not many rookies can solve major-league pitching well enough to reach the

magical .300 plateau. Moon homered in his first major-league at-bat—
and, ironically, in his last at-bat—of a magnificent rookie season.
Moon, a lean, six-footer, batted left and played the outfield with speed
and natural ability. Until Orlando Cepeda, Moon was the only NL
Rookie of the Year to bat .300. Rookies of the Year who did not breach
that lofty batting mark in their first major-league season include Willie
Mays, Junior Gilliam, and Frank Robinson, as well as Bill Virdon, the
West Plains, Missouri, product who won the rookie award while
batting .281. Even the great Willie Mays batted only .274 in his rookie
season. Frank Robinson batted .290 (but with 38 homers).

Spring training in 1956 held an extra measure of fun and exposure
for the young Smiths. Arlene Francis hosted *Home*, an hour-long NBC
television "magazine" show directed toward women viewers, and while
the Cardinals were in Florida, Francis invited Carolyn to appear on the
show and flew her to New York City, Carolyn's first plane trip. Carolyn
and Arlene had a wonderful day shopping along Fifth Avenue the day
before the live show. The human interest side of Carolyn as a young
wife of a young player determined to reach the major-league level was
a popular airing. Hal said his taped appearance in which he explained
the daily routine of ball players was "kinda corny." But it certainly
appealed to the audiences of that era, one of those illustrations that
Americans lived in a "simpler age" perhaps. After this family
excitement and after the exhibition games, the Cardinals returned to
St. Louis for two days of practice at Busch Stadium, the former
Sportsman's Park, on Grand Avenue. Hal was thrilled to see balls lift
off Musial's bat and zoom into the right-field screen or onto the roof of
the "pavilion," familiar landing zones for Musial's shots. Boyer and
Moon launched drives of their own. Pitchers and back-up catchers like
Hal didn't get many swings in the batting cage, before indoor facilities
were installed at ballparks. Most of the practices found Hal down in the
bullpen, catching heat from Mizell and Jackson and McDaniel, all hard
throwers. Hal kept a tiny sponge inside his Rawlings catcher's mitt,

placed just over the bone of his index finger. The sponge softened the
impact only a little. Fastballs from these big, Cardinal pitchers could
tenderize the toughest hand, even if it was still callused from winter
ball. The bare, throwing hand of the catcher is subjected to foul tips
and other abuse. As the season progresses, the major-league catcher
frequently cannot secure a firm, or at least, pain-free grip on the bat.
This problem tends to result in catchers having the lowest batting
average for any position player on the team. Permanently bent fingers
and gnarled hands distinguish catchers from other players. Bullpen
wags scoff at catchers, with their cumbersome chest protectors, shin
guards and face masks—the "tools of ignorance." Slow running is
another result of years of squatting behind the plate. Great catchers
come along once in awhile to break these molds—a Bench, a
McCarver, or a Berra—but such exceptions among those brave-
hearted men who don the "tools of ignorance" only prove the rule.

The club that Hutchinson would field in 1956 seemed strong
enough to contend for the pennant and replace the Brooklyn Dodgers
as the National League's entry in the World Series. Stanky told a
reporter that he would have "managed this club for nothing next year.
That's how good I think it will be." To complement his veterans,
Hutchinson now had the promising newcomers, Hal and Blasingame.
Tom Alston, a tall fielder good with the glove but a light hitter, would
contest Stan Musial for the starting job at first base. Schoendienst was
at second and Alex Grammas, nicknamed the Golden Greek because
of his graceful athleticism, was at short. Boyer had been moved to
third base from centerfield because of an abundance of good
outfielders that included Moon and Virdon. With Brandt on the
roster, the Cardinals had a player with a chance to be the Cardinal's
third straight outfield winner of the NL Rookie of the Year award.
Brandt was a twenty-year-old phenom from Omaha, Nebraska, who
had batted .312 with twelve home runs and 70 RBI's for the Rochester
Red Birds in the AAA International League in 1955. Graceful in the

outfield, Brandt smacked hard line drives and had an innocent, if off-beat, sense of humor. As it happened, Brandt didn't stay long with St. Louis. Instead, the Cards' leftfielder turned out to be Rip Repulski, a holdover from the Cardinals' early 50's "Polish Brigade."[19] The pitching staff had the young flame throwers, along with crafty junk ballers Stu Miller and Harvey Haddix. Ellis Kinder depended on his breaking pitches and guile to get hitters out. At catcher, the Cardinals penciled in Sarni, who had batted .300 in '54 before falling off to .255 in '55. As a 15-year-old, Sarni began his career in 1943 with Los Angeles in the Pacific Coast League. In his eight minor-league years, Sarni had been up and down as a hitter. After making it to St. Louis in 1951, Sarni was returned to Triple A three times for more "seasoning." Finally, the Cardinals thought Sarni ready to take over for Del Rice, their venerable catcher since 1945. The Cardinal brass saw a younger man who could hit .250 or better and decided to trade Rice to Milwaukee. Yet, Rice's long-term replacement turned out to be Hal Smith rather than Sarni. Hal, who was four years younger than Sarni, had a better arm and a gift for settling down pitchers so they wouldn't unravel in big games.

On April 17th, in a night game against Cincinnati at Crosley Field, the Cardinals opened the 1956 season behind Vinegar Bend Mizell. He beat the Reds, 4-2, and Sarni caught the game. However, Hutchinson replaced Schoendienst at second base with Blasingame. It was an ominous sign. Frank Lane was the new Cardinal general manager. Lane, an ex-car salesman, had been hired by owner August Busch to bring a pennant to St. Louis. Lane was the polar opposite to Branch Rickey in his approach to providing players for the ball club. Lane believed in trading for talent, as opposed to developing it in the farm system. He shuffled players in and out at a dizzying pace. For example, forty-five different Cardinals got into the lineup sometime during the 1956 season. Even before Lane arrived, the Cardinal front office had proved that no player's job was safe. This included "ol'

No. 9," Enos "Country" Slaughter, one of the most popular Cardinals of all time. Many fans, who loved Country's hustle on the field,cried when they heard he'd been traded to the Yankees in 1954. Slaughter had achieved Olympian stature among St. Louis fans because of his dash from first to home on a single to right-center in the 1946 World Series against the Red Sox. That play has been analyzed over and over, but the best account of it was written by David Halberstam in his book, *Teammates.* Johnny Pesky, with whom Hal coached at Pittsburgh in 1965, is forever linked with Slaughter in this memorable play. As he rounded third base, Slaughter saw Pesky "drop his arm," as the players say. Slaughter turned on the jets and slid into home, just ahead of Pesky's throw, which was late because of his hesitation. Many fans and virtually all writers believe it was that one play that turned the series in the Cardinals' favor.

The 1946 Cardinal outfield of Slaughter, Terry Moore, and Musial was one of the club's best ever and has remained quite dear to Cardinal fans. The St. Louis *Post Dispatch* ran a photograph of Slaughter weeping as he heard the news of his trade to the Yankees. Casey Stengel had wanted Slaughter because of his tough play and hustle. Slaughter played in three World Series with the Yankees. The Cardinals explained that they had to make room for Wally Moon. In the exchange, they also got Bill Virdon, a promising Yankee outfielder from southern Missouri.

Two weeks into the 1956 season, on a Wednesday night, May 2nd, the Pirates were at Sportsman's Park. Harvey Haddix was on the mound for the Cardinals. In the fifth, Haddix ran into trouble and the Pirates scored three times before McDaniel relieved him. Hal started warming up Larry Jackson, who would be the next pitcher if Hutch needed him. In the bottom of the fifth, the bullpen phone rang. Hutchinson told Walker Cooper to send Hal up to the dugout. Hal arrived from the bullpen looking rather dubious while Brandt, who was pinch-hitting for Virdon, grounded out. Hal said later, "I didn't even know Hutch knew my name. I felt like I should introduce myself." The next batter was Repulski, who got a base hit. "Get up there, Smith," Hutch barked. "Tell the ump that you're batting for McDaniel." Hal strode to the plate carrying Musial's bat, hastily plucked from the bat rack. In those pre-batting helmet days, batters often inserted a plastic liner under their felt caps to protect a little more against wayward fast balls. Hal, who wore a short crew cut, forgot all about the liner and faced his first major-league pitcher with very little insulation for the ol' bean. The Pirate pitcher, Jack McMahan, was an Arkansan from Hot Springs. McMahan threw the rookie pinch-hitter a fast ball and Hal laced it into left-center for a stand-up double while Repulski scored from first base. Hal stood on second, adrenalin pumping. In his first at-bat in the major leagues, he had an extra-base hit and an RBI. Moreover, he started a rally. Following him in the order were Blasingame and Schoendienst. Both reached and, with the bases full, Musial stepped up. The great star drove the ball high over the screen in right field and onto the pavilion roof for a grand slam. The crowd went wild. Hal's heart was pumping as he waited at the plate while "the Man" rounded the bases in that smooth stride. The five runs driven in by Smith and Musial put the Cards in front, but the Pirates came back to tie and the game went into extra innings. The Cards won in the bottom of the tenth after a perfectly executed squeeze bunt by Grammas. Thus, Hal's major-league debut had more to do with offense than defense, but it was a wonderful ending. Now, he finally believed that he belonged and could help the Cardinals. After all, the win put the team in first place.

Two weeks later, Lane traded Grammas to Cincinnati for Chuck Harmon, a back-up third baseman. The trade meant that the Cards had decided that Blasingame could play shortstop. Schoendienst had second base all to himself again. A big change happened at the catcher position, too. On May 6, 1956, four days after Hal's first appearance, a runner collided with Sarni on a play at the plate. The next day, Hal recalled that he "was out in right field shagging balls during batting practice and I saw Hutchinson come walking out toward me. I said, 'Oh, no. I'm going back to Houston.'" Instead, Hutch said, 'You're catching tonight. Go on in and take batting practice with the regular line up.' And last week I didn't even think he knew who I was!" In that May 6 game, which the Cards lost, 5-4, to the Giants, Willie Mays had swiped four bases off the Mizell-Sarni battery. This offensive display by the spectacular Mays convinced Hutch that Hal had to be his starting catcher. He might be able to stop opposing base runners from taking such liberties. Hal thus drew a release from his duties in the bullpen.

The bullpen got its name early in baseball history because the Cincinnati field had what was described as the "bull pen" in foul territory area just beyond first and third base.[20] In the Polo Grounds, the bullpens were carved out of the playing area but stuck so far out in left and right-center that they weren't in anybody's way. Out there, Giants' fans exchanged barbs with the visitors in the bullpen, but the players could exit to the nearby clubhouse to escape the razz and get a sandwich or a smoke. Joe Garagiola once said that "a bullpen is supposed to be a place for warming up pitchers. That's what it is a little bit of the time. Mostly, it's a place for eating peanuts, trading insults with the fans, second-guessing the manager, and picking all kinds of silly all-star teams like the All-Screwball team or the All-Ugly team, or the All-Stack-blowing team."[21]

Hal made his first major-league start on Wednesday May 7, 1956, at Busch Stadium. Not only did Hal hit well in the next month, the Cardinals continued to win. By the end of May, they were still in first place, a game ahead of the Braves. Sportswriter Jack Herman, in a feature article headlined, "Hal Smith Crowding Sarni for No. 1 Job," noted that Hal "didn't break in under the most favorable circumstances, either." That is, he faced Robin Roberts. In his first at-bat against the Phillies' future Hall-of-Famer, Hal ripped a single to center that drove in a run. In the sixth inning, Smith "belted his first homer as a big leaguer, winding up with three RBI's for his debut."[22] Since Carolyn, Sharon, and Sandra were not at his first game (it was a surprise start), Hal repeated the excitement for them as they sat in the stands the next night. He hit a 400-foot drive off of Phillies' right-hander Herm Wehmeier. In an ironic twist, Wehmeier became Hal's battery mate two days later because of a five-player swap engineered by Lane.

Family Misses Smith's First Home Run, But He Encores

ST. LOUIS, Mo.—Hal Smith wore a big smile in the Cardinal's clubhouse, May 8, following the 9 to 1 victory over the Phillies, but the excited rookie catcher still was a bit disappointed—his wife and two small daughters had missed Papa Smiths' first major league home run by just one night.

Wife Carolyn had taken Sandy, 4½ years old, and little Sharon, 1½, to watch the Redbirds beat the Giants the night before. It was chilly, the game lasted 2:47, and the best Pop could do was ground out as a pinch-hitter. It was too cool, May 8, so the three Smith girls took in the game by apartment radio.

So what happens? With Bill Sarni out because of a knee injury, Smith started his first major league game, drove in a run with a sharp single the first time he faced Robin Roberts, then followed with his four-bagger with a man on, giving him three RBIs in his starting debut.

Hal didn't disappoint his family the next night, for he whacked another home run against the Phils.

Hal's auspicious start may have caught some sportswriters by surprise, but Joe Garagiola had been claiming all along that Hal was ready for the major leagues. He said as much in an article that appeared in the April 9, 1956, *Sports Illustrated* special issue on baseball. Garagiola shared the Cardinal broadcasting booth with Harry Caray and Jack Buck and had been a major-league catcher from 1946 to 1954. Garagiola said that what set Hal apart was his cannon arm and daring, "something that you can't teach a kid."

With a tight race in the National League shaping up in 1956, Lane decided to deal with the Giants for players who could help the Cardinals win a pennant. Lane was convinced that Hal "had a fine future," only he didn't say with which club. A blockbuster trade soon sent Sarni to the New York Giants, leaving the starting catcher job to Hal, who thought to himself, "They're giving me every chance to make good."

The trouble that fans and sportswriters had with that trade concerned another player Lane included in the nine-player package deal—Schoendienst. The great second baseman, along with promising outfielder Brandt, pitcher Dick Littlefield, and infielder Bobby Stephenson, completed the list of those Cardinals going to New York in exchange for Alvin Dark, Whitey Lockman, catcher Ray Katt, and pitcher Don Liddle. Schoendienst in later years reflected that he didn't want to be traded. "One day," he said, "Stan came out walking slowly with head down to the car where Lil and Mary and I waited. 'Red,' Stan murmured, 'they want to trade me.' Later, after we dropped them off— we lived around the corner from them in south St. Louis—it dawned on me that I might be on Lane's trade list, too. And, I was."[23]

Though Dark had a glittering background and had played in three World Series, the Cardinals did not seem that much improved by the trade and finished the season in fourth place with a won-loss percentage of just under .500. But Dark hit .290 after the trade, enough so that the Cardinals wanted to keep him as their shortstop for the next season. Over the winter, Lane traded Lockman back to the Giants for Hoyt Wilhelm, while the Giants traded Schoendienst to Milwaukee for three players. Many baseball men believed that when the Braves' acquired Schoendienst—a salty, knowledgeable competitor—the final piece of the championship puzzle was found for Milwaukee. With Red on board, the Braves put together back-to-back National League championship seasons. In 1961, Schoendienst returned to St. Louis as a part-time player. He was elected to Baseball's

Hall of Fame in 1989. Sarni finished out the 1956 season with the Giants, his last year in the majors. He had a mild heart attack, which ended his playing days. Out of baseball, Sarni moved back to St. Louis and became a successful stockbroker. Brandt batted .291 for the Giants, one point higher than Frank Robinson's average for 1956. Sportswriters selected Robinson, not Brandt, as the Rookie of the Year. The U.S. Army, however, selected Brandt. He was drafted in the winter of 1956 and spent the next two years at Fort Chaffee, Arkansas, just outside Hal's hometown of Barling.

Many Cardinal fans, then and now, still want to know why Lane traded Schoendienst. Hal didn't know either but, he recalled, "Frank Lane was the general manager and Frank Lane traded everybody. He even traded managers one time." That was true. Two-thirds of the way through the 1960 season, Lane was at Cleveland. He sent his manager, Joe Gordon, to Detroit in exchange for their manager, Jimmy Dykes. With Detroit, Gordon won 26 and lost 31. At Cleveland, new manager Dykes went 26 and 32. You can't make up these kind of stories!

For road trips to the east coast, the Cardinals traveled on trains. In New York, players stayed two to the room in downtown hotels like the Waldorf. Back then, players wore a jacket and tie and typically had on a fedora when checking in. Hal and his roommate, Repulski, had a routine of eating a late breakfast or early lunch in the hotel dining room, then catching a cab to the ballpark. Hal usually stayed in at night while on the road. He arose fresh and arrived at the ball park early. On June 19th, he and Repulski arrived at Ebbets Field four hours before the game. Hal caught a jewel of a game that day, hurled by the old master, Murray Dickson. The line score read:

St Louis	4	0	0	0	0	0	2	0	0	–	6	9
Brooklyn	0	0	0	0	0	0	0	0	0	–	0	3

This win over the Dodgers pulled the Cards into a first-place tie with Cincinnati. Mizell lost to the Dodgers the next day and the

Cardinals dropped all the way to fourth place in the standings. They would stay there for the rest of the season.

In 1956, Cincinnati had a powerful team that could blow more than their stacks. They had Frank Robinson, who hit 39 home runs in his first season. They had Gus Bell and Ed Bailey. They had left-handed slugger Ted Kluszewski, on his way to hitting 35 dingers that year. Hal remembered that "you could not throw a fast ball by him. You could throw him change-ups and he'd chase them all day long." He recalled a story he'd heard when the Reds were playing Brooklyn with Kluszewski at the plate. "Hodges, the first baseman, went over to the pitcher, Preacher Roe, and said 'Preacher, why don't you pitch this guy outside and let him hit out to left field.' Then Cox, the third baseman, came in and said, 'Preacher, why don't you pitch him inside and let him pull that ball.' So, Preach told 'em, 'I'll just throw it up there and we'll all scatter!' Kluszewski was a strong guy. He had a couple of brothers who were as big and Ted said, 'when we go in, we fill up a room pretty quick.' That's when Cincinnati started cutting the shirts off at the shoulder 'cause they couldn't get Kluszewski's arms in the sleeves."

Kluszewski at 6-2, 225 pounds exuded strength and looked huge in his day. But in comparison, modern home run hitters like Frank Thomas (6-5, 255) or Mark McGwire (6-5, 255) are bigger.

There were some rarities for the Cards in the '56 season. They pulled off two triple plays, both coming with the bases loaded and both starting with line drives to the first baseman—Moon in one case, Musial in the other. On the down side, they set a major-league record when *four* Cardinals, Hal and Brandt included, struck out in *one inning* against the Cubs.[24] They stunk against the champion Dodgers, and against Milwaukee and Cincinnati. These lopsided results against the contenders cost the Cards dearly in 1956. Their 76-78 record endangered Hutchinson's job, although the Cards competed hard under his leadership. The Brooklyn Dodgers won the NL despite frequent injuries to their superstar Jackie Robinson. Handsome

Ransom Jackson from Little Rock, Arkansas, often substituted at third base for Robinson, who retired after the 1956 season. In a subway series, the Yankees beat the Brooklyn Dodgers four games to three in the World Series.[25]

Though the Cardinals finished in the middle of the eight-team league, Hal had what baseball men like to call "a good year." The Cards had found a regular catcher. Hal played in 75 games, almost double that of any other catcher on the roster, and hit .282 with five home runs and 23 RBIs. He even had a stolen base. Moreover, he had developed excellent relationships, both on and off the field, with Cardinal pitchers McDaniel and Dickson. He had a friendship with Jackson that dated to their Omaha days and, of course, with Wilmer Mizell, the left-hander who posted a 14-14 mark in 1956 and was considered the "stopper" on the staff. Another promising young pitcher, Bob Blaylock from Muldrow, Oklahoma, was well known to Hal. In the off-season, Blaylock attended Fort Smith Junior College, where he was the leading scorer on the Lions' basketball team. Bob was no relation to Marvin Blaylock of the Phillies. Like Marvin, however, he had a large following in Fort Smith. Fans marveled at his athletic ability. At 6-1, he could easily dunk a basketball and he had that major-league caliber fastball. At the time of his call-up on July 22, 1956, he was with Rochester in the International League and had posted a 9-4 record with a 1.67 ERA. Blaylock started six games for the '56 Cardinals.

The first of those was against the Dodgers, who were in St. Louis for a Sunday doubleheader in Busch Stadium. Blaylock, with Hal behind the plate, was pitted against Dodger ace, Carl Erskine. In the first inning, the Dodgers loaded the bases with nobody out. Over KMOX, Harry Caray described the scene as Hal went out to settle down his hometown battery mate. Those listening to the broadcast in Arkansas held their breaths. Whatever Hal told Blaylock, it seemed to work for the moment. Blaylock got out of the jam without Brooklyn scoring and went on to complete the game. He lost, 5-3, but proved that he could pitch in the majors. Blaylock picked up his first major-league win four days later against the Phillies in Philadelphia.

Earlier in the season, on Sunday, July 15, the Phillies were in St. Louis for a doubleheader. Hal's American Legion coach, Clarence Higgins, was in the stands to watch him and the Cardinals take on the Phillies, who had Fort Smith native Marvin Blaylock at first base. Thus, Higgins was treated to seeing two of his former American Legion players take the field in a major-league game. Blaylock batted second in the Phillies' order and got two hits that game to raise his BA to .268. Hal batted eighth in the line-up and went one for three, raising his batting average to .328, *highest of the starters on either team*. More than 18,000 fans attended this July doubleheader that put the Cardinals over the one-million attendance mark for the year—third best in the league. A serious fan shortage plagued the New York Giants in '56. Games at the Polo Grounds averaged only 8,171 paying customers and season attendance would slip to 629,000. It had been two years since the Giants' four-game World Series sweep over the Cleveland Indians (highlighted by the sensational catch by Willie Mays of a drive off the bat of Vic Wertz some 500 feet from home plate in that cavernous centerfield). On June 29, 1954, 51,464 fans had jammed the Polo Grounds for a Tuesday night game with the Brooklyn Dodgers. The Giants won, 4-3, in thirteen innings. More than 100,000 filled the seats for that three-game series. Those were heady days, but it is not far from the penthouse to the outhouse, a politician once remarked. Giants' attendance dropped so quickly that the stunned owners took out newspaper ads warning "fair weather" fans that the franchise was in trouble. Despite the undertones of this announcement, New Yorkers could not imagine that Mays and company would pull up stakes as the Boston Braves and St. Louis Browns had done previously. Few could dream that the NL team would soon be playing home games in California some 3,000 miles west of New York. Yogi Berra said, "that if people didn't want to come out to the ball park, nobody's going to stop them!" Ironically, nobody did stop those people who didn't want to come out to the Giants' games and the games themselves stopped, at least in the National League in New York. People who didn't come out caused a seismic change in the game of baseball and consequently in the country itself.

In a smaller matter, Cards' GM Lane acquired Bobby Del Greco, who would soon be a regular in the Cardinals' lineup. Lane had been impressed with Del Greco after seeing him play one game at Pittsburgh. Del Greco made a sensational catch in centerfield and rapped two long hits. It may have been his best game ever and Lane happened to be there and decided to trade Virdon for Del Greco. For good measure, Lane threw in Dick Littlefield, the pitcher who had just unpacked his bags after coming to St. Louis in the big trade with the Giants. Without Virdon, Hutchinson either had to play the aging Lockman or put Del Greco in centerfield, which is what he did. Del Greco responded by hitting a dismal .214. "He couldn't hit me if I walked across the middle of the plate," Hal once remarked.

Since Hal was now a regular in the lineup, even more people in Arkansas were attracted to St. Louis and became Cardinal fans. The broadcasts of Harry Caray had long been a staple in north Arkansas radio stations. Fort Smith's senior station, KFPW, had its studio in the Goldman Hotel and carried every Cardinal game. Caray was an entertaining announcer with a distinctive style. His stock of pet phrases and his pitch for Greisedick Brothers beer were as familiar to listeners in this area as any voices on radio, including those of *Lum and Abner*. In January of 1954, Caray and big band singer Phil Regan visited Fort Smith and put in an appearance at the Boys Club. The trip was part of a promotional tour known as the Cardinal Caravan. Entering the Boys Club building, Caray warmly greeted Hal, who was working at the Boys Club that winter. Awaiting the announcer, hundreds of boys sat spell-bound on the gym floor, eager to hear

Caray's magic words. After Regan's songs and the Caravan's baseball anecdotes, Caray did not disappoint those boys. He recreated an exciting finish to a Cardinal game in which Stan Musial hit a home run to beat the Dodgers. With his trademark, "it might be, it could be, IT IS a home run!" call, Caray thrilled the youngsters, one of whom was Buddy Blair. Blair later became a state senator of considerable influence in the Arkansas General Assembly. Blair said that his greatest boyhood memory was of Harry Caray and his visit to Fort Smith. A twelve-year old boy who traveled in from the edge of town for this great occasion missed his bus afterward and started the long walk home. He remembered that Hal Smith generously offered to go out of his way and give him a ride. For that boy, Jim King, the act further affirmed Hal as his hero. King played ten years in the NBA, mostly with the Los Angeles Lakers, and was a 1968 NBA All-Star game selection.

With Hal generating local interest, Caray called the action over a large network of AM stations with his gifted side-kicks in the broadcast booth, Joe Garagiola and Jack Buck. The Cardinals became entrenched as the favorite team of Arkansans. The starting Cardinal catcher from Barling gave a personal hello to many local fans who traveled to St. Louis. Ted Skokos, a Fort Smith dentist, took his large family to St. Louis to attend a Cardinal series. Skokos contacted Hal and asked for one enormous favor. Could Hal arrange for him to shake hands with Stan Musial? Hal took Doc Skokos through the player's entrance and into the runway of the dugout. Skokos stood anxiously while Smith went out to find the Cardinal great. Soon, Hal returned with "the Man" in tow. It was a moment that Skokos recalled with great delight fifty years later. "I had played prep basketball against Musial in the Pittsburgh area and wondered if he remembered those games. He did," exulted Skokos. "I was pretty good in those days, but Musial was just a great athlete. I'm glad that he chose baseball for his career." Musial signed with St. Louis as a 17-year-old, left-handed pitcher. Like Boyer, he made the switch to a position player because of the greatness of his bat. One day, as Musial sat in front of his locker before changing from street clothes into his uniform, Hal remembered this prophetic quote. Musial said, "I *know* I'm going to get two hits today!" Hal was thinking, "Boy, I wish I *knew* that."

A photograph taken at Busch Stadium in1956 depicts Hal with a group of young fans from Fort Smith. It is easy to determine the year of this photograph because of Hal's unique Cardinal uniform. The logo with the Redbirds facing each other along a baseball bat is missing. Lane approved of the sans bird design, but it only lasted for one year. Fans hounded the general manager until the Redbirds re-appeared the next spring, once again perched atop the bat.

Caray remembered Hal and his hometown. One night, Hal's roommate, Rip Repulski, hit a game- winning homer. Caray heightened the enjoyment in Rip's Wisconsin hometown by announcing that "they are dancing in the streets of Ripon!" A couple of weeks later, Hal hit a similarly dramatic home run and Caray burst out with, "Now they're dancing in the streets of Barling!" They were indeed dancing in Barling, and Fort Smith as well, after that home run. By most accounts, it was Caray who gave Hal the nickname of "Barling Darling." That was the fourth nickname pinned on Harold Raymond Smith. First, there was "Smitty," from his American Legion days in Fort Smith. Then, there was Cura, from the Mexican League. As he progressed in baseball, sportswriters shortened Harold to Hal. Most people today know him as Hal. The last nickname created a slight identity problem because another Hal Smith—Harold Wayne Smith—was playing in the major leagues at the same time.

Hal Smith's batting average plummeted fifty points in the last two months of the 1956 season. Major-league pitchers know how to "get a book" on young hitters. Seemingly endless road trips and double-headers take their toll, especially on catchers, in the long season. Hal ended up with a .282 batting average, second among NL catchers to

Ed Bailey of the Reds at .300. Even with a successful year, Hal had a lot riding on the next season and decided to continue playing over the winter. Lane helped him land a position on a Cuban team. This didn't cost the Cardinals anything at all, but the miserly Lane deducted Hal's winter ball salary from what he planned to offer him on next year's contract with the Cardinals!

Cuba had a winter league that involved no travel for its four teams. Cuba offered a resort climate, a family atmosphere and keen baseball competition. Hal wanted to go and would be joined by friends Bob Blaylock and Wilmer Mizell. Hal remembered how winter play in Mexico had sharpened his batting eye for the 1955 season at Houston. It would work for his next major-league season, too.

One young player in the majors did not to go to Cuba or anywhere else to play winter ball. He only wanted to relax and bask in his accomplishments of the past summer. That player was Mickey Mantle. He had such a great year that he later co-wrote a book entitled *1956*, in which he declared it to be his favorite year of all.[26] Mantle had helped the Yankees win the '56 World Series. During the season, he had hit .353 to lead the league. He had blasted, and in his case that word is not mere hyperbole, 52 home runs and 132 RBIs to lead the league. For good measure, he scored 132 runs and led the American League in that department, too. He was named the Most Valuable Player. No wonder he thought so much of 1956! He was twenty-five years old, the same age as Hal, who relished 1956 as well.

8

Cuba

In September of 1956, after his first season in the major leagues, Hal and Carolyn bought a house in Florissant, a suburb of St. Louis. They moved in at 2370 Hudson Drive, arranged the furniture, and relaxed in their new home for all of five days. Then, they loaded up their daughters—six-year-old Sandra and three-year-old Sharon— and all the luggage their Ford Fairlane could carry and set out for the Florida Keys. Their neighbors in the Hathaway Manor development took turns parking their cars in the Smith driveway to make it look like someone was home. Hal and his family would be away for four months of winter baseball in Cuba, where Lane had recommended him to Club Marianao in the Cuban League. Marianao was a middle class, baseball-crazy suburb west of Havana and a charter member of the Cuban Professional League. The team won the first Cuban League championship in 1922-23. By now, Club Marianao had not won a pennant since the 1936-37 season and its legacy for fans was fourteen years of disappointment. The owners, Dr. Alfredo Pequeno and Jose Rodriguez, signed Hal for $1,000 per month for the four-month Cuban baseball season. The St. Louis Cardinals had paid Hal the major-league minimum salary of $6,000 in 1956. That came to $500 a

month. He would make twice as much per game in Cuba. Club
Marianao, the Tigres, were hungry and had signed one of baseball's
premium players, Orestes "Minnie" Minoso, a native of Havana.
Minoso had hit .316 for the White Sox in the 1956 season and led the
American League in triples.

From Key West, the Smith family drove the car onto a ferry boat
and headed for the "Pearl of the Antilles," ninety miles away over a
choppy sea. At the time, Fulgenco Batista ruled Cuba by relying on
muscle and his control over the army. Cabarets and dinner clubs with
floor shows and marvelous entertainment attracted the world's
"glitterati" and chunks of tourist dollars, but the Batista government
fretted, more than a little nervous about its hold on the island.
Rebellion was in the air and on the mind and lips of the populace.
Sugar prices had plummeted in the past few years, bringing financial
hardship to Cuba's working classes. Fidel Castro, a former law student
and sometime baseball pitcher, was the large, spoiled son of a sugar
plantation owner. He plotted to overthrow the Batista regime from his
hideaway in the Sierra Maestre Mountains in the eastern part of the
large island. Castro's message did not persuade many students at the
University of Havana. They opposed Batista but had different
objectives and a different agenda for democracy. Campus radicals
sought to bring about a "free Cuba" with their continuous schemes to
assassinate President Batista.

At age 29, Castro had returned to Cuba from his Mexican exile
at the head of an "invasion" which landed in what is now Granma
province in eastern Cuba in October of 1956. It was the same month
that Hal and his family arrived in Havana harbor. The invasion
failed to inspire the peasants and Castro's actual following was small.
He had maybe 140 guerrillas in his camp but Castro's prospects
improved after the addition of Argentine Marxist and medical
doctor, Ernesto "Che" Guevara to his rag-tag band of
revolutionaries. Guevara had organizational skills and a clear

revolutionary agenda, two elements sorely lacking in the young and boisterous Fidel, who mainly brought the charisma.

Castro's success, which lay three years down the road, was hard to envision in 1956. The Batista government felt more pressure and received more threats of violence in the capital from the student radicals. During his stay in Cuba, Hal heard the unrest and saw evidence of it as he passed sandbagged pillboxes on the way to the ballpark. Troops in combat attire, armed with submachine guns, watched crowds carefully from atop the stadium roof. Still, the revolution seemed to be only a vague threat. Batista had guns, troops, the American mafia, and support from the Eisenhower administration and other Latin American dictatorial governments.

Since 1878, when one of the first baseball games was played at Havana's Palmar del Junco stadium, the game had become ingrained in Cuban society. Baseball and politics were passionate topics of conversation in Cuba, especially during the four-month "winter season," when major leaguers joined Latinos to field high-powered teams. When the Havana Sugar Kings participated in the AAA International League, a sports writer described the Cuban fan as "a complete extrovert and does everything but get right [down on the field and] into the ball game."[27] The fire of Latino baseball leapt from Cuba to Puerto Rico and to the Dominican Republic. On these islands of the Greater Antilles, beisbol became the dominant sport. Soccer soaked into most Latin American cultures, but in these islands, youngsters and older fans lived and breathed baseball. Now, the people of Venezuela, Panama, and Mexico share their passion for soccer with a rising passion for baseball.

The rivalry between nationalities over baseball grew fierce. Fans needed a method of settling arguments and establishing concrete bragging rights, thus the *raison d'être* for the Caribbean World Series. Moreover, it had to be played in Havana, where else? The CWS would be unique in that it would feature teams from four countries—Cuba,

Puerto Rico, Venezuela, and Panama. Each would send its best professional team to compete for the title of Baseball King of the Caribbean. The Cuban League champion, Almendares, had won the initial series in 1949, led by the home runs of Giants' African-American star Monte Irvin. By 1957, Puerto Rico had emerged as a baseball power and won four Caribbean World Series. One Puerto Rico team alone, Santurce, had won three of those, matching the Havana club's total of three. It didn't hurt that Santurce had American star Roberto Clemente. For good measure, Santurce once had Clemente *and* Willie Mays together in the same outfield.

Obviously, the Marianao Tigres had their work cut out for them in order to satisfy Dr. Pegueno's dream. First, they had to win the Cuban Professional League and then, as Cuba's representative, win the Caribbean World Series. A tall order, indeed, but with Hal catching and power pitchers Jim Bunning and Bill Werle tossing darts, they did just that! Hal played well over the four-month season and, of course, so did Minnie Minoso.

It didn't hurt that the Tigres had Bunning. Hal said he "was tough on right-handed hitters and you really had to make up your mind to stay in the batter's box because he could get you out of there real quick." Bunning's four months in Cuba obviously got him in gear because the right-hander went on to a 20-8 year with Detroit in 1957. It was his second year in the majors and the best year of his sparkling career. Hal and Bunning established a good rapport in Cuba. Whenever the Cardinals played Detroit in spring training, Hal remembers how Bunning, his old Marianao buddy, "always laughed when he struck me out. Oooh, yeah. It was a lot more fun *catching* him!"[28] Bunning, now a United States Senator from Kentucky, had 182 strike-outs in 1957 and was second to Early Wynn in the American League. Jim Bouton wrote that Ted Williams used to imagine it was Bunning's pitch coming at him during batting practice and would psyche himself up by snarling: "OK, Bunning. You're not going to come in here with that little-shit slider!" Although he is known as a conservative in Congress, Bunning was one of the first and most fervent supporters of the baseball players' union at a time when the idea seemed radical to most observers and even a few players.[29]

Playing in the Cuban League in 1957 differed for Hal from the winter ball in Mexico in 1954-55. For one thing, Hal faced Cuban pitchers like Chico Carrasquel and Camilo Pascual, who compiled excellent records in the major leagues. Scouts knew that the Latino players were as good as players anywhere. Like African-American players, the Latinos offered a new pool of talented and hungry young players for the major leagues. In Mexico, teams traveled sometimes long distances to play games against league rivals on sparsely maintained fields. In Cuba, all games were played at the same well-groomed stadium. It was a short ride in Hal's Fairlane from the pleasant cottage he and Carolyn rented for their four-month stay in the Caribbean. In Cuba, the games started as late as 9 or 10 p.m. On off-days, Hal and Carolyn would take their girls on sight-seeing trips to old Havana. At the harbor where Moro Castle stood, the wreckage of the U.S.S. *Maine* sat at the bottom of the bay. The U.S.S. *Enterprise* aircraft carrier often anchored in the harbor and was a comforting sight to Carolyn.

Havana had plenty of nightlife, like the extravagant floor shows at the Tropicana Cabaret, and it attracted lots of fans and some players after the games. As usual, Hal just went out to eat, sometimes at a small family café with an outside veranda that served black beans and rice. Carolyn and the girls liked going there, too. Night life was not Hal's forte. He "let the other people do that. I'd head back to the house." Minoso, a fun-loving guy, was friendly to Hal, as he was to everybody on the team. Hal practiced his Spanish, which was mostly "si and no," with Minnie and other Cubans. As long as the topic was baseball, he could mostly understand. A regular delivery man, "a real baseball nut," used to stand on the front porch and talk with Hal in

Spanish for long periods about the previous night's game. Carolyn was amused because of "how much Hal would just stand there and try to talk to the guy! Hal would name names and would tell the delivery guy that he got two base hits or a base hit or whatever."

Even though it was the Cuban winter, the weather was warm and the Smith family slept with the screened windows open. They experienced no hurricanes but a tropical disturbance raised waves high enough to be seen from their cottage near the beach. Sometimes, Carolyn would take the kids to the water's edge, where they stood and watched the ocean come in and peer longingly toward Florida. In those days, overseas telephone calls were not easy to make. Typically, it took an hour or so to get a call through. At Christmas, Hal and his family put up a little tree and decorated it. Marianao houses were all decorated, some in a big way, for the holidays.

Some of the fascinations of Cuban life—rum drinks and the famous cigars—eluded Hal, the family man. He had no bad habits it seemed, except for baseball. On off-days, Tigre manager Napoleon Reyes, a former New York Giant third baseman, might schedule a practice. Hal got a chance to bat against Cardinal pitchers, too. Bob Blaylock and Billy Muffett were playing for Havana. To his great delight, Hal collected a few hits off of his St. Louis teammates. Marianao clinched the Cuban League pennant with a win over the Havana team—Jim Bunning over Bob Blaylock. Hal still smiles at the thought.

At the end of January, the Caribbean World Series began in Havana. Over a ten-day period, the Cuban representative, Marianao, posted five wins and lost one game to claim the championship. Hal, Bunning, and Minoso played quite well in the series, but the Most Valuable Player award for the 1957 Caribbean World Series went to teammate, Solly Drake, a centerfielder. Born Solomon Louis Drake in Little Rock, Arkansas, in 1930, Drake was an African-American who never got the chance to join the all-white Little Rock Doughboys. In 1956, Drake had played in 65 games with the Cubs and batted .256

with two home runs. The Cubs' management thought winter baseball experience might develop the young player into a true major leaguer. Despite his great winter season with Marianao, however, the Cubs released Drake in 1957 and he finished his baseball career in the minors. Perhaps the high-water mark of Solly Drake's career *was* that 1957 CWS, though he did have a fine 1958 season with Montreal in the International League. He batted .301 with nine home runs and 68 RBI's from the lead-off position. Drake had another shot at the big leagues with the Dodgers in 1959. They thought his great speed was just what they needed to help track down drives in the spacious Coliseum centerfield. He was considered as the replacement for Duke Snider, who would be moved to right field. Nine games into the season, however, the Dodgers traded Drake to the Phillies and Walter Alston put tall, skinny Don Demeter in center. Hal recalled that Drake's blazing speed led the team to a good series. Drake always seemed to be on base, waiting for Minoso or Hal to drive him in.[30]

Dr. Pequeno and the Marianao fans were ecstatic about the team's great baseball achievement. Hal remembered Pequeno as being a quiet man who stayed in the background. Once, he made a trip to St. Louis to visit Hal. After that, however, Hal never saw him again. He does not know what happened to the doctor after the revolution, which thrust Castro into power on January 9, 1959. The 1960 Caribbean World Series was the last in which Cuba participated. The Castro regime eliminated professional baseball and the CWS ended, at least, for a decade. In 1970, it was revived by three original members, plus the Dominican Republic. Cuba still does not participate.

Marianao, under manager Reyes, would repeat as Caribbean World Series champion in 1958 without Hal's help. By then, he was finished with winter baseball. It was the last time a Cuban team won the series.

Carolyn, who had wistfully watched the ferry boat pull out from its berth bound for Key West many times during that winter season, finally was able to board it herself with Hal and the children. It was mid-February of 1957 and they were headed home. Hal drove the Fairlane up the 250-mile-long chain of small Florida islands on U.S. 1 to Miami, then across the peninsula of Florida and from there on to St. Louis. Hal had only a few days free before he was to report to St. Petersburg for spring training. He was, nevertheless, curiously refreshed. He was mentally and physically prepared to nail down the job as the starting catcher for the St. Louis Cardinals. Just like his first winter baseball season, he had reached new levels as a hitter and catcher. The next year, the Marianao fans and the owner fretted about their chances because they were not able to re-sign two key players to the club—Jim Bunning and Hal Smith.[31]

Now, Hal felt ready for the National League and its demanding fans. The upcoming season, 1957, would be Hal's best with the bat and would earn him a spot on the NL All-Star team, a high honor for a second-year man. He would become a long-term, stabilizing force and hold his job for five straight years—the longest term of any Cardinal catcher since Del Rice.

9

Fighting for the NL Pennant

Big Fred Hutchinson came to spring training ready to work and that meant he was ready to work his players, too. The Cardinals were hungry. Since having won NL pennants and World Series championships in each decade of the 20's, 30's, and 40's, the Cards had come up short in the fifties. It was a tragic dearth for the team that comes closest to the New York Yankees in winning tradition in all of major-league baseball. In fact, the Cardinals hold a 3-2 edge in World Series play with the Yankees. The 1926 World Series, which may have been one of the grandest and most dramatic of all, ended with Babe Ruth being thrown out while trying to steal second base. That last out in the seventh game sealed the 3-2 Cards' win and gave Grover Cleveland Alexander a save to go with his two wins in the series. It was Gehrig's first full year in the majors and, in the World Series, he had batted .346.

Despite such a heady, all-time record, the Cards had little to show for their efforts in the fifties. It was a trying time for St. Louis' other major-league team, the Browns, and part of this involved simple market economics. The American League Browns shared their stadium with the Cardinals in the major leagues' smallest city to have two teams. The Browns had slipped in the league standings each year since their 1944 war-time championship. They had lost to their National League counterpart, the Cardinals, in the only World Series ever played at Sportsman's Park on Grand Avenue. The Browns finished in seventh place in 1950 and dropped into the cellar the next year when Bill Veeck (as in wreck) purchased the team. In 1948, Veeck had put together an excellent team at Cleveland while helping set a major-league attendance record of two million. To manage his newly acquired Browns, Veeck brought in Rogers Hornsby but replaced him in '52 and '53 with Marty Marion. Neither of these St. Louis baseball legends could turn the club around, nor could the exploits of iconic pitcher, Leroy Robert "Satchel" Paige. The 45-year old Paige had a winning record in 1952, going 12-10 with an ERA of 3.07 and 10 saves. Veeck signed a 3-7, 65-pound midget, Eddie Gaedel, who wore No.1/8 on his jersey. Despite such efforts, the Browns attracted less than 300,000, about 3,100 paying fans per game, and lost their final game of the season to make their record 54-100 in 1953. A group of Baltimore businessmen bought the team and called it the Orioles. The next year, the Baltimore Orioles lost a hundred games, too, but did so in front of a million fans. In St. Louis, the Browns played in "Busch Stadium," the new name of old Sportsman's Park. The management never bothered to change the name on the tickets. Still, the Browns had left some good memories in St. Louis. Browns' pitcher Ned Garner was quoted as saying that Browns' fans never booed the players. "They wouldn't dare," he said. "We outnumbered them!" Some of the few Browns' fans may have remembered seeing the Yankees, with Lou Gehrig and Babe Ruth, play in Sportsman's Park. It was there that Gehrig broke the existing record of 843 for consecutive games played by a major-leaguer. By the end of his career, he would push that record to 2,113, a mark eventually surpassed by Baltimore Oriole Cal Ripken, Jr. One day in St. Louis, Ruth homered in his first two at-bats. In his third trip to the plate, a wary pitcher gave the big lefty an intentional walk. In his next at-bat, Ruth batted right-handed.

Managers like Fred Hutchinson probably would not have been amused at Ruth's light-hearted antics. Hutch didn't believe humor belonged on the field, although it might be shared in private with teammates. When the players were winning and in a good mood, they liked to mimic each other and kid around, but around Hutchinson players limited the horseplay. All signed autographs patiently and wore their pants bloused just below the knee. The uniforms had numbers but no names. The players dressed conservatively in sports coats on road trips and usually traveled in the company of their roommate. The room pairings were assigned by the traveling secretary. There were no "boom boxes" or personal trainers in the locker room. When music was played, it was most often the country-and-western songs of Porter Wagoner, Lloyd Price, Ernest Tubb, or Patsy Cline. It was a simpler time. Eisenhower threw out the first ball in 1957. Elvis had just switched from Sun Records to RCA, where he recorded "Heartbreak Hotel." Ford and GMC were marketing their brand new sports cars, the Thunderbird and the Corvette.

Approaching the new season, Hutch and his coaches were sure they had improved the Cardinal lineup. Bobby Del Greco, who had hit .202 in the Cuban League that winter, was gone. Bobby Gene Smith, just off an outstanding year in Houston, might be a candidate for the Rookie of the Year award. If he won, it would be the third in four years for the Cardinal outfield. Ken Boyer was moved to third base and Musial to first, with Wally Moon stationed in left and veteran power-hitter Del Ennis looming in right. The defense up the middle looked good, anchored by Bobby Gene Smith in center. Hal was behind the plate. Blasingame and Dark provided a strong combo at second and short and insured that the Cardinal defense showed strength up the middle. Hutchinson told St. Louis sportswriters that this team could win the National League pennant in 1957.

Because major-league baseball recognizes the Cincinnati Redlegs as the historic first professional ball club, the commissioner granted that franchise the permanent privilege of playing the major-league season's first game. So, St. Louis and Cincinnati opened the 1957 season at Crosley Field on April 16th. The Cards started big Herm Wehmeier. For the Reds, it was Johnny Klippstein, who tossed warm-up pitches to his catcher Ed "Strawberry Plains" Bailey while Hutchinson and Reds manager Birdie Tebbetts gave their line-ups to umpire Jock O'Conlin, who always wore a bow tie.

In the first inning, before 32,554 fans, Dark doubled with one out. Musial, playing first and hitting third, lined a double to deep right-center to score Dark. Klippstein got out of that inning but the Cardinals scored in the third, fourth, and sixth innings to seize a commanding 8-2 lead. Musial was four for four. Hal went two for five with two runs scored and one RBI. Blasingame stole a base. The Reds didn't attempt a steal. The Cardinals pounded out seventeen hits and scored thirteen runs. Hal made a sliding catch of a foul ball in front of the Cincinnati dugout. The play reinforced the respect that Tebbetts, a former catcher, had for Hal's defensive skills. Tebbetts once told Hutch that "the little buzzard reminded him of one of Knute Rockne's watch charm guards at Notre Dame, both in compact size and in spirit."[32] Amidst happy bantering with their "little buzzard," and while munching on sandwiches, the Cardinals packed their gear. Later in the evening, they boarded a train for St. Louis. After an off-day, they played the Cubs in their second game of the season. Hutchinson stayed with the same lineup but got totally different results. Although the '57 Cubs spent most of the season mired in the second division, they did have the great Ernie Banks in their lineup. Banks doubled twice and scored three runs while Cub starter Moe Drabowsky baffled Card hitters. Of the four Cardinal hits, Hal had two of them, but committed one of his rare errors to take some luster off the base hits. A William Schmidt sinker got by Hal, allowing Banks to score from third.

In the next day's game, Hal grounded into a double play in the second inning. Hutch benched Hal, who had injured his hand. For the next ten days, Hal sat out. He and the weather were equally miserable. When it wasn't raining, Hal warmed up relievers in the bullpen as Hobie Landrith and Walker Cooper shared the catcher position. Hutch put Hal back into the lineup at Forbes Field in Pittsburgh on April 30 to catch curve-baller Sam Jones, who pitched a terrific game against Luis Arroyo. The Cards, feasting on a monumental 425-foot-home run by Wally Moon, led 5-0 going into the bottom of the ninth. Three straight hits by Roberto Clemente, Dick Groat, and Frank Thomas ended Jones' outing. Hutch brought in Hoyt Wilhelm, who eventually made it to the Hall of Fame on the mastery of his knuckleball. Wilhelm got Bill Mazeroski to hit into a double play but the Pirates still were not finished. Freeze singled and Virdon hit one off the wall. He scored on an error by Dark and the game was tied at five. The Cardinals changed pitchers and got out of the inning. Hal stayed in to catch the rest of the game, which was won in the 13th on a Musial home run. It was his second of the season and came off the Pirates' ace reliever, Elroy Face. Hal, happy that the team was back to .500, slept well in his Pullman berth while the train sped through the nippy Allegheny night en route to New York City's Grand Central Station.

During road trips in those days, players were responsible for their own transportation from their hotels to the ball parks. On the second day of May, Hal and his roommate, Mizell, stepped outside the Biltmore Hotel near Grand Central Station and hailed a Yellow cab. To get to Brooklyn, one had to negotiate the streets of what one sportswriter called "the seethingest metropolis in the world." The previous year, Cards' reliever Ellis Kinder, who was from Atkins, Arkansas, decided to catch the subway out to Ebbets Field. He finally made it to the ballpark in a cab just as the 8 p.m. game started. He'd boarded the wrong train and got hopelessly lost.[33] Hal wanted to arrive in plenty of time because he anticipated being in the line-up that night and getting a chance to bat against lefty Johnny Podres. Podres had won two for Brooklyn in the 1955 World Series, including a shut-out of the Yankees in Game 7 for which he had been named the MVP. Hutchinson sent his big right-hander, Wehmeier, up against Podres in this first meeting of the season between the rival clubs. Wehmeier had been acquired by Lane, but sportswriters couldn't figure out why. Wehmeier had a career record of 0-14 against the Cardinals. Against the Dodgers, he did well enough but the game went fifteen innings, lasting four hours and 55 minutes. Larry Jackson relieved and got the win, 3-2. The Cards showed they could play tough in the Big Apple against the National League champs. Junior Gilliam, the base-stealing threat, never reached base, so Hal didn't get a chance to cut him down.

On the next day, the Dodgers turned it around as 14,000 fans at Jersey City's Roosevelt Stadium saw Don Newcombe pitch a five-hit, shut-out. Hal got one of the hits but the Cards were unable to put a scoring inning together against the powerful Newcombe, who blanked the heart of the Cardinal batting order—Moon, Musial, and Ennis. The Cards had dared to think about the pennant. This rubber game in Ebbets Field might give them an indication of their strength.

Hutchinson rested Hal while Hobie Landrith caught. The Cardinals stayed in the game behind Lindy McDaniel until a two-run blast by Charlie Neal in the bottom of the ninth sealed a 4-2 Dodger win. Roy Campanella homered and Musial, off to one of his hottest starts, doubled twice in a battle of great players.

Early the next morning, the Cardinals gathered in the lobby of the Biltmore before boarding a bus for the trip to Philadelphia and a Sunday doubleheader with the Phillies at Connie Mack Stadium. Hal caught both ends, had a triple and a home run against Curt Simmons, and the Cards handled the Phillies twice. The team rode the bus all night back to New York to take on the Giants the next day. The Polo Grounds, home of the Giants, was famous in baseball history for Willie Mays' magnificent over-the-shoulder catch of Vic Wertz's drive in the

1954 World Series. It was 500 feet to center, a vastness that weakened the knees of visiting centerfielders. If the ball got by them, some coaches warned, it would take a day-and-a-half to get to it. In contrast, the leftfield line was a short 250 feet. Giants' player Dusty Rhodes, a veteran of the Class-C Western Association, specialized in hitting pop flies right down that line and out of the park. He didn't seem to mind that needlers scoffed at these "Chinese homers." The dressing rooms at the Polo Grounds were in dead centerfield and made for a long walk. During the games, the Cardinals would be on the look-out for the Giants' "pitch signaler." This guy often was posted in the bleachers over the dressing rooms. After picking up the catcher's signs using a telescope, he would wave a white towel or use a telephone to tell Giant hitters what the pitcher was going to throw next.[34] The Cards relied on no such foolishness. After all, they had Dark on the infield and he was one of baseball's great sign stealers. When he flashed Hal a sign that the runner was going to steal, the catcher trusted him. Once, Hal even called for a pitch-out on a two-ball, no-strike count. Dark, who eventually became a fine manager, knew how the wheels of baseball turned!

Hal went three for five with six RBI's in the opening game of the 1957 Giants' series in New York, but only 3,500 fans showed up to see his break-out day. One guy who noticed Hal's performance was Frankie Frisch, the Hall-of-Famer who had played much of his career with the Cardinals. Frisch hosted a post-game TV show sponsored by Brille-Crème, a popular hair gel of the early Rock n' Roll era. If Elvis or Little Richard didn't use the gel, it surely looked like they did. The product had a well-known advertising jingle that went, "Brille-Creme, a little dab'll do ya ... " When Frisch sent word down that he would like Hal to appear on the program, Hal got excited. He didn't really care that he'd been picked as the "star of the game." He was more interested in what he might make for appearing on the show. The producers usually paid each player a small sum, maybe twenty-five dollars, or gave them a memento like a new watch. It was the first time he had ever been invited to one of these interviews and it was brief. After it was over, the production manager handed Hal his gift for being on the show. It was a six-pack of Brille-Creme. Later, as he looked at his balding head in the mirror at the hotel room, Hal thought that "sure enough, a little dab will do me!" Fifty years later, he claimed that he still had five tubes of the stuff left.

Dismal attendance for Polo Grounds games had Giant owner Horace Stoneham threatening to move his franchise out of town. Few fans took him seriously, even though there were the examples of the Braves, who had moved to Milwaukee, and the Browns, who had found new surroundings and bigger crowds in Baltimore. It didn't seem to New Yorkers that the Giants could fit in anywhere except the Big Apple.

Still, the Giants were obviously on hard times in 1957 while the Cardinals were flexing their muscles. When the Cardinals left New York sporting a 6-4 record on the road trip, they were pleased to have won a 16-inning game, a 15-inning game, and a double-header. The wins moved them into third in the National League standings. Recovered from his hand injury, Hal caught all of these games and threw out Willie Mays trying to steal second. It marked the first time in the season any catcher had nailed Mays, who already had twelve stolen bases. He swiped four in one game against one of the league's premier catchers, Smokey Burgess of the Reds. Hal's throw was made more remarkable because Mizell's slow, exaggerated delivery showed the batter the spikes on the bottom of his shoe while offering the runner a great jump.

Helped along by Dark, Hal sought to "read" the idiosyncrasies of opposing pitchers and catchers so he could gain an advantage at the plate. Once, against the Cubs' Bob Rush, a 6-4, hard-throwing right-hander, Dark told him to watch the catcher's feet because the near-sighted Rush couldn't see the finger signals very well. Hal recalled that each Cardinal on-deck would closely observe the catcher when he prepared to give a sign. Soon, they were able to spot a trend. "If he had his heels together, that meant a fast ball," Hal said, "and if he got down and then spread his heels apart, he was going to throw a breaking ball. So, now the guy in the batting circle would watch that and tell the guy at bat. He'd kinda' tip him off with a word—'c'mon' or whatever voice signal we settled on." Hal wanted in on the tip-off, if possible, but one guy who refused any such help was Stan the Man. With his superior vision and concentration, Musial preferred to watch the ball intently as it came out of the pitcher's hand. He could tell what kind of pitch it was by seeing the "spin pattern" created by the seams on the ball as it rotated toward him. Then, he could make up his mind about swinging or holding up. Evidently, his system worked, since he was leading the league in batting average and got three hits off of Cub pitching without using the tip-off. Still, the "read" on the catcher's feet must have worked because Hal had two hits off of Rush. He also threw out Walt Moryn at third base and the Cards beat the Cubs, 6-2.

The swing through the Atlantic coast cities brought a rush of success for Hal and the rest of the team. Moon was in the middle of a hitting streak that would run to twenty-four games. It was the longest in the majors in 1957, edging out a 23-game streak by Schoendienst, who was now the lead-off hitter of the Braves. The writers began to include the Cards, along with the Dodgers, the Reds, and Milwaukee, as one of the teams with a shot to play in the World Series. On May 26th in Cincinnati, the Cards were down four in the eighth but rallied to tie the score. To hold the Reds in the bottom of the eighth, Hutch went to his big right-hander, Wehmeier, normally a starter. Hal Jeffcoat, the Reds' pitcher and a pretty good hitter, was leading off the inning. Reds' manager Tebbetts opted not to pinch-hit for Jeffcoat, although he was 0 for 3 at the plate and had just given up four runs. Obviously, managers had a bit of a different take on relievers, pitchers as hitters, and pitch counts in those days. With Jeffcoat hanging over the plate, Hal called for a fastball. Instead, Wehmeier served up a slow ball. Larry Jackson had been doing that same thing to Hal—that is, throwing a change-up instead of the fastball his catcher had signaled. Jackson expected Hal to recognize the pitch and not be fooled by it. Apparently, Jackson had lectured the other pitchers about the need for bringing such a surprise and this is exactly what Big Herm did. Hal was not the only one who saw it coming. So did Jeffcoat and he hammered it out of the park. On a home run by their pitcher, the Reds took a 7-6 lead into the ninth. Jeffcoat set down Cunningham, Hal, and pinch-hitter Landrith to finish the game with a win. In the clubhouse at Crosley Field, the door to the manager's office had solid-wood paneling. As the Cardinals filed silently into the locker room after the game, Hutch put his fist right through that oak door.

Such a loss to another contender, however, did not finish his club. Maybe the punch to the door got Hutch's point across because the Cards won five of their next eight games. In early June, they went on a winning streak that reached eight games. Hutch had his fielders hustling and the pitchers were just good enough to out-do their opposing numbers. The Phillies finally ended the eight-game win streak and the Cards bused back to the Big Apple to face the Dodgers for another four games at Ebbets Field, intent on starting a new streak. On June 14, Don Newcombe and Lindy McDaniel locked up on a fine Brooklyn night, each giving up just one run in nine innings. Although the Cards got two hits in the tenth inning, Big Newk got Joe Cunningham out to end the threat. Matching the Dodger pitcher inning for inning, McDaniel went out in the bottom half and walked Junior Gilliam, the first hitter. McDaniel then retired Pee Wee Reese and Duke Snider on ground-outs. Gilliam advanced to third base. With a 1-1 count on Campanella, Gilliam broke for home. He slid in under Hal's tag and his score won the game. It was only the 26th time that a game-ending steal of home had happened in a major-league game. Some fans hold that the most exciting play in baseball is the grand slam. Others believe a squeeze play with the game on the line tops all else. Some veteran baseball men, however, view stealing home as the single, most exciting event that can occur in a baseball game. It is certainly one of the rarest.[35]

The Cardinals regrouped the next day, however, and reeled off three straight wins against the Dodgers. Furthermore, the Cardinal pitching staff got a boost from an unlikely source. Eighteen-year-old Von McDaniel, brother of Lindy, joined the team. The McDaniels were from Hollis, a small town in western Oklahoma near the Red River. When the Cardinals signed Von, they paid him a record bonus of $50,000. Hutch had seen Von in two relief spots. One of them was in a tight ball game at Ebbets Field in which he had pitched four shut-out innings and picked up his first major-league victory. Hutch decided the kid had the moxie, the velocity, and the precision to help the rotation. On June 21st in St. Louis, Von started against the Dodgers. In the pre-game session with the young pitcher, Hal and pitching coach Howie Pollet talked about the tendencies of the Brooklyn hitters. Hal described his signals—one for a curve, two for a fastball, three for a change. Von reminded his catcher that he had a slider, too. Hal smiled and said, "OK. That'll be four fingers." When Pollet pointed out into centerfield and asked, "You know who they got out there?" Von replied, "Yessir. That's Mr. Snider." The youngster refused to be awed, however, and sailed through the Brooklyn lineup for the first five innings without allowing a hit. In the sixth, the Dodgers loaded the bases with nobody out. Hal went out to the mound, thinking he needed to settle down the youngster and remind him that there was a play at the plate if he got a ground ball. Von looked as cool as a veteran pitcher. On the next pitch, McDaniel got an easy come-backer from Elmer Valo and threw out the speedy Gilliam on a force play at the plate. Hal completed the double play with a rifle throw to Musial at first. The next batter, Gino Cimoli, was having an All-Star year but went down on a meek grounder. Von trotted to the dugout as if he were still pitching for his high school team on an all-dirt infield. He went nine innings, walked none, and shut out the fearsome Dodgers. The 2-0 victory pushed young Von's record to 2-0. Obviously, the Cardinals had a phenom. The next day, the Cardinal front office called Dizzy Dean and invited him to St. Louis for a photo session with the McDaniel brothers. Sportswriters reminded their readers of Dizzy and Paul, the last pair of brothers to grace the Cardinal pitching rotation. They had led the Cards to the 1934 pennant. In one season, the Dean brothers had combined to win 49 games. Now, Dizzy was the broadcasting partner of Buddy Blattner in Mutual Radio's Game of the Week program. When Dean posed for photographs with Lindy and Von, he told them that they, too, might win 49 games between them.

Everything was going right for the Cardinals. Their pennant hopes were high because of the McDaniel brothers and the red-hot bats of Musial and Moon, who had gone on another hitting binge. Steady play from Joe Cunningham, Blaze Blasingame, and Hal delighted St. Louisians, who came to the stadium in droves and had begun scouting tickets for the Major League All-Star game scheduled on July 9th in Busch Stadium.

On July 3, a huge crowd filled Busch Stadium for the match-up between one of the major-league's oldest pitching stars, Warren Spahn, and one of its newest, Von McDaniel. Musial, Ennis, and Hal each got two hits off "Spahnie," as the players called him. The Cardinals scored four runs while young Von shut out the Braves. This was no small task, considering the Braves' line-up. Bill Bruton was the lead-off man, followed by the big bats of Eddie Mathews, Henry Aaron, Joe Adcock, and Del Crandall. Von was just as good as ol' Diz' had inferred. After the game, Hal and Carolyn went out with their neighbors for a little celebration at a quiet restaurant with red-checkered table cloths and candles stuck in wine bottles. Hal's friend, a salesman by vocation and an animated fellow, talked a lot and was always gesturing with his hands. At one point in the meal, his napkin caught on fire. The guy jumped up, slapping at the blaze. "You know, I like atmosphere," he roared, glancing around the room where all eyes were on him, "but this is ridiculous!" Hal and Carolyn laughed until tears came. The steak was good, the company even better, and the Smiths were feeling jubilant. A good day at the ball park can do that. Hal had two hits off Spahn and caught every inning in the shut-out of a contending team.

On July 4, 1957, the Cards were in second place, just a half-game behind the Reds. The Reds, as it turned out, would fade quickly after the All-Star break. Still, the early excitement and dedication of their fans was revealed in the huge vote that Reds' players garnered in the All-Star balloting. Until 1946, managers had selected the players for the All-Star squads. In the afterglow of World War II victories over dictatorships, democracy was on everyone's mind. It even seemed to reach major-league baseball, at least, where the All-Star selections were concerned. In this natural progression, the fans now got to pick the players. A Cincinnati newspaper distributed forms that were already filled out with Red players for each position. Reds' fans flooded the National League office with these pre-printed ballots. Under the rules for selection, this was all legal. However, it became apparent that the American League All-Stars would be playing an NL team mainly comprised of Cincinnati Reds. In the final tally, Musial, the league's leading hitter, edged out Cincinnati first baseman, George Crowe, but the rest of the Reds' lineup had finished first in the fan poll. Their second-year leftfielder, Frank Robinson, certainly was an All-Star, along with their catcher, Ed Bailey. Even a dyed-in-the-wool Cincinnati fan might flinch at a line-up that had Gus Bell over Willie Mays in center and Wally Post instead of Hank Aaron in right field! National League commissioner Ford Frick certainly was not pleased. He stepped in and overrode this entire "democratic process." Frick complained that the All-Star "team would not be typical of the league and ... would not meet with the approval of the fans the country over."[36] The commissioner thereupon ordered that Post and Bell be benched. Frick further instructed National League manager Walter Alston to replace two other Reds'starters, Don Hoak at third and Roy McMillan at short, after one at-bat with Ed Mathews and Alvin Dark.

Despite this serious hitch, the 24th All-Star game was to be a "gem," so said banner headlines in the All-Star issue of *The Sporting News*. The "Dream Tilt" featured Stan Musial and Ted Williams in their 14th and 13th All-Star games, respectively. Cardinal announcers Harry Caray and Joe Garagiola, along with Cleveland's Bob Neal, were selected for the play-by-play. It would be carried by 194 NBC radio stations and beamed overseas by the Armed Forces Radio Service. The All-Star game would be telecast by NBC, in black and white, of course.

Reds' catcher, Ed Bailey, placed second in overall votes behind Frank Robinson. Hal was the second highest vote-getter among National League catchers. He called his parents in Barling to say that he had tickets for them, so Ronald and Katherine Smith drove to St. Louis for the game. Ronald Smith, however, wanted to avoid the big crowd and stayed behind at the Smith house, even though he had never seen Hal play in the big leagues. He watched the game, with Mel Allen's call, on television. Carolyn, who was pregnant, and Katherine took in the great sights and watched the famed baseball players that graced Busch Stadium that day. They were disappointed, though, that the National League lost and that Hal didn't get into the game. Hal was disappointed, too. One newspaper noted that he was in pretty good company, since Johnnie Antonelli and Warren Spahn, who was on course to win the 1957 Cy Young award, sat out, mostly in the bullpen with Hal. Alston said he was afraid to use his other catcher too soon in the tight game. Behind Hal's former Marianao battery mate Jim Bunning, who had three shutout innings, the American Leaguers won it 6-5.

In another season, Ronald Smith finally got a chance to see Hal play in the major leagues. At the park, Mr. Smith "got a beer and my mother almost had a fit," Hal recalled with a chuckle. Ronald and Katherine took in another great St. Louis attraction, the Forest Park zoo. Hal and Carolyn always liked to take their guests out to the zoo. It was a popular place and was one of Hal's favorites. He especially liked seeing the chimpanzees perform their show and enjoyed the way they mocked the on-lookers.

The Cardinals had a rule that no more than four players could fly in the same airplane. After the All-Star game, Hal and his teammates—Musial, Boyer, Dark, and Jackson—flew out to rejoin the team in New York after getting special permission from the Cardinal management, which approved the exception because air travel was becoming safer and far more common. That marked the only time Hal flew to a game during the 1957 season, but extensive air travel for National League teams came suddenly in 1958.

When the Cardinals played the Giants on July 11 at the Polo Grounds, they led the National League by three games. Although Antonelli shut them out, 1-0, Lindy McDaniel pitched almost as well as Antonelli. The Cardinals' record in July was 21-10 and they were winning on the road. In Philadelphia a couple days later, Von McDaniel took his first major-league loss. Vinegar Bend Mizell couldn't win the next day either and his record plummeted to 3-7. Back in Brooklyn, the Cardinals lost their third in a row despite a hit by Hal, his first since the All-Star break. Hal scored after he alertly stole second base when Dodger pitcher Danny McDevitt used a full windup, but it wasn't enough and Lindy McDaniel's record fell to 8-6. The Cardinals struggled on this visit to the eastern clubs. In Pittsburgh, the Pirates got to Von McDaniel early and his record dropped to 4-2. The McDaniel brothers were taking their lumps. The Cards rebounded to win the next two in the Pittsburgh series. In the last game, Hal threw out Roberto Clemente on his attempted steal of second. Before the year was out, Hal would add Henry Aaron to the list of those he nailed and that throw ended

Hammerin' Hank's streak of 28 straight steals. Hal said Hank was as fast as Willie, just not as spectacular.

The Cardinals came home to a near-record crowd of 29, 416 for a Tuesday game with the Brooklyn Dodgers. Hutch started Sam Jones, who was mowing down opposing batters with his curve ball. Acquiring Sam Jones had been one of Frank Lane's happier deals. Hal said Jones had a curve that "would make you sit down." Dick Groat once said that Jones had "a dozen curves—fast curves, slow curves, about six different speeds and they all break quick." The recent losing streak dropped the Cards to third place, but they were still just a half-game out of first. In a one-hour, 54-minute game, however, Johnny Podres shut out the Cardinals while the Dodgers scored one run off of Jones to win the series opener. The next night, Jackson returned the favor by shutting out the fearsome Dodgers, 3-0, before 24,000 Cardinal fans. Showing the resiliency that had come to characterize this team, the Cards won the rubber game and this series with the Brooklyn club. St. Louis was in the middle of a streak in which they won fifteen games and lost only three. Cub skipper Bob Scheffing assured sportswriters that the Cards would win the league. Milwaukee second baseman Red Schoendienst thought so, too. Maybe the one-hitter Von McDaniel threw against the Pirates on Sunday, July 28 in a 4-0 Cardinal victory impressed them. Schoendienst knew that the Cards had an outstanding catcher who was totally focused and a steely competitor despite having that big smile on his face.

On August 3, Von McDaniel beat the Phillies to pick up his sixth win. The Cards held first place in the National League, a game-and-a-half up on the Braves, and were making prophets out of Schoendienst and Scheffing.

There were troubling signs, though. Hutch had to call on Landrith to handle more of the catching duties. After the season was over, Hutch remarked that Hal was worn out from having played continuously for 18 months. Once, Hutch asked Hal why he was holding the bat with one finger raised. Hal said, "Well, Skip, I can't close it down on the bat." Hal had been above .300 until July 6, but his average had begun to slide in the second half of the season. In early August, Musial was leading the league in hitting but sustained a shoulder injury. Hitters were catching up to the sliders of the McDaniel brothers. Boyer was having one of his worst years at the plate, slumping so much in the late season that Hutch benched him. Milwaukee, with Aaron and Mathews pounding the ball every game, went on a ten-game winning streak to open a commanding lead.

Yet, this curious mix of players that Lane had assembled dogged the Braves and took three out of four from them in mid-August before their last swing to the Big Apple. On August 20, the Cards faced the Giants at the Polo Grounds with Sam Jones on the hill. Musial homered in the first inning and Boyer followed with a long shot into the left-centerfield stands. In the Giants' half of the third, Mays tripled over Boyer's head in deep center to drive in two runs and tie the score. The next batter, Hank Sauer, shot one into the hole and third baseman Eddie Kasko made a dive for it. Mays, the best base runner in the game, broke for the plate. Kasko scrambled to his feet and fired to Hal at the plate to nip Mays. In the next inning Kasko blasted a home run, the Cards' third solo of the game and the rookie Kasko's only one of the year. It was enough. Jones and Hal worked complete games, with Hal throwing out Daryl Spencer. The 3-2 victory kept the Cards five games behind the Braves as Spahn picked up his 15th win the same day over the Pirates. Later in the week and still knocking on the door, the Cards moved over to Ebbets Field to take on the Dodgers. In a heartbreaking 6-5 loss, the Cards faced a parade of great Dodger pitchers—Don Drysdale, Ed Roebuck, Sandy Koufax, and Sal Maglie—*all in one game!* With two men in scoring position in the top of the ninth and the Cards behind a run, Hutch pinch-hit Hal for the left-handed Cunningham. Koufax walked Hal to fill the bases. Brooklyn manager Walter Alston then brought in Maglie to face Boyer, who struck out swinging.

The Cardinals put on a final kick down the September stretch. A sudden surge by Cardinal hitters in September fueled the drive. The Braves did not clinch the pennant until Hank Aaron's 11th-inning home run off Cardinal reliever Billy Muffett on September 23 before a County Stadium crowd of 40,926. Hal was behind the plate when Aaron hit the blast that put the Milwaukee Braves into the World Series for the first time. Especially dangerous in such situations, Aaron settled into the batter's box waving his thin-handled bat, identical to the model preferred by Musial. Muffett somehow got two strikes on Aaron. Hal said at that point, "Alvin Dark called time-out and beckoned for me to come to the mound. Dark asked Billy if he could throw a fastball that rises. Billy said, 'Well, I'll try.' I went back there and Muffett threw a fast ball and boy did it rise after Aaron hit it! It rose out of sight and clinched the pennant for them."

For the Cardinals, it was a season of such close games, several being decided by a dramatic home run. Gil Hodges had hit a grand slam in Brooklyn in the bottom of the ninth, for instance, to win a come-from-behind game for the Dodgers and hand the Cards another heartbreaker at Ebbets Field. The Cards had won some close ones with their own heroics. Hutchinson believed in his players. He stayed with Mizell in the first half of the season when the rustic Alabama right-hander was off his game and overweight. Mizell came back to post an 8-3 record after the All-Star break.

Dark, Ennis, Musial, Walker Cooper, and Murray Dickson provided the steady hands of seasoned veterans. Teammates saw Blaze Blasingame as their fastest runner and the hardest to catch in a run-down. Big Coop, who once said of the nervous Jackie Brandt that he chewed off so many fingernails in left field that he might trip over the pile of them, was named best bench jockey and heckler on the Cardinal team. The well known "holler guy," little Solly Hemus, easily garnered the bench jockey and heckler awards in the Phillies' dugout. Hal ended 1957 by having played in 100 of the Cardinals' games. Back then, teams played a 154-game schedule. After the major leagues expanded, they went to a 162-game schedule (the reason why Baseball Commissioner Bowie Kuhn put an asterisk by Roger Maris' name after his 61 homers in 1961). Hal had batted .279, one of the highest averages for catchers in the majors. He had thrown out 35% of the runners who had tried to steal. In the batting order, he had batted third once, fifth once, and seventh most of the time. One revealing stat was that Hal hit .333 with runners in scoring position. Hal came to bat 87 times with runners on second or third and drove in 33 of them. It was enough to prove that he was a hitter who delivered in the clutch. Hal handled pitchers as well as any catcher in the majors. His one flaw was having too many passed balls—17 during the season. He had learned much in the minors, but catching Hall of Fame knuckleball pitcher Hoyt Wilhelm (the 1957 Cardinal save leader) and veteran junk pitchers like Murray Dickson had proven to be hard chores for the young catcher. Gus Triandos caught Wilhelm in his 1-0 no-hitter against the Yankees in 1958. Next time out with Wilhelm, Triandos had four passed balls in five innings. When reporters asked him why he had so much trouble catching Wilhelm's knuckler this time, he simply stuck out his catcher's mitt and said, "You go try." Once, Hal was warming up Wilhelm in the Ebbets Field bullpen and finally caught one of the knuckleballs. Dodger fans gave him an ovation. Hal had learned a lot about stance, footwork, and positioning from Del Wilbur at Houston. Now, he studied Del Crandall and, in the process, became the top-rated defensive catcher in the Cardinal organization.

In Hal's second season, the '57 Cardinals won 87 games (twenty games over .500) and finished second in the tough, eight-team league. As the Braves beat the Yanks in the World Series, Cardinal players received a $1,636 check as their share—$600 more than if the Yankees had won. *The Sporting News* selected Stan Musial the NL's Most Valuable Player. Frank Lane vowed to bring a pennant to St. Louis the next year. August Busch told a banquet crowd at the

Knights of the Cauliflower Ear that Lane had better deliver or "he would be out on his bleep."[37] Busch also let Lane know that Musial was off the trading block. So was Boyer. Lane floated Hal's name from time to time, but that stopped when Hutchinson released the veteran catcher, Walker Cooper. Hutch wanted Hal and Hobie Landrith to stay. They were the two catchers that the Cardinals had decided they needed in order to make a run for the championship in 1958. Hal's negotiations with new Cardinal general manager Bing Devine were more satisfactory. Hal's contract showed a nice raise to $10,000—as much as the governor of Arkansas made in 1958. There would be no Cuban baseball for the Smith family in the winter of 57-58. Instead, the Smiths would stay in St. Louis and Hal would let his injured hands heal. Carolyn was pregnant again and, over the winter, their son Dennis was born. Hal and Carolyn now had three children to enliven their home and their lives.

10

Celebrity in St. Louis

In Florissant, Hal and Carolyn lived on a nice street and the houses in their subdivision bordered a wooded area with a small stream running through it. The setting reminded Hal and Carolyn of Arkansas. They formed a close friendship with the couple next door. Their children were about the same ages as Sandra and Sharon. Hal and Carolyn enjoyed picnicking in the backyard near the woods with the girls and their baby son, Dennis. Such gatherings attracted other couples and children in the neighborhood. It was a pleasant time. Hal was writing songs. KMOX wanted him as a deejay for a Sunday morning radio show. He enjoyed the work and sometimes played songs that he had written. His songs came with wry titles like "Sittin', Spittin', and Whitlin'," "Purt Near It, But Not Plumb," "I Got a Churn Full of Chitlins and A Belly Full of You." Others included "Thirty Yards of Petticoat and a Nickel's Worth of Gum," and "I'll Never Forget What's Her Name." They should have caught the attention of Roger Miller, a humorous songster of that time. Hal liked the engineer at KMOX, who handled the technical side of broadcasting. A true fan, he and Hal would talk baseball all the time.

One Sunday morning, the 6 a.m. Hal Smith Show caught up with Dixie and Harry Walker, who were 600 miles away from St. Louis on a fishing trip. In the middle of an Alabama lake, they were trying to find a country music station on a cordless radio that was powered by two "D cell" batteries. By accident, they tuned in their teammate on KMOX. "Now, who's going to listen to that on Sunday morning?" Hal chuckled, as he recalled the event. The Walker brothers thought they had one on Hal and made a "collect" call to him from the first pay phone they found on their way home.

Hal never had musical training but he had an ear for music and played boogie-woogie songs on the piano during his high school days. As a college student, Hal joined a bluegrass band—he played a washtub fiddle—and his piano playing and singing had been featured at times on the Fort Smith Boys Club Saturday Morning Radio Show.

Local arrangement committees asked Hal to speak at charitable and civic organizations at fund-raising events and bowling and golf tournaments. On this banquet circuit, Hal found that people liked his stories and he could make them laugh. His folksy, self-depreciating style of humor combined well with his excellent sense of timing as he delivered the punch line to delighted audiences. Like previous Cardinal catcher Joe Garagiola, Hal had the natural traits of a toastmaster. Also, he had an ideal source for humorous stories and good, clean fun. Garagiola had his Yogi Berra, the Yankee catcher. Hal had his teammate, Vinegar Bend Mizell. Berra once reminded a writer "that he never said all those things that he said." That much was true. Garagiola invented many of the sayings and attributed them to Berra, who often came up with a few of his own. Once, during spring training at St. Petersburg, Hal and Berra and some of their Yankee and Cardinal teammates decided to go out to dinner after a long day of practice. Someone suggested a popular restaurant, but Berra objected, "Aw, that place's got long lines and you gotta' stand and wait 20 or 30 minutes. That's the reason nobody ever goes there." Garagiola and Berra had been childhood friends. They grew up together and played as teammates in a sandlot league in one of St. Louis's Italian neighborhoods. Yogi once told Garagiola that he went out and bought two sweat shirts, "one navy blue and the other one is navy brown."

Hal perfected the Mizell stories. The two were good friends and had been together in baseball since they were eighteen years old and playing in the Georgia-Florida league. They lived close to each other in St. Louis and took turns driving to the stadium for games. Their wives were friends, too and attended games together. Over the winter, Hal and Vinnie, as Hal called his friend, worked out at the YMCA and attended Cardinal functions and publicity events. In January 1958, they were invited to the plush penthouse of the Anheuser-Busch Company. There, they previewed a documentary film that highlighted Cardinal greats and the history of the team. Hal was inspired by the stories, especially those about Dizzy Dean.

Hal, Mizell and another teammate, Joe Cunningham, were personable sorts. They stayed in St. Louis during the winter and the popular trio was in demand for appearances all over the city. At one appearance, someone asked Hal how he and Mizell met during their days in Class D ball in Albany. Hal recalled that when Mizell joined the club from the farm in Vinegar Bend, Alabama, he was pretty wild. "How wild?" someone asked. "Well," Hal replied, "they sent him down to the bullpen to warm up for relief and the fence behind the backstop in that ball park in Americus, Georgia, had sheet iron. He was throwing and all of a sudden, you'd hear this terrific clanging noise down in the bullpen. Mizell's throws were so high the ball would clear the backstop, hit the sheet iron, and make all that racket. Before long, everyone is looking down at the bullpen. The manager brought him in to pitch and the guys in the other dugout are saying, 'they're not gonna' bring him in, are they?' The first pitch he threw went over the grandstand. I called time and went out and asked him, 'Wilmer, are you nervous?' He said, 'No, you go on back and do the pitching and I'll do the catching!' I started back there and I looked up in the stands and people are hiding behind their seats! I finally realized that I was in the safest spot in the ballpark because he didn't come close to me all night."

Mizell helped with such mirth. He told the urbane St. Louis sportswriters in one interview that when he went home in December to hunt rabbits, his folks put him to work on the farm. He showed them the blisters on his hands to prove it. In many ways, Garagiola's stories enhanced Berra's legend as well as his career. Hal probably did the same for Mizell, who rose to become well-known both in baseball, American folklore, and politics. After being traded by the Cardinals, the big lefty had a banner season with the Pirates, who claimed the pennant in 1960 and beat the Yankees in a dramatic World Series, four games to three. After his retirement from baseball, Vinnie settled in Midway, North Carolina, home of his wife's family and, he thought, a good place for rabbit hunting. But he had little time for that as it turned out because Vinnie was elected to the U.S. House of Representatives. Mizell served in Congress for three terms from 1968 to 1974, representing North Carolina's 5th District during the Richard Nixon and Gerald Ford administrations. In 1989, President George H. W. Bush named Mizell Executive Director of the President's Council on Physical Fitness and Sports. Mizell immediately appointed his old friend and teammate Hal Smith to the Council. Stan Musial had chaired the Council during the LBJ administration and Arnold Schwarzenegger would follow Mizell as its director. While in Washington for Council business in seeking ways to improved physical fitness and awareness for the American people, Hal met President George H. W. Bush and toured the White House. In 1999, the death of Wilmer "Vinegar Bend" Mizell at age 68 left the Smiths with great sadness and the sort of void one feels for a life-long companion with whom so much was shared.

Fred Hutchinson felt that St. Louis had a good chance to win the National League championship in 1958. Instead, the team plunged into an early nose-dive and never recovered in a disappointing season. Only

Boyer improved his batting average from the previous season. Moon, Blasingame, and Ennis had off-years and Hal's batting average dropped fifty points in 1958. Musial started the year with injuries. When he returned to the lineup, his famous swing was shortened and a bit slower than normal. The Cards were helped by the arrival of Curt Flood, although he sustained an injury late in the season. Without much run support, the pitching rotation—Jackson, Jones, Mizell and Lindy McDaniel—took many losses despite a decent earned-run average.

Von McDaniel never regained his winning form or the mastery over hitters that he had displayed as an 18-year-old rookie. In one of those enduring mysteries of baseball, Von McDaniel found himself washed up before he was old enough to vote. After a 7-5 record in 1957 that included nine-inning shutouts and the near no-hitter against the Pirates, Von pitched in two games—a total of two innings in which he walked five, struck out none and allowed five hits—in 1958. He never got a single batter out. It reminded Hal that there was a fine line between the major leagues and the minors. Lose just a little stuff or timing or location and, all of a sudden, hitters are on to you and you just can't get them out.

A Saturday night game on June 7th against Philadelphia epitomized the frustration of the 1958 season. The Phillies started Curt Simmons. Hal and his teammates ordinarily hit well against him, but not on this night. Instead, the Phillies hammered Cardinal pitching in a long game and scored 13 runs. The Phillie lineup had Hal's former roommate, Rip Repulski, hitting in the clean-up spot. Repulski hit a three-run shot off Card starter Lindy McDaniel in the first inning, driving in Solly Hemus and centerfielder Richie Ashburn. Ashburn, a future Hall of Famer, was on his way to the 1958 National League batting championship with a .350 average, and led the league in triples with 13. Ashburn, Hal said, "used to have a stomach problem that would get him every once in awhile." Busch Stadium had a little toilet room right behind the dugout. Leading off in the first

inning against Sal Maglie, "Ashburn hit one off the wall and stretched
it into a triple. As Ashburn slid into third base, he was calling time.
He bounced up, trotted to our dugout and went into that john. They
held up the game until he finished his business. Ashburn came out,
bent over and deliberately adjusted his stockings, and stepped back on
to the bag. Third base umpire Tom Gorman said, 'Play Ball'" The
batter, Solly Hemus, stepped in and on the first pitch promptly singled
in a grateful Ashburn.

Perhaps the greatest moment of the 1958 season came early in
the season—May 13th—at Wrigley Field, a day game, of course.
Hutch had Stan Musial riding the bench, reluctant to use his injured
star who had 2,999 hits going into this last game of a road trip.
Nevertheless, Hutchinson had to ask Musial to pinch-hit in the sixth
inning because the game was on the line. Musial doubled and
registered the 3,000th hit of his career. Hal singled for his eightieth
major-league hit, driving in a run. (Hal finished his career with 437
hits in 570 games over five years and two months). Flood replaced ly
Moon in the sixth inning and doubled when he came to bat. It was
his tenth career hit. (Flood had 1,861 hits in 1,759 games over fifteen
years). Hutch had wanted Musial to get that 3,000th hit at Busch
Stadium in front of 30,000 fans rather than the 5,692 who saw it in
Chicago, but the pinch-hit helped the Cards to a much needed win—
only their ninth victory of the young season.

Hal and the rest of the Cardinals swarmed their teammate, one of
the most productive, stylish, and beloved players in baseball history.
After the game, amidst much joyful teasing and back slapping, the
Cardinal players showered, dressed, and packed their bags. They
boarded the Illinois Central train bound for St. Louis. In the twilight,
crowds gathered at the Springfield stop to hail Musial. As soon as he
made his appearance, they burst into cheers for "The Man." Later that
night, when the train pulled into St. Louis's Union Station, it was
packed with well-wishers for Musial. He assured all the children that

there would be "no school tomorrow!" And, the next day in the city of St. Louis, there was no school. City officials had declared it a holiday!

Musial became the eighth man in major-league history to collect 3,000 hits and the first to do it since Paul Waner in 1942. Four of the eight were still living. To celebrate Musial's feat, the Cardinals succeeded in bringing two of those four—"Big Poison" Waner[38] and Tris Speaker—to St. Louis on a day of celebration, where they congratulated Stan Musial and posed for pictures with him. Ty Cobb, at 72 years old, was too sick to attend. Napoleon Lajoie, age 84, was not up to the trip, either. It would be twelve years before another player joined this elite club. Hank Aaron on May 17, 1970, and Willie Mays on July 18, 1970 reached 3,000 hits and Roberto Clemente did it in 1972.[39]

The next day, 20,000 fans filled Busch Stadium as the Cards faced the San Francisco Giants. It was the Giants' first *eastbound* trip to St. Louis and the first in which they arrived at Lambert airport instead of Union Station. With their ace lefty, Johnny Antonelli, on the mound, Hutchinson inserted Flood in the line-up, replacing the left-handed hitting Moon. Musial was at first and Hal was behind the plate with Mizell pitching. Thus, the game was set up for some classic matchups. In the top of the first inning, Mays reached on a force-out, just beating Blasingame's relay. Taking advantage of Mizell's high kick and deliberate delivery to the plate, Mays stole second and then third on two successive pitches. Hal's hurried throw to third eluded Boyer and Mays scored. It was an unearned run, due solely to the speed and base running skill of Willie Mays, and the only one the visitors from California would get in the game which ended 2-1.

Musial's 3,001st hit came in his first at-bat. He homered over the right-field pavilion to tie the score. Hal scored the winning run on Blasingame's double in the sixth inning. Mizell, showing his best form, held the Giants to two runs for nine innings.

The Cardinals had little else to boast about in this season. They finished 10 games under .500, mired in sixth place behind the Chicago

Cubs. Ten games from the end of the season, Hutchinson got fired. The front office replaced him with interim manager Stan Hack. Hutchinson stayed in town and watched three more games from the press box before leaving for an interview with Seattle of the Triple-A Pacific Coast League. The next year, the Cincinnati Reds picked up Hutchinson and in 1961, he took that club to the World Championship.

Considering his hitting slump in the '58 season, Hal might have thought his days as a Redbird starter were over. In the final three games of the season, Hal collected five hits. It was a good way to end a disappointing season for a team that was supposed to challenge the solid Milwaukee Braves. But the Cards finished in the second division, in fifth place overall, and players got none of the "share money" from the World Series.

11

Solly Takes the Team ... to Japan!

August Busch wasted no time in naming Solomon Joseph Hemus as his new manager. Busch liked Solly for his "short man's" aggressiveness and his "holler guy" persona. Hemus had the same style as some legendary managers—Casey Stengel, Leo Durocher, and Eddie Stanky—but he wasn't quite as talented on the field. He razzed opposing players as a way of seeking an edge. Though he could hit stinging line drives, he preferred to bunt or draw a base on balls. Once, he fouled off 13 straight pitches on a 3-2 count before the pitcher yielded the walk.

Hal, Moon, Blasingame, Ennis, and Lindy McDaniel had letdowns in 1958. Musial, Boyer, and Cunningham had all played well. The ace pitcher on the staff had been Sam Jones, who finished with a 14-13 record. In his last start of the season with Hal behind the plate, Jones had a no-hitter going against the Dodgers in the LA Coliseum. With two outs in the eighth, Gilliam bounced one off the pitcher's glove to spoil the bid.

Yet, Solly talked about turning the club around without too many personnel changes. Given the lack of prospects in the farm system and the odds against pulling off a truly helpful trade, Hemus and Devine thought that "wholesale comebacks" were the biggest hope. Hoping to augment this idea, the Cardinals scheduled an Asian tour in which the club would visit Hawaii, Japan, Korea, Okinawa, and the Philippines. It would be the first exhibition tour of Asia by a major-league club since the Dodgers in 1956 and the Yankees in 1954. On the first of November, 1958, the Cardinals were in the best of moods as they boarded a long-range Lockheed Constellation to cross the Pacific. These four-engine, propeller-driven airplanes—nicknamed Super Connies—were state-of-the-art and designed for global travel. Some wives traveled with the team, including Musial's wife, Lillian. In order to care for her growing family, Carolyn Smith had to pass up this great excursion to the Far East.

The Cards opened their 16-game goodwill exhibition tour on November 3rd against the Japan All-Stars at Osaka. Between games, the major leaguers traveled the country, played golf, and took sight-seeing tours. Their hosts staged open-car parades and arranged Japanese baths. Large crowds attended—50,000 at Osaka and more than 20,000 in other cities—but acted strangely by American standards. Lillian observed that "everyone watches so silently and intently. There is no yelling, shouting, or booing like at home. Maybe it is due to Japanese politeness." Hal said that, instead of scrambling for a foul ball like U.S. fans, the Japanese fans would just sort of move over and let the ball hit. Then, they would pick it up and calmly toss it back to a ball boy. Moon complained that the Japanese baseball "just didn't go. It's dead." Mizell added that the "Japanese ball is heavy and harder to pitch...." Hal didn't mind the quiet crowds or the heavy baseballs. He continued his onslaught from the end of the previous season. Bing Devine lauded Hal as being loose [relaxed] and "stinging the ball and looking better than he had in a long time." Hal's rival for the regular catching job, Gene Green, was hitting the ball well, too. Hal and Green were friends and roomed together on the Japan tour. During one stretch, Green hit five long home runs—almost one a day. Solly Hemus liked what he saw in the huge Green, not that Hal worried about it too much. Hal was getting his hits, too and developing rapidly as a consistent hitter. Hal's defensive skills and rapport with the pitchers rivaled or superseded any catcher in the league. Besides, Hal knew that Gene habitually stayed out late. He chuckled when recalling how often his carousing roommate got into bed just before the crack of dawn. Japan is, after all, the land of the rising sun!

Hal was loose because he enjoyed the tour. "Just twelve years after the war and the Japanese showed us around royally. We went from one end of Japan to the other. Before every game, we'd line up across the infield and geisha girls would bring us out a bouquet of flowers or some kind of gift." The Cardinals ate well in Japan, too. Although Hal avoided the sushi, some of his teammates relished it. One buffet included chrysanthemums and bowls of fresh, raw eggs into which the diner dipped his morsels of meat. Their hospitable hosts treated the Americans to steaks from cows that were fattened on beer.

Most of the time, the team dressed in ballpark locker rooms. In one town, however, they had to dress at the hotel and then take Cadillac touring vehicles to the stadium. The hotel had public baths but no showers in the rooms. In order to reach the baths, the players had to walk through the lobby with terry cloth robes. The robes were too skimpy for some of the big guys like Brosnan, Mizell, and Jones, who put them on backwards like hospital gowns. They'd walk to the bathhouse in front of the little guys, who covered their rears.

In the bathhouse, guys sat on little stools and used sponges and a pail of water to soap up. Giggling geisha girls brought in towels and spread them around on the floor. The Cards were not used to that kind of public attention, so the modest players would dive into the bath water and stay under until the geishas had retreated.

After the bath, the guys would put on their robes again for the parade through the lobby—big guys in front, little guys in back. Hal said that people were standing outside looking through the windows at the big American baseball players as they traipsed about the hotel.

Garagiola, the Cardinal broadcaster who had accompanied the team on the tour, invited Hal to a televised talent show in which five Cardinals and five of the Japanese All-Stars appeared in a sort of audience participation contest. Garagiola emceed the show and asked Hal to play the piano and sing. Hal gave them "The Chattanooga Shoeshine Boy." When asked if they liked his performance, Hal said, "Well, they clapped., but maybe it was because they thought I was through singing!" As a gift for this gig, Hal received a Sony transistor radio—a new invention at the time and the first such radio Hal had ever seen.

The majestic Mt. Fuji, of course, provided a great background for several stops on the tour. For Hal, the most moving moment came at Hiroshima at the Peace Memorial. The memorial museum is near the site where the first atomic bomb exploded on August 6th, 1945. As an American standing in the midst of hundreds of Japanese visitors to the memorial, Hal remembered feeling strange but awed.

Japanese baseball diamonds typically had dirt infields. Oddly enough, there was no grass in the outfields either. The Japanese teams took batting practice with two cages going at the same time. "They'd have a pitcher here and a pitcher there and balls flying everywhere," Hall recalled. "I never saw anyone get hurt." The Japanese people love baseball, which preceded American occupation after World War II, and consider it a national pastime. In fact, the Japanese professional league, like its American counterparts, continued regular play during World War II through 1944. Only after American war planes began to bomb the homeland in 1945 did the Japanese leagues cancel their schedules.

The Cards won fourteen of the sixteen games in Japan. On a couple of occasions, Hemus put himself in. Once, he dropped a pop foul near the dugout. In the final game, he replaced Blasingame in the eighth and made two successive errors. "Don't do what I do, but do what I say," Solly yelled to his laughing players in the dugout. One game that got away was against the Japanese All-Stars at Osaka. That 9-2 victory was highlighted by a grand-slam home run by one of Japan's premier players, Futoshi "Big Buffalo" Nakanishi, a 220-pound first baseman. He hit the shot off Bob Blaylock. Nevertheless, Blaylock had what Hemus and Devine considered a good exhibition season. He was on the roster for 1959 and, as one of the hardest throwers on the team, was considered to be a good "long relief" pitcher. But, Blaylock never made it through the spring with the Cards, who sent him down to Triple-A Rochester. Hal thought Blaylock had a setback when Terry Moore thought he spotted a flaw in Blaylock's delivery and tried to correct it. Worse, Blaylock listened. Moore was a centerfielder, a great one to be sure, but not a pitching coach.

Nakanishi played for the Nishitetsu Lions, a Japanese League club that showed interest in signing Phil Paine, one of the Cardinal pitchers on the tour. Paine had pitched for Nishitetsu in 1953 while stationed there with the U.S. Army during the Korean War. At the time of the 1958 Cardinal tour, no Japanese players were in the major leagues and the Japanese teams had signed hardly any American players. Musial thought that the outstanding Japanese player he saw was Shigeo Nagashima of the Yomiuri (Tokyo) Giants. Hemus said that Shigeo was "good enough right now to play in the U.S. major leagues." He may have been that good, but he never did play in the U.S. Devine stated that the Cardinals were not interested in signing Japanese players. Neither was anyone else. Forty-three years after this 1958 tour, Ichiro Suzuki became the first Japanese-born, everyday "position" player in the major leagues in 2001. Before him, two Japanese-born players—Masanori Murakami (five games with the Giants in 1964 and 1965) and Hideo Nomo (1995-2005)—pitched in the majors. In 2004, So Taguchi became the first Japanese-born player to sign with the Cardinals.

Had Devine and Hemus scouted a few young, local prospects while on their tour of Japan, they might have stumbled across

Sadaharu Oh. In the 1959 season, Oh broke in with Yomiuri and over the next 22 years hit 868 home runs. Oh is the Babe Ruth of Japan.

Before going to Japan, the Cards had visited the Philippines, Okinawa, and Korea, playing national all-star teams and one team from the armed forces. After a month and 22 games in four countries, Hal and his teammates were more than ready to fly back to their families and homes.

On the return trip, Ken Boyer recruited Hal to help him with his highly publicized School of Baseball in Tampa that operated during the month of February 1959, just before spring training began.

Back in St. Louis, Hemus summed up each player's performance for the sportswriters. Wally Moon "looked better" to the new manager (Moon would be traded to the Dodgers the next week). Bobby Gene Smith: "hits in streaks and is as good a centerfielder as just about anybody in the National League (which had Mays and Snider)." Curt Flood: "We've had conflicting reports on him, although most people in our organization are high on him." Flood was in the Army for a six-month hitch at the time and missed the Japan tour. Flood grew to dislike Hemus as he sat on the bench for most of the 1959 season. Hal Smith: "Hit the ball well [in Japan] and is one of the best defensive catchers in the league." Ken Boyer: "One of the top five players in the National League." Bob Blaylock: "Blaylock was very impressive and has a good chance to make it." Stan Musial: "Stan seems to think he can help the club more in the outfield. He may not have the greatest arm, but he gets rid of the ball well." At the start of the season, Hemus moved Musial to left field and installed Joe Cunningham at first. Pitching was still a question mark. Lindy McDaniel did not make the trip. Larry Jackson went and pitched well. Much depended on Jim Brosnan and Ernie Broglio, a new acquisition.

Photographs

Seventeen-year-old Hal Smith poses in Houston uniform at a spring training camp in Seguin, Texas.

(Right) Hal's Houston Buff teammates congratulate him at the plate after a home run.

(Below) Photographed in front of the Fort Smith Boys Club, this team took the powerful Little Rock Doughboys to the wire for the state title in 1948. Hal is second from the left on the first row and future LSU baseball coach Jim Smith is second from the left on the top row.

(Above) Hal Smith on the right poses in front of Ronald Smith's home in Barling in an off-season visit. With him are Clarence Higgins and Jackie Brandt in the uniform of his country. Brandt, drafted into the army after his rookie season in 1956, spent two years at Fort Chaffee.

(Left) Freddie Hawn, shown here with Lindy (left) and Von (right), signed the McDaniel brothers. Hawn also signed Hal Smith, Wally Moon, and Jim King for the Cardinals.

(Right) Hal Smith
signs an autograph
for a young fan while
former umpire Dusty
Boggess watches.
Boggess, who
switched to scouting,
carried two sets of
eyeglasses in his shirt
pocket, and told Hal,
"Now I can see at
last!"

(Below) One winter
day, Ken Boyer arose
early to join in on
Hal's country music
show on KMOX.

In January 1954, Hal Smith and broadcast announcer Harry Caray share a laugh in front of the Cardinal Caravan poster at the Fort Smith Boys Club. Two years later, Hal was in his rookie season with the Cardinals and when he became the starting catcher, Caray nicknamed him, "The Barling Darling."

Hal Smith greeted boys and volunteers from the Fort Smith Boys Club in 1956 as they attended a game during Hal's rookie year. Hal arranged an autograph session for them with Stan Musial, Ken Boyer, Wilmer Mizell, and Wally Moon.

Brooklyn Dodger fans nicknamed Stan Musial, the Man, after the 1946 season when his bat dented the Dodger pennant hopes. Here is his graceful swing caught by a photographer at Ebbets Field. Roy Campanella is the catcher.

Sportsman's Park received a new name after Anheuser-Busch purchased the team in 1953. Buses catering to fans lined Grand Avenue and buildings surrounded the stadium. Home owners and businesses rented out parking spaces on game days.

Phillies shortstop Granny Hamner watches as rookie catcher Hal just misses bare handing the pop-up on the bunt attempt.

Hal delights his teammates and the audience, if not the host behind him, while on the Japan tour with his piano rendition of "Chattanooga Shoe Shine Boy."

Catcher Hal Smith in tense mound meeting with manager Solly Hemus (left), third baseman Ken Boyer, and pitcher Gary Blaylock (right).

Wearing number 2 before Schoendienst rejoined the Cardinals, Hal got a deep spike cut on his ankle from Dodger catcher John Roseboro in this play at the plate.

The Cardinal Special, a Douglas DC-4, after landing in Japan in November 1958. Hal is on the far left of the group. Fifth from the left is Wally Moon with camera. Moon was traded to the Dodgers after the tour. Joe Garagiola is squatted in the right foreground aiming his camera at the presentation. Stan and Lillian Musial are standing under the engine.

(Right) Manager Harry "The Hat" Walker greets his friend, coach, and protégé Hal Smith on a Pirate spring training field.

(Below) In this August 11, 1959, game with the Giants, Hal tags hustling Jim Davenport a little too high to save a run giving the Cards a heartbreaking loss in their run for the pennant.

In a July 1959 game at Crosley Field, Hal chased a pop foul into the Cincinnati dugout winding up in the lap of George Crowe, in the middle wearing glasses. Johnny Temple is to the left of Crowe.

Cardinal first basemen Joe Cunningham and Stan Musial.

Hal tags Don Hoak of the Pirates after blocking the plate in the 1959 season.

Hal, Wally Moon, Herm Wehmeier, and Stan Musial share a moment in the locker room after a 1956 Cardinal victory.

Hal R. Smith, the Barling Darling, is on the left. His contemporary, Harold Wayne Smith, is on the right. The Kansas City Athletics traded Hal W. to Pittsburgh in time for the Pirates 1960 pennant and World Series winning season to which the "other Hal" contributed mightily.

Hal hustled to cover the bag and tagged out Tony Taylor after the Cubs' second baseman made too big a turn at first.

(Right) Hal in the
hospital following his
diagnosis of a heart
condition that ended
his playing days with
the Cardinals.

(Below) The 1961
Cardinals team
photo. Hal is third
from the left on the
top row. Curt Flood
and Bob Gibson are
on each end of the
top row, and Stan
Musial is on the left
end of the first row.

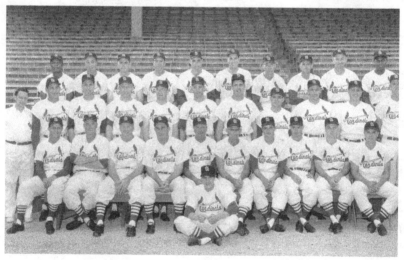

Bob Gibson (left), Julian Javier, and Red Schoendienst pose for the photographer.

Left to right are Stan Musial, Ernie Broglio, Hal, and Walt Moryn standing in front of Musial's locker after Broglio's twentieth victory in 1960.

Hal Smith (L) and Johnny Pesky (R), Pirate coaches in 1965.

Hal's teammate, battery mate, and his close friend Wilmer "Vinegar Bend" Mizell.

Wally Moon. The Bay-Truman product had five good years with the Cardinals before his trade to LA in 1959.

Coaches Hal Smith and Jimmy Bragan with Reds manager Dave Bristol in his Cincinnati jacket.

Hal Smith pictured in 1998 with his Barling friend of youth (but no relation), Lawrence "Squeaky" Smith. Squeaky coached the Kerwin's American Legion team in Fort Smith for thirty years. Both have been inducted into the Arkansas Sports Hall of Fame.

Hal and Carolyn with son Dennis and daughters Sandra and Sharon at Busch Stadium at a ceremony announcing his retirement for medical reasons in 1961.

12

The 1959 Season

Bespectacled Jim Brosnan kept a journal while the Cardinals were in the Far East and sent frequent articles to newspapers describing the culture and events on the tour. Brosnan wore a blazer and smoked a briar pipe. He read books and earned the nickname of "The Professor" from his Cardinal teammates. Brosnan continued keeping his diary in 1959 and Harper & Row published it in 1960 as *The Long Season*. The book was advertised as, "*The* classic inside account of a baseball year." Brosnan began his book by expressing his extreme disappointment in his contract negotiations. Bing Devine only offered him $16,000, when he expected at least $20,000. Actually, he thought he was worth closer to $25,000. Brosnan held out for a month before signing for $18,000. *The Sporting News* reported that Brosnan and Hal signed on the same day. Hal's contract was for less than that of Brosnan. Mizell held out a few days, too, but Larry Jackson signed his contract almost as soon as he got it in the mail. The contract issue behind him, sort of, Brosnan went on to have solid outings in spring training at St. Petersburg. Hemus thought the Professor could have a 20-win year. It was an improved prognosis for Brosnan, especially since Bing Devine had said in Japan that Brosnan and Blaylock were his picks for the long-relief jobs. "Long man," Brosnan's friends said to him, "that's the lowest form of pitching there is, isn't it?"

In April, just before the club headed north, the St. Petersburg *Times* ran an article beneath a headline that read: "Brosnan, Mizell, Hal Smith Brightest For Cards." Hemus assured the team that they would win more than they did in Florida once they got north. With great anticipation, the players, Cardinal fans, and sportswriters awaited the opening day on April 10th. The Giants would be in town. Word was that Hemus would love to start Green at catcher, particularly since he'd led the Cardinals in home runs during their tour of the Far East. Johnny Keane knew better, though. Coach Keane pulled Hal aside and assured him that during spring training, Hal had won the job by proving that he was the best catcher and a reliable major-league hitter. Eventually, Hemus came over and told the press that he rated "Smitty right up with Del Crandall. With that strong, accurate arm of his, Smitty isn't going to let many runners steal on him this season. He can hit .220 or .230 and still be my regular catcher."[40]

The San Francisco Giants were in their second year on the west coast. Before the game, Brandt walked by the batting cage where Hemus had just looked at a pitch instead of swinging. "What are you doing, Solly," Brandt called, "taking 'take' practice?"

Jackie Brandt's 1957 and '58 seasons had been spent at Fort Chaffee, wearing the uniform of a private in the U.S. Army. Those were actually good years for Brandt. He made lifelong friends, both in the barracks and in downtown Fort Smith. Over the winter, Hal had visited his parents in Barling and had a chance to introduce Brandt to Clarence Higgins, Jim Charles, and Clair Bates—all baseball men. Through them, Brandt met a lot of people in Fort Smith, a town that quickly discovered his wit and big heart. Of course, Brandt played baseball for the post team, which had other professional ballplayers like Tom Borland, who pitched for the Red Sox in 1960 and '61. Gene Wofford and Gene Trotter, good basketball players at the college level, gave the Chaffee team capable athletes to go with the pro ball players. Mason Rudolph, the PGA golfer, was at Chaffee too, and he and Brandt became lifelong friends. The draft brought people together from all walks of life. One member of Brandt's company, Jim Bexley, married the daughter of the baker/owner of Slack's Sweet Shop in Fort Smith. Bexley, who stayed on to live in Arkansas, keeps these old army buddies in touch by arranging an annual get-together. At the core of this group of post-Korean War veterans is their hero, Brandt, who also is quite a storyteller. A lot of stories are told about him, too. During hand grenade practice, the instructor non-com told the men to pull the pin and throw the grenade at an earthen mound about 30 yards in front of them and then duck. Brandt threw his so far that the officer in charge on the tower yelled down to "send that trooper up here!" Brandt climbed the wooden stairs to the top of the platform and the major yelled, "What the hell are you doing?" Brandt said, "Well, I just threw it as far as I could." The major shook his head and replied, "We've never had anybody throw one *over* the mountain!" Brandt had a great arm! In his second year in the minors at Columbus, Georgia, he had more than forty assists from centerfield.

Major-league baseball pundits said Brandt never quite played up to his potential and labeled him a "flake." In spring training, he once loaded teammates into his jalopy and drove fifteen miles to an ice cream stand because it offered 27 flavors to choose from. After pondering the choices for ten minutes, Brandt ordered a vanilla cone. Flakes, by definition, are people whom other people can't figure out. Brandt's army friends prefer to think of him as a solid pal and a quick wit. He won the Gold Glove award while playing for the Giants. As a Baltimore Oriole, he drove in 75 runs from the lead-off spot and had the highest, late-inning batting average on the team. During one winter, Brandt reminded the Orioles' general manager, Paul Richards, of that fact while trying to negotiate a better contract over long-distance telephone. Richards went silent on his end for a minute or so and then came back with this concession, "Okay, you get a thousand more this year!" In 1962, Brandt took it. What else could he do? At spring training in 1960, a young lawyer named Marvin Miller was there on a mission. He visited the clubhouses, including Baltimore's, where he gave the Orioles a stirring talk about unionizing. Miller was trying to start a players' union over the objections of almost everybody, especially ownership and the man on the street. If he succeeded, they said, it would be the "end of baseball as we know it!" The Oriole players gave Miller a distinctly cool reception, even though salaries on the club were low and uneven. At the end of the speech, Miller asked for those in favor of a union to raise their hands. Brandt's hand went up. His was the only one. Well, what else to expect from a "flake?" Maybe Brandt was ahead of his time, like W. C. Fields and Eleanor Roosevelt. The ballplayer's union didn't come into existence until 1969.[41] When it did, salaries for the Orioles and other major leaguers began to rise and even out. Brandt's salary was never close to that of Roger Clemens, for example, who received more money for one start in 2007 than Brandt *totaled* in his 23-year span with professional baseball. That included eleven years in the majors, four years in the minors, two years in the Army, five years as a coach, and one year as manager of the Oklahoma City Eighty-Niners. Brandt was ejected from one game in all those years. While coaching first base, he saw a balk by the left-handed pitcher. "Charley," Brandt said to the umpire, "he balked." Charley, a short, heavy-set umpire, said nothing and didn't even look at Brandt. "Charley, he balked," Brandt repeated. Again, nothing from Charley. "Hey, Midget!" Brandt hollered. "You're outta' here," Charley responded. Brandt was fined, too. It cost him twenty-five dollars.

Brandt's two children were born in Fort Smith while he spent his two years in Army khaki. He and his young wife, Jan, rented a small house on Greenwood Avenue and enjoyed playing bridge with their friends and neighbors. In his time off from the post, the 24-year-old

Brandt umpired American Legion games in Fort Smith and put on a few hitting exhibitions. He joined up with the Shadehunters, a local semipro team made up of local coaches and a few ex-minor leaguers. The Shadehunters were a tad over the hill, but knew the game well and still wanted to be out there making those wisecracks and waiting for their moment. They all appreciated the marvelous talent of Brandt, who liked to catch for the Shadehunters (he said he was the only one of them who could still squat) and show off his arm. Jim Charles recalled how Brandt tried to pick off a runner at third in a semi-pro district tournament played at Andrews Field. His throw plunked the guy in the back and knocked the breath out of him. Three pitches later, Brandt fired it to third again. This time, Brandt's rocket throw cracked the runner in the side under his arm as he dove back in. The guy called time and got to his feet, grimacing. He stumbled toward his dugout saying, "My rib's broke. Get somebody else out here. "I've had enough of this sh*t!"

When his army obligation expired, Brandt went to Puerto Rico for winter ball so he could shake out the kinks for the 1959 major-league season. In his journal, Brosnan described the Cardinal clubhouse meeting before the 1959 opening-day game with the Giants. Cunningham, the Cardinal starting rightfielder, and "Blaze" sat on stools next to each other. Jackson, the starting pitcher, covered each Giant hitter and outlined the game plan for the visitor's batting order. Brandt hit second in the lineup in front of Willie Mays. "I like to pitch Jackie down and try to make him go for the curve ball. He'll chase it once in awhile," Jackson commented. Hemus asked, "How do you want him played? He's got pretty good power." Jackson decided he wanted his defense to play Brandt straight-away. Harry Walker reminded Hal and third baseman Boyer that Brandt would bunt, too. Hemus and Jackson went over their "book"on Mays and Orlando Cepeda. It was depressing subject for opposing managers and pitchers since there was no good way to pitch to these future Hall-of-Fame hitters. As the players filed out of the locker room after the meeting, Johnny Keane was hollering "five minutes to infield!" and Hal walked alongside Jackson. "When I give you the fist, that's the pitch-out, just like last year," Hal told his tall, right-handed battery mate. "And when I take my cap off and scratch my head, that means I'm lost—or at least that I'm thinking."

The Giants' starting pitcher was Johnny Antonelli, the lefthander, who had won 21 games in 1954 for the New York Giants and 20 in 1956. Ace Antonelli got the win, 6-5, on opening day in St. Louis before 21,000 fans. Brandt, who was two for five, drove in the winning run with a double off Brosnan in the top of the ninth. Hal went 0-3. Mays went 0-4. The Cards' hitting star in the opener was Grammas, the "Golden Greek," who went three for four, drove in a run and scored one.

The Cards dropped the next two to San Francisco. They were off to an 0-3 start for the Hemus era. After the short and not-so-sweet opening homestand, Hal and his teammates hugged and kissed wives and girlfriends at the St. Louis airport before boarding a chartered DC-6 for the trip to Los Angeles to take on the Dodgers. The ball players were air travelers in 1959, but the novelty of it still created a few apprehensions in Hal that were slow to fade.

The Dodgers played in the Memorial Coliseum from 1958 through1961. Their state-of-the-art baseball stadium was being built in Chavez Ravine and would not be ready until the 1962 season. The Coliseum, constructed in the early 1920's, showcased the track and field events for the 1936 and 1984 Los Angeles Olympics. The Coliseum lent itself well to football but had an odd shape for a professional baseball layout. The left-field fence was a short distance away from home plate, while center and right fields stretched out of sight. Of course, the Dodgers equalized the field somewhat by adding a high screen in left and a partition to bring the right field in to 370 feet. Right- handed hitters like Hal enjoyed the idea of playing in a stadium with the "short porch" in left, except that they had to think about facing Don Drysdale.

Going into the fourth game of the 1959 season, Hal had not had a hit and the Cardinals had not won a game. Prospects of a change in either condition didn't look too good either. In LA, Johnny Podres was going for the Dodgers in the first game, which would be their home opener. Drysdale was scheduled to pitch the second game and Sandy Koufax would wind up the series. In spite of this array of good arms, and with more than 60,000 fans packing the stadium, Hal was undaunted. Four of his outs came on sharp line drives that went right at someone. Hal got his first hit of the year in the second inning. Pumped, Hal tried to steal second but Dodger catcher John Roseboro threw him out. In the sixth off of Podres, Hal hit a home run—a two-run shot over the left-field screen that sealed the Cards' first victory of the year. Lindy McDaniel went the distance to get the win. The Dodgers came right back the next day with Drysdale, who hurled a nine-inning shutout. In the final game, Hal's second-inning double off Koufax after Boyer's homer helped send the great left-hander to an early shower. The Dodgers had acquired Wally Moon in December after the Cards returned from their Far East tour. Moon, a left-handed hitter, was mastering the art of stroking the ball "inside out" to the opposite field. His style of artful hitting in the Coliseum enabled Moon to lead the National League in triples in 1959. He told the press after the deal that sent him from St. Louis to L.A. for Gino Cimoli that the Dodgers had made a "heckuva good trade." But, in an April series with the Dodgers, Cimoli looked good in nailing Ron Fairly at the plate in the top of the tenth with the game on the line. Hal took the throw on a difficult hop and, as Harry Caray described it over the radio, made "a magnificent tag" on the sliding runner![42]

The Cardinals flew the short leg up to San Francisco where Willie Mays, Orlando Cepeda, Matty Alou, and Jackie Brandt awaited. Vinnie Mizell quieted those fearsome hitters in the first game, allowing one run in nine innings. Mizell got a base hit and tried to advance by stealing second but was thrown out. Hemus had them all running. Hal hit his second homer to seal the Cardinal victory.

The next day, Antonelli was on the mound for the Giants. Hal and Grammas had reached on base hits and the pitcher, Jackson, was at the plate with nobody out. Hemus pulled the double steal and it worked! Yet, the Cards did not score and lost the game. After nine games with the Dodgers and the Giants, the Cards flew into Chicago's O'Hare Field with a 2-7 record. Hemus decided to bench Flood, who had been starting in centerfield.

In Chicago, Hemus shook things up to get the team going. The Cards had acquired first baseman Bill White from the Giants, who had a surplus in that position with Cepeda and Willie McCovey on the roster. Hemus put White in centerfield, put himself in to pinch-hit (he walked), used rookie bullpen pitcher Bob Gibson as a pinch-runner, and pinch-hit Flood (he homered). Mizell teamed up with his catcher and roommate, Hal, to win a one-run, complete-game beauty at Wrigley Field. The Cardinals left windy, cold Chicago for home with a 3-9 overall record. While talking to his Gibson, his roomie, Flood confessed his doubts about Hemus. The Professor wrote the same thing in his diary: "Harry Walker, who'd had loads of minor-league success, or Keane, the knowledgeable third base coach, were waiting in the wings and would do better if provided the chance."

Hal, Cunningham, "Blaze" and Boyer were off to humble starts at the plate. Musial was hitting .225 with no homers. Devine, perhaps thinking his team would lack for offense, had traded Sam Jones, the Cardinals' best pitcher in 1958, for White. The GM also had acquired George Crowe, an African-American player who spanned the years between Jackie Robinson (with whom he had played on an amateur basketball team) and Flood, White, and Gibson. Crowe was a tall man, quiet-spoken, and could hit a baseball out of sight. As an indicator of the respect that he had in the Cardinal clubhouse, the players had made him the "judge" of the kangaroo court. As such, he meted out fines for misplays, boo-boos, bad jokes, bad songs, embarrassments, bad advice, bad haircuts, and so on. Kangaroo courts are the player's "parallel world" for the official rules and disciplinary policies of major-league baseball. If theatrical and literary folks recognize seven forms of humor, then baseball players must have eight, counting the kangaroo court.

One day, Hemus gave a pep talk and told his team to "stay with them, boys. Keep swinging those bats. We're better than we've shown and they are going to start falling in." Despite such confidence by the skipper, the Cards lost the first game of the homestand to the Dodgers, 2-1, on an April Saturday night. Hal got no hits. Flood did not play. Gibson was used as a pinch-runner. Hemus pinch-hit in the bottom of the ninth and grounded out. Clem Labine got Hal to ground out to end the game.

When Hemus brought out the line-up card on Saturday, the umpire and the sportswriters were surprised. Hemus had Boyer replacing Grammas at shortstop and the little manager started himself at third. The outfield had Cunningham, Bill White, and Irv Noren, a guy who was with the '59 Cards for all of eight games. Crowe started at first base, putting the slumping Musial back on the bench. The new-look Cards knocked Drysdale out in the first inning when Hemus singled, Cunningham singled, White doubled and Crowe and Boyer each got base hits. Hal drew an intentional walk. The Cards won, 6-5.

In the rubber game, Hal responded by getting two hits and caught Ron Fairly stealing. The Cards chased Koufax again and scored 11 runs, but it wasn't enough. They lost, 17-11, as Mizell, Broglio, Jackson, and two other Card pitchers had their troubles in getting anyone out.

Hal went one for three against Lew Burdette at Milwaukee. The starter, Larry Jackson, lost to go 0-3. Milwaukee catcher Crandall caught White stealing. Hal watched Crandall with great intensity, trying to pick up tips. Although Hal was a fine defensive catcher, he thought Crandall was the best. Jim Weigand, a baseball statistician and researcher, agrees. Weigand devised a scale for comparing catchers. According to his scale, Crandall was the best in the major leagues for 1959 and 1960.[43] Hal had a lot of memories of County Stadium. In the opener between the one-two teams of 1957, he saw Aaron hit his fifth homer of the year—the 145th of his career. From the field of this same stadium in 1976, Hal was coaching first base for the Brewers. He watched as Aaron launched the last home run of his career—Number 755.

During the next game of the series in 1959, Aaron blasted his sixth of the year and the defending NL champions beat the Cardinals 1-0 behind Spahn. Hal was held hitless, although he batted .247 lifetime in 73 at-bats against the Hall-of-Famer. Musial, who had 81 at-bats against Spahn, had a .321 lifetime average. Hal did as well as Musial in one department. Each had one triple off of Spahn. In Milwaukee, Flood was deep in Hemus' doghouse and had been used only as a pinch-runner.

Brosnan wrote that Hemus didn't like him, either. Brosnan also thought that, "Pittsburgh is not a bad town!" After Pirate games, Brosnan usually went to a Pittsburgh joint called Danny's for good food and good booze. A lot of ball players liked that kind of atmosphere. Brosnan did not mention what pals accompanied him, but Hal was not among them. He usually joined his roommate Mizell, Lindy McDaniel, and Blasingame for dinner and a movie when on the road. On the first of May, 1959, the Cardinals could take a moment to relax. Blasingame, who'd had two hits, was feeling good. Mizell picked up the win—his third of the year—and Brosnan had saved it for him. Hal went two for three, including a triple that scored Musial from first base. The Cards won, 7-6. In the ninth, with Clemente on first, clean-up hitter Dick Stuart sauntered to the plate. Hal went out to talk with his pitcher. He reminded Brosnan of the plan for pitching Stuart—

hard, up and in. Hal went back and called for the inside fastball. Brosnan shook him off, twice. He wanted to throw his slider, or slide ball, as he called it. The pitcher got his way. (They always do. It's their game, after all). By Brosnan's own account, he knew "when the ball hit the bat that it was in for a long ride." That was an understatement. The ball soared over the *120-foot tall light tower behind* the scoreboard that was 405 feet away from the plate. Forbes Field was so big it was called the best park in the league for pitchers. This drive, according to news accounts, traveled over 500 feet. Hal was shaking his head when he got a new ball from the umpire as Stuart rounded the bases. Brosnan came halfway in to take the toss from Hal and said, "I think that was the wrong pitch."

Despite the gargantuan blast, Brosnan saved the win for Mizell, who congratulated the Professor in the clubhouse. "Thanks," Vinnie said. "Gave 'em a thrill, didn't ya?" Cunningham, one of Brosnan's pals—the other was his roommate Gene Green—came over and shook Brosnan's hand. "Wonder if they're getting any signals at Canaveral yet? That thing's got to be in orbit." Brosnan walked into Danny's a little later to polite applause. His fame in chunking this wonderful gopher ball had preceded him. Somebody told his girlfriend, "This is the guy who threw the pitch!" A complete stranger, who was sitting on a bar stool, glanced at Brosnan and said loudly, "You guys won't believe this, but I was coming into the airport on an American Airlines plane ... " Brosnan got up and went to the restroom.[44]

On a drizzly Sunday on May 3, 1959, the Pirates and the Cardinals played a double-header. The Pirates had a good club under Danny Murtaugh. (They were in fourth place and a year away from winning an NL pennant and defeating the Yankees in a memorable World Series). In the first game, Brosnan relieved and gave up a base hit to Bill Mazeroski that scored Don Hoak and gave the Pirates a 4-3 win in extra innings. Hal lined the ball hard twice right at an infielder. Hal referred to those kind as "at 'ems." His defensive play, however, kept the Cardinals in the game. In the third inning, Pirate centerfielder Bill Virdon led off with a single. After Vern Law struck out in an attempt to sacrifice the runner over, Virdon tried to steal second but Hal nailed him with a perfect throw to Blasingame. In the Pirate fourth, Clemente reached on an error and tried the same thing. Hal threw Roberto out, too. In the fifth inning, with the score tied 2-2, the Pirates had runners at the corners and no outs. Hoak lined to rightfielder Smith and Virdon tagged at third. Hal blocked the plate, caught the ball, and applied the tag to the speedy Virdon to keep the score even.

The pitching in this Sunday game was good for both clubs as Jackson and Brosnan matched Vern Law and Elroy Face. "Deacon" Law was so good that Smokey Burgess, the Pirates' catcher, actually told Hal what pitch he would throw. "Smokey said to me this one time at the plate, 'I'm just going to tell you what's coming! Fast ball, here comes a fast ball.' And it was. He wasn't lying. Then, I started to wonder why I couldn't hit it." Jackson was about as tough on the Pirates. Burgess hit third in their line up but went 0 for 4. In 1959, Burgess was the only full-time catcher in the National League to hit for a higher average than Hal. Smokey hit .297 with 11 home runs and 59 RBI's, slightly above Hal's .270 with 13 home runs and 50 RBI's.

The second game of the double-header was remarkable for a stunt pulled by Hemus. The manager had inserted himself into the Cardinal lineup, which by now had a sort of patched-up look. Musial, Hal, Blasingame, and Flood watched from the bench as Hemus, batting second, was hit by a pitch from Pirate hurler Bennie Daniels. Brosnan wrote that Hemus stuck his leg out intentionally. The fiery little manager veered off the base path on his way to first to shout a racial slur at Daniels, an African-American. The two came together and the benches emptied. A couple of players threw punches. There were no ejections, although Cunningham was tossed later in the game for arguing a close call. The event has been chronicled in at least four books written by or about Cardinal players. The incident happened at a time when there seemed to be a turning point for better race relations in baseball. The Cardinals felt a lot of sensitivity to the issue, since they were the southernmost team in the 1950's major leagues and one of the last clubs to integrate.

The next day, Hemus had a clubhouse meeting and told the team what he had called Daniels. Crowe, White, Curt Flood and his roommate, Bob Gibson, were embarrassed. Hemus said he yelled at Daniels to fire up his team and made no attempt to apologize for his remark. Flood confided to Gibson that Hemus' true colors were out. Flood's biographer, Alex Belth, wrote that prior to the Daniels incident, Flood and Gibson disliked Hemus. Now, they came to despise him.[45] White thought that a bridge had been crossed. In later years, Hemus explained that he was in the wrong place at the wrong time. When he was a young player, veterans often used caustic ethnic and racial epithets against opposing players. He himself had experienced name-calling. Spahn and Burdette had called him a "cheap hitter" and a "little Jew." (Hemus was not a Jew, but some players and fans may have had that impression because his first name was Solomon). Hemus defended himself and reminded people that he had convinced August Busch to house white and black players together at spring training in otherwise segregated St. Pete. Before 1961, Hal said that "when we'd go to spring training, all the black players would have to stay in one part of town while white players who were there without their families would have to stay at the Bainbridge Hotel. On road trips, they wouldn't let black players come in the restaurants. It was really sad, you know, and I just could hardly take it. It always bothered me ... I didn't know what to do about it." Many white players did not want to be separated in situations from their African-American teammates. Hemus claimed that he didn't like segregation and had tried to do something about it. If he was ever an instrument of progressive change, however, few seemed to recognize it. Hemus hatched from the rough-and-tumble, confrontational school of baseball. After the Daniels incident, Bing Devine began to doubt Hemus' ability to adjust to societal changes or understand modern ballplayers. If he couldn't adjust, then Hemus couldn't manage effectively and wouldn't win games.

Hal experienced the uneven way in which Hemus treated his players. In a game at home against the Reds, Hemus sent George Crowe to pinch-hit for Hal when the bases were loaded, only to have Crowe hit into a double play. A day later, Hemus brought up the subject and said to Hal, "you thought I was wrong there?" Hal replied, "Yes, Skip. You had confidence in me to hit me up in the order, but then turned around and pulled me when I could have helped the team." Flood and Gibson could have understood Hal's confusion.

Hal recalled that Hemus kept things stirred up in other ways, too, particularly when it came to brawls. "Yes, I saw quite a few. When Solly Hemus was our manager, for a little guy he had a knack of getting brawls started. I'll never forget one time against Cincinnati. Ted Kluszewski had Solly up under his arm while Solly flailed away. I don't even know what the fight was about, but Solly could cause them real quick."

It was a tough series in Pittsburgh and leaving town was tough, too. The Sunday night turned foggy as the Cardinals boarded their charter plane for the short hop to Philadelphia. The weather broke enough to allow a departure, but soon after liftoff the pilot feathered an engine. The Cardinals were startled. Hal remembered that "Lindy McDaniel and I were sitting side by side and I was looking out the window. All of a sudden, the engine on the end stopped! I said, 'Lindy, look!' He said, 'Aw, this thing can run on three engines.' And I said, 'If it didn't need four, they wouldn't have put four on it.'" The fire trucks lined the runway as the plane banked, returned to Pittsburgh, and landed safely.

In 1876, the New York Mutuals had boarded a passenger train to get to their series of games with the St. Louis Brown Stockings. Thus began the use of rail by major-league baseball teams. It was an arrangement that lasted for eighty years and dictated an off-day set aside for travel between series in cities of the league. Major-league cities were grouped in the northeastern quadrant of the country, where the population was concentrated. Given the nineteenth-century pace of travel via railroads back then, distance determined the belt of major-league cities.

The Cincinnati Reds, the first professional baseball team, was the first to fly to a series. In 1934, Reds' general manager Larry McPhail chartered a plane for the team to fly to Chicago. After World War II and the vast advances in air technology it inspired, the New York Yankees flew on a regular basis to their most distant games in Chicago, Cleveland, St. Louis, and Detroit aboard a chartered DC-4.

The development of jet airliners in the post-war years made it feasible for Horace Stoneham and Walter O'Malley to move the Giants and Dodgers west to rapidly-growing California. Since 1876, the geographical center of baseball had been located on the Pennsylvania-Ohio border. With the dramatic shift to the west coast in 1958, baseball truly became the "National Pastime."

As commander of Allied Forces in Europe during World War II, Dwight David Eisenhower marveled at the German autobahns and the effective internal lines for military defense that the high speed, limited access roadways created. That impression carried into Ike's presidency and, by 1956, he had guided the Interstate Highway System Act through Congress. While these highways were designed for multi-purpose use, the system came under the supervision of the Defense Department, which could dictate traffic flow in case of a national emergency. The civilian sector, however, soon claimed primacy of use. Thus, the emerging transportation infrastructure of the country led to increased commuting from outlying residential areas to downtown offices, ballparks and other recreational facilities. Where the business of major-league baseball was concerned, the interstates meant that more and more fans arrived at games by automobile. Previously, fans walked to the ballpark or rode subways or city buses. Almost by accident, and certainly without full recognition of the far-reaching consequences, Congress' funding of an interstate highway system profoundly impacted American society and culture.

Hal's knuckles turned white as he gripped the armrests while the crippled plane landed in Pittsburgh, but he was aboard for the second take-off. All engines worked to perfection and the team arrived in Philadelphia for a two-game series. Hal shook off any nervousness from the flight (or maybe his adrenaline was still pumping) to hit a two-run home run off Robin Roberts in the opener. The Cards split this series as Hal went three for seven with a home run, a double and three RBI's.

Back at home against the Cubs, Hal continued his hot hitting streak. On Saturday, May 9th, the Cubs started Glen Hobbie against the Cards. Hal hit a home run in the fourth inning with two on and two out to chase Hobbie, the Cubs' best pitcher. Hal hit another one in the eighth inning—his only multi-homer game in the majors. The two-homer day was made memorable in another way, too. Tending to a growing family limited Carolyn in the number of games she attended. On this Saturday, she stayed at home while her two daughters attended a neighborhood party. As Hal walked into the dugout after the two-homer game, an excited stadium security guard said, "Hal, both of your daughters have broken their arms!" Down the dugout ramp a clubhouse attendant said, "Hal, one of your daughters has broken both her arms!" Hal didn't know which story was right, but he knew either way it was not good. As it turned out, Hal's oldest daughter, Sandra, then eight years old, had fallen out of a swing at the party. She had swung so high that she slipped off the seat. When she hit the ground, the impact broke both arms right above the wrists. Hal went from Busch Stadium straight to the hospital where Sandra was having one of her arms immobilized and the other placed in a regular cast. "Some celebration for the two home runs," Hal said. Sandra recovered fully at home and pursued her school work while being nursed by Carolyn. Hal knew that Sandra was feeling much better when, one afternoon, he saw her "playing football in the front yard with all these neighborhood boys!"

Hal hit another home run in May and three in June of 1959 to bring his total to eight by the All-Star break. The Cards won all of those games in which Hal hit home runs, but otherwise were not winning enough to climb above sixth in the standings. Tension generated by an upset Hemus further strained his relationships with Gibson, Flood, and Brosnan. Brosnan, normally a reliever, made a rare but disastrous start on June 7th. He retired a single Phillies' batter en route to giving up a homer, a triple, a double, and four runs in the first inning. Evidently, Brosnan had trouble that day with his slide ball. Hal, catching the game, remembered George "Sparky" Anderson getting a line-drive hit up the middle on the last pitch Brosnan ever threw for Hemus. Sparky didn't get many hits in his lone season (1959) in the majors, batting only .218 for the Phillies. This hit, however, chased Brosnan and was the last straw for Hemus. In a giveaway trade the next day, the Cardinals shipped Brosnan to the Reds in return for Hal Jeffcoat. Thereafter, Hemus hardly ever called on Jeffcoat, who was soon released by the Cards.

The Cardinal record after beating the Cubs on June 30 stood at 35-38. The Cubs were in fifth, one game ahead of the Cards. The Pirates were in fourth, three games ahead. The Braves were at the top of the standings. The pennant fight was a three-way scrap with the Braves, the Dodgers, and the Giants all clustered within a game of each other as the first All-Star break neared. This season, there would be two All-Star games.

When Reds' fans had stuffed the ballot box on All-Star voting, Ford Frick mandated a significant change in the selection process for the game by taking the ballots out of the fan's hands. After 1957, players, coaches, and managers selected the best at each position, with one provision—each team had to have at least one player on the All-Star roster. Moreover, two games would be played. Players wanted an extra game to bolster a player pension fund entirely dependent on proceeds from the All-Star games. The two-game experiment lasted four years.

Under the new peer selection process, Hal was named to the National League squad for both of the All-Star games in 1959. Hal arrived at Forbes Field for the first of the two, along with fellow Cardinals Musial, Boyer, White, and Cunningham. Mizell, at 9-3, had been named to the squad but, suffering from back pains, did not make the trip. Crandall of the Braves started behind the plate and stayed in for the entire game. Manager Fred Haney of the Braves did not play Hal nor did he call on the other catcher, Burgess. The AL's Yogi Berra didn't get in the game either. Musial and Boyer pinch-hit and were the only Cardinals to play. Moon, the former Cardinal, started alongside Aaron and Mays in the National League outfield. Moon's Dodger teammate, Drysdale, pitched three perfect innings as the National League won the game, 5-4.

Afterwards, the Cardinal All-Stars took cabs to the airport and boarded a commercial flight for Philadelphia to rejoin their team. The next day at Philadelphia, Hal caught both games of a doubleheader, going one for four in the nightcap against Robin Roberts as the Cards beat the future Hall-of-Famer to split the two games. The next day, the Cards won again behind Mizell, who ran his record to 10-3. Hal supported his roommate with the bat, going three for five with a home run that Hal thought might have been his longest. "Turk Farrell was pitching for the Phillies and the player before me [Gene Oliver] hit a home run. So I was the next hitter and I swung and hit the ball and actually thought I popped it up. But it went on the roof at that old ballpark in Philadelphia [Connie Mack Stadium]. When I came back in, George Crowe was standing there with his hands on his hips and he was looking at me and said, 'Where did that come from?' I kidded him back and said, 'how far did that one go, George?'"

The Cards took three out of four from Philadelphia in a series that began a grueling, 27-game stretch. It was bookended by the two All-Star games with only one day off (July 13). Hal started behind the plate in 23 of them and played in all but one. The Cards boarded a charter flight to Pittsburgh for their second double-header in four days. The Pirates and the Cards tussled with each other to stay out of the second division. Both games on July 12 at Forbes went ten innings, with the teams splitting. That night, the Cards flew home to St. Louis and Hal spent the day with family, his only day off in July.

The home stand opened with Cincinnati, another team battling with the Cards to gain fourth place in the standings and thereby enter the first division. Hal collected a hit off big Don Newcombe and the Cards won, 6-5, but lost the next two despite Hal nailing speedster Vada Pinson trying to steal second.

Pinson had 21 steals that year to lead the Reds. (Mays led the league with 27). Between the All-Star games, Hal threw out three runners in 12 attempts—he got them 33 percent of the time. All but two of the attempts were by league leaders in stolen bases, indicating that only the fastest dared test his arm. A modern researcher calculated that strong-armed catchers with good defensive skills like Hal's *intimidated* the opponents' running game. In other words, teams attempted fewer steals. During that stretch where opponents had 12 attempted steals, the Cardinals attempted 27 against opposing catchers—more than twice as many. By this measurement, Hal was quite effective in controlling the base- running offense of the National League teams.

The hot weather, intense schedule, and long road trips of July wore Hal down. Facing pitchers like Robin Roberts, Roger Craig, Harvey Haddix, Don Drysdale, Mike McCormick, Warren Spahn, Vern Law, and Bob Buhl did not help, either. The Cards struggled to stay in the top division of the league. Two games on July 22nd and 23rd at San Francisco, however, killed their hopes. In a windy Seals'

Stadium, Hal gave up three stolen bases—one each to Mays, Cepeda, and Brandt—without throwing anyone out. In one game, Hal tripled-in the only run the Cards could score. Of 23 Cardinal players polled that week by sportswriters, 16 of them, Hal included, were convinced that the Giants would win the pennant. Hal's roomie, Mizell, voted for Milwaukee to repeat. Cunningham, a close buddy to Hall and Vinnie, chose the Dodgers. He was correct.

Hemus and Devine sent Gene Green to Rochester and acquired the services of journeyman catcher Jay Porter from Shawnee, Oklahoma. Porter caught the game on July 29, the only time between the two All-Star games in which Hal sat out the entire nine innings. Hal started the other 26 games and played 200 of the 244 innings during this stretch. Hemus told *The Sporting News* that "Smitty's been getting a little tired." The manager indicated that his All-Star catcher had lost some of the old snap in the swing, even though his batting average hovered around the .290 mark.

The day of rest must have helped Hal because he had a memorable game the next night at Crosley Field against the Reds. Hemus started Bob Gibson, who had just returned to the St. Louis club from a stint in Omaha where Hemus had sent him to "work on his control." With Hal behind the plate calling pitches, Gibson continually worked out of trouble. Gibson went the nine innings and posted his first major league win, 1-0, providing a glimpse of the masterful pitching he would show later on a consistent basis. The last out came with two Reds on base. Johnny Temple rifled a shot to centerfield. Flood, who had just come into the game, tracked it down to save the Cardinal victory and Gibson's first as a major-leaguer. The game took two hours and 22 minutes. Hal was two for four at the plate, but the only Cardinal run came in the second inning when Boyer doubled and Cunningham singled him in. Hemus let his opinion be known that neither Flood nor Gibson would make it in the big leagues. "Gibson throws everything at the same speed," he said, leaving Tim McCarver, who caught Gibson after Hal's retirement, to wonder "but who could match his speed?"[46]

On August 2, Hal caught the last three innings of the opener in a Sunday doubleheader in Milwaukee's Miller Stadium against the Braves and the entire second game. The Cards split with the defending NL champions. Hal flew out that night bound for Los Angeles and his third All-Star game—the second of this season. This time he would play.

Game No. 2 contributed a substantial amount to the player's pension as 55,105 fans jammed into mammoth L. A. Coliseum on a hot Monday afternoon. They paid a record six dollars for reserved seats and eight dollars for the box seats. These high-priced tickets keep fans away, complained one National League All-Star, Eddie Mathews. Superstars Musial and Ted Williams started—Stan the Man at first base and Williams, the Splendid Splinter, in left field. Hemus fumed that his ace, Mizell, didn't get picked for the second game. Still, the National League had a commanding array of pitchers ready to challenge Williams and his fellow American League sluggers—Frank Malzone, Mantle and Berra of the Yankees, Roger Maris of the Kansas City Athletics, and Cleveland's Rocky Colavito. Malzone, Berra, and Colavito homered in the game, which was won by the American Leaguers, 5-3.

One Red Sox player who did not accompany Williams and Malzone to Los Angeles for the All-Star game was Pumpsie Green, a second baseman. Called up from Minneapolis in the American Association where he was hitting over .300, Green entered a Red Sox game on July 21 as a pinch-runner and earned the distinction of being the first African-American to play for Boston. In so doing, he made "the Negro cycle now complete" for major-league baseball, twelve years after Jackie Robinson broke the color line.[47]

In the ninth inning of the All-Star game, Hal made a plate appearance and bunted foul on a sacrifice attempt and then went down swinging. After the game, Hal told an interviewer, "I didn't want to show up Ted Williams," Playing in the All-Star game had been a great thrill. Ernie Banks felt the same. Banks rushed to the airport right after the game ended and boarded a plane for Chicago. Arriving Tuesday morning at 7 A.M., Banks was in uniform for the afternoon game at Wrigley Field. "Let's play two," he told reporters.

Hal and Musial took a TWA flight to St. Louis on Tuesday morning and that night Hal was behind the plate for Gibson's second start, a rough outing. The Pirates, led by Clemente, were on him in the first inning for three runs. Musial got one back with his ninth homer, but Hemus pulled Gibson in the fifth inning. He had struck out three, walked two, hit one batter and had one wild pitch. Gibson's record fell to 1-1. Uncharacteristically, Hal dropped a pop foul.

Four days later, Hal caught Bob Miller, a 23-year-old "bonus baby." Miller pitched a complete game against the Phillies and won, 4-3, infusing the Cards with new hope for the season. Musial's eleventh homer with a man on tied the game in the fourth, erasing Robin Robert's early lead.

Ernie Broglio had emerged as a dependable starter for the Cardinals. Though his record at mid-season was a meager 5-5, he led in shut-out innings. Hal thought his curve ball was equal to that of Sam Jones, the former Cardinal who was on his way to winning 21 games for the Giants in 1959. Five years down the road, Broglio, of course, became a party to one of the Cardinal's most heralded trades ever. In 1964, Bing Devine dealt Broglio for the Cub's Lou Brock. Broglio, who won 21 games for the Cards in 1960, said at the time that "the Cubs got quite a deal." As it turned out, it was the Cardinals who got quite a deal. Brock blossomed as a great star in St. Louis and played a pivotal role in the Cardinals' 1964 championship year. Broglio never regained the form he'd shown in 1959-60.

But in 1959, Broglio established himself as a Cardinal ace. After Broglio beat Bob Friend, 3-0, in August, the Cards' pitching had reappeared. Mizell seemed to be over the back problems that had beset him. Steady Larry Jackson led the team in ERA. Lindy McDaniel had worked his way to 10-10. Perhaps, Hemus thought, his team might make a run for the first division after all.

When the Giants visited in mid-August for a two-game series, Hemus had Mizell and Jackson ready. The Cards fought hard in trying to punch their way up to the first division, but the Giants had a scent of the pennant. They beat the Cards in two one-run games, the second in ten innings. At least, Brandt didn't do any damage this time. Hal handled his pitchers well and threw out two of three runners. Only Mays slid in under the tag at second. Encouraged by good crowds, the Cardinals looked forward to facing another contender as the Dodgers came to town. Hemus had his rookie sensation, Bob Miller, matched against Koufax. The Cardinals played well and Hal doubled off Koufax and later threw out his Dodger counterpart, Johnny Roseboro, by ten feet. The game and the season, however, belonged to the Dodgers. Koufax survived extra-base hitting by Hal and Flood and home runs by Boyer and Oliver to run his record to 6-2.

After the short series with the West Coast powerhouses, the Cardinals flew to Philadelphia. They split the two-game series with the Phillies and were on to Pittsburgh. The Pirates had given them trouble all year. Hemus had his two rookie right-handers, Bob Gibson and Bob Miller, scheduled for the mound in Forbes Field. Gibson lasted six innings and lost, 4-2. The next night, Friend avenged his earlier loss to Miller. The Cardinals took the short trip to Cincinnati by bus and dropped three in a row to the Reds. A loss the next day to Milwaukee in County Stadium ran their losing streak to six games. Gibson pitched in the last of these, losing 3-1 in nine innings against Spahn, who mastered Musial, Boyer, and Hal on this day. Gibson had a wild pitch high over Hal's head and a fielding error that cost him a run. Once Hal settled him down, his late-inning pitches matched those of Spahn. There was a pattern developing around Gibson that gave substance to the old warning about facing good pitchers: get them early or forget it!

The losing streak ended and the Cards won four in a row against the Braves and Reds, showing that the Cardinals refused to give up. The three-team pennant race kept the whole league involved. On September 19 at San Francisco, the Giants and the Dodgers began a three-game series. The pitching matchups with a National League championship at stake drew capacity crowds to old Seals' Stadium for the day-night doubleheader. In the first game, the Dodgers' Roger Craig out-dueled Johnny Antonelli and in the nightcap, Don Drysdale beat Mike McCormick, 5-3. Johnny Podres finished the Dodger sweep the next day by defeating Giants' ace Sam Jones.

The Dodgers were peaking at the right time. But, the Cardinals pinned a loss on them in St. Louis on September 22nd in the 149th game of the 154-game season. In the top of the first, the red-hot Dodgers scored three runs off Cardinal pitcher Larry Jackson. With a comfortable lead, Sandy Koufax took the mound but walked Cardinal leadoff hitter Blasingame in the Cardinal half. Cunningham, batting second and the only real challenger to Aaron for the NL batting championship in 1959, grounded into a force play. Cimoli, who was nearing his last game with the Cardinals, grounded out. Koufax worked around clean-up hitter Ken Boyer, who was on a tear. Gene Oliver, a rookie back-up catcher who started in left field, squibbed a grounder just beyond Junior Gilliam's reach for an infield hit. With the bases loaded, Hal stepped into the batter's box, the No. 6 man in the lineup. With two outs and down three runs, Hal took one strike. On the next pitch, he blasted a Koufax fastball out of Busch Stadium and into the night sky. His grand slam gave the Cardinals a lead over the Dodgers. Typically, Hal downplayed his feat. "You could tell he didn't have his best stuff," Hal explained. "After all, he had loaded the bases!"

For the season finale, the Giants were one-and-a-half games back and came into St. Louis, where they had opened the season back in April. Holding a big advantage in head-to-head meetings between the two clubs and featuring a powerful lineup with Mays, Cepeda,

McCovey, and Brandt, the Giants liked their chances to sweep and gain ground on the Dodgers. The Cardinals wanted to salvage something out of this grueling and disappointing season. The Giants started their ace, Sad Sam Jones, in the opener. Jones had all of his stuff and no-hit the Cards for eight innings when the game was called because of rain. Jones got his 21st victory and the Giants still had their chance to win the pennant. But, the Cards swept the doubleheader from the Giants on the last day of the regular season, September 27. Hal did damage to the Giants with his defense—a perfect peg to Blasingame on a "strike 'em out, throw 'em out" double play—in the first game, which the Cards won, 2-1. At the end of the day, the Braves and the Dodgers were tied for first. A playoff between those two clubs ended with two straight Dodger victories. For the first time, Los Angeles would host a World Series. Their Dodgers would battle the Chicago White Sox, who squeezed by Cleveland to gain the AL spot in the fall classic. Los Angeles won the 1959 World Series, four games to two.

Earlier that October, the Cardinal players cleaned out their lockers and started for their off-season homes. For many of them, it was family time again. As Brosnan said, the end of the season is a bittersweet time. Hal liked being at home with Carolyn and the children. He knew that he had recovered from his mid-season injuries and had begun to hit better as the cooler weather arrived. His performance at the end of the season had matched his great start in May and early June. He finished with a .270 batting average and his home run (No. 13) against Koufax put him third on the team in that category. Musial had 14 in 1959. Ken Boyer's 28 led the Cardinals. Bill White, acquired for power in the trade that gave up Sam Jones, had 12.

The pitching staff could have used Jones in '59, but the trade for Bill White paid great dividends for the Cardinals. White became an All-Star first baseman with the Cardinals and a key player in the 1960's championship years. He and George Crowe, with their calming influence and dignified presence, counseled budding stars Gibson and

Flood during some difficult times in 1959. Jones' absence hastened the development of Gibson, who picked up the victory in relief in the last game of the year against the Giants. His nine-inning shut out of the Phillies in his pitching debut previewed the incredible 12, nine-inning shut-outs that he would pitch in 1968. Bob Miller's debut showed him to be a pitcher of promise for the next year. Jackson and Mizell led the team in victories and in ERA. Lindy McDaniel proved to be effective in coming out of the bullpen. Broglio had that great curve ball, which would help him fashion a 21-9 record in 1960.

The source of the Cardinals' real confusion seemed to be the outfield positions, where Hemus had tried no less than ten players. Much to Flood's anguish, he had played only part-time. Hemus seemed to downgrade Flood's speed, bat, and competitiveness. The other two catchers, Green and Oliver, couldn't match Hal's defensive skill and pitch-calling know-how but Hemus wanted their bats in the line-up and rotated them in the outfield. Two others who played outfield, Cunningham and White, actually were first basemen but first base belonged to Musial. Ironically, former Cardinal outfielders traded to other clubs galvanized their new teams. Bill Virdon had a big role in the Pirates' pennant season of 1960. In Los Angeles, writers said the acquisition of Wally Moon was a "huge" factor in the 1959 pennant-winning season for the Dodgers. While playing for San Francisco, Jackie Brandt won the Gold Glove for leftfielders in 1959.

Brandt and Virdon had been traded away by Frantic Frankie Lane. Dismissed by Gussie Busch, Lane continued his GM career at Cleveland. Sportswriters credited Lane with making a pennant contender out of the Indians through key trades, namely those that brought in Woodie Held, Vic Power, and Jimmy Piersall. Power was a pioneering, Caribbean player who influenced Clemente and other Latinos. He brought a flashy glove, a flashier batting stance, and a hot bat to the Indian lineup. Piersall battled mental illness and gave an account of it in his autobiographical book, *Fear Strikes Out*. The good news about the book: Hollywood picked it up and made a movie with the same name. The bad news: they cast non-athletic Tony Perkins in the role of Piersall. In between his headaches, Piersall was a funny man. Clubhouse comedians fostered good relationships and good humor over the long season. Piersall came up with the Red Sox and rapidly became a fan favorite in Boston. Thirty years later, one Red Sox fan remembered with great delight a game he attended at Fenway Park in Boston. As Dom DiMaggio, who was somewhat paddle-footed, walked out to his position, Piersall followed in the great centerfielder's shadow, imitating his peculiar stride step for step. DiMaggio suddenly became aware of this and chased away his teammate with the odd sense of humor. Hal remembered that once, in a spring training game, Piersall hit one out of the park and circled the bases while running backwards.

In assessing the roster after the 1959 season, the Cardinals seemed solid in only three or four positions. Boyer, at third, was a perennial All-Star. Musial told the management and the reporters that he had another super year looming ahead of him. Hal, a two-time All-Star, was at catcher. He had hit more homers and had more at-bats than any catcher in the National League except for Crandall. At second base, there was Blasingame, the steadiest of players and a worthy successor to former Cardinal legendary second baseman, Red Schoendienst. Blasingame appears to be an earlier version of Houston's Craig Biggio—both got more than 540 at-bats each year they played. In 1957, "Blaze" played in *all 154* games. In 1959, he appeared in 150 games. Sure-handed in the field, the little guy showed up to play hard, play fair, and win. Although he wasn't a power hitter, Blasingame had a .289 batting average in 1959 and led the team in stolen bases. Despite all of this, the Cards traded him to the Giants in December of 1959 for Daryl Spencer.

Cunningham, the rightfielder, had been a big producer for the '59 Cards. His .345 batting average came in second to Aaron's .355.[48] Over in the American League that year, Harvey Kuenn (.353) and Al

Kaline (.327), were one-two in batting average. Tito Francona, who hit .363, was one at-bat shy of winning the AL batting crown in 1959. He had 399 at-bats instead of the 400 necessary to qualify.

Hal gained a ringing endorsement in the *The Sporting News* after the season. One writer editorialized that *only* four Cardinal players deserved increases in their contracts for the next season and Hal was one of them. The Cardinal front office agreed. When Hal met with Devine, the general manager raised Hal's salary to $21,000 in his 1960 contract.

On November 11, the 1959 Rawlings Gold Glove winners were announced as selected by the National League players, coaches, and managers. Brandt, along with Mays and Aaron, made up the best-fielding NL outfield according to their peers. Crandall, at catcher, won the first of his four Gold Glove awards. The news article mentioned that Hal was the *only* other contender for Gold Glove catcher. Hal received 52 votes to Crandall's 118, enough to put Hal on the NL Gold Glove runner-up team. The group included Banks at shortstop, Johnny Temple at second, with Clemente, Pinson, and Moon in the outfield.[49] Though the Cardinals finished a disappointing seventh in the eight-team league, Hal and some of his teammates received recognition for their outstanding individual performances.

13

Those Changes!

The end of the 50's proved to be momentous in the history of the United States. Rock 'n Roll had changed the tempo of America. Imported automobiles took to American roads. Jetliners streaked overhead. Cold War tensions spilled into the Western Hemisphere and affected Caribbean winter baseball. In Cuba, Castro took power. His autocratic government confiscated the property of affluent Cubans and sent many of them into exile in south Florida. Castro's appropriations of private property and vicious purging of his opponents led the Eisenhower administration in 1960 to restrict imports of Cuban sugar. On January 2, 1960, a young, energetic senator from Massachusetts, John F. Kennedy—a Catholic, an athlete, a World War II veteran, and a lover of Cuban cigars—announced his candidacy for president. Later, Kennedy promised to put a man on the moon in ten years during his inauguration speech, the same time that major leaguers from the U.S. were playing their last winter ball season in Cuba.

In that same month, Hal and Joe Garagiola were on goodwill tours for the Cardinals, putting smiles on the faces of fans, especially with their stories about Vinegar Bend Mizell and Yogi Berra. Garagiola traveled treacherous U.S. Highway 71 south to DeQueen, Arkansas, to emcee a banquet for chicken producers, while Hal ranged northward to Waterloo, Iowa.

The Smiths enjoyed frequent visits with their new neighbors, Joe and Cathy Cunningham. In St. Louis, Joe had met Cathy Dillard of Mammoth Springs, Arkansas. They hit it right off and decided to get married. Since Joe spent much of the time on the road during the season, Cathy's apartment worked out well as their residence. In the fall, however, the couple began to shop for a house to buy. It happened that a nice house came up for sale near Hal and Carolyn, who notified Cathy and Joe and encouraged them to buy it. The newlyweds bought the house and moved in near their dear friends. Hal and Carolyn loved to see Joe, who often dropped over for coffee or to borrow some tool or a ladder. He hadn't had time to accumulate all the things one needs to care for a house.

One Sunday afternoon, however, Hal and Carolyn drove by a house with a "for sale" sign planted in the yard that really caught their eye. Out of curiosity, they contacted the realtor about it. Before they knew it, they had purchased the house. With little fanfare, Hal and Carolyn signed papers and called the mover. Throughout this flurry of real estate activity, they avoided telling the Cunninghams for fear of their reaction. Forty years later, Joe brings up the subject every chance he gets. "I can't believe that as soon as you got us to move here, you moved out!" Joe exclaims, each time the couples get together. For years, according to Carolyn, "Cathy Cunningham drove one of Mary K's pink Cadillacs as a top saleswoman in the cosmetics firm. Joe works for the Cardinal organization in community relations. His trademark sign-off to a telephone conversation is, "Keep swinging!" As Dizzy Dean used to say, "You're always dangerous when you're swinging!"

Today, free agency and drug test results often rule baseball headlines in the winter months. In 1959-60, reporters covered meetings where general managers busily tried to improve their clubs through trades. Once traded, a player had no option but to play for the team that had obtained his contract. Congress was suspicious of this "reserve clause," which was standard in all player contracts. The reserve clause permitted absolute control by owners over the careers of professional ballplayers, yet Congress still had done nothing about it. At the same time, Branch Rickey talked constantly of starting up the Continental League. He wanted to challenge the 16 club owners who steadfastly refused to expand major-league baseball beyond the eight National League cities and eight American League cities. Major-league baseball opposed Rickey and acted to freeze him out. This monopolistic attitude attracted the attention of Senator Estes Kefauver of Tennessee, chairman of the Senate Anti-Trust and Monopoly Subcommittee.

Warren Giles, the National League commissioner, and Senator Kefauver, who had presidential ambitions, weren't exactly fond of each other. But it was an attack that arose from the dugout, not the halls of Congress, that wounded and eventually killed the absolutism of baseball's owners. Hal's teammate, Curt Flood, sued major-league baseball over the reserve clause. Flood's refusal to be traded to Philadelphia effectively ended his career. His stance, however, ultimately led to revolutionary changes in the relationship between players and owners, in the financial landscape of baseball, and in the greater American society as well.

Before the end of "baseball as we know it" came about, there were a few trades that reflected a sort of random genius on the part of the execs who labored tirelessly to mend roster weaknesses or cut expenses. Sometimes, a sort of serendipity luck surfaced in all the trading madness. Hal and Carolyn read newspapers and watched the sports news, where player trades often were announced before the players involved had been told. In just this way, they learned that their friend Jackie Brandt had been traded to Baltimore in the American League. Hal thought that it could be a good move for Brandt because he might be able to regain his position as a centerfielder—a position Willie Mays owned with the Giants.

One day, Hal and Carolyn picked up the paper to find that Hal Smith had been traded to the Pittsburgh Pirates! Fortunately, the news referred to Harold Wayne Smith of the Kansas City Athletics. The baseball world also had shortened his name to Hal. With two Hal Smiths playing in the major leagues, this resulted in more than a little confusion. The two Hals were a year apart in age (Hal R. was a year younger). They were both catchers, although Hal W. played third base much of the time in Kansas City. Their professional careers started in 1949. In 1954, Hal W. hit .350 for the Columbus, Ohio, Jets, a farm team of Kansas City, to lead the league. Hal W. got his major league call in 1955. In his rookie year, he hit .271 with 4 home runs and 52 RBI'S for the Baltimore Orioles. In 1955, Hal R. hit .299 for the Houston Buffs. It was a great year and helped send him to the majors in 1956, where he hit .282 with five home runs and 23 RBI'S as a rookie. The two Hals were aware of each other. Since they played in different leagues, however, they had little contact. At any rate, the confusion about these players with the same names was compounded when they both ended up in Pittsburgh wearing Pirate uniforms. When Hal R. went to Pittsburgh as a player/coach in 1965, Harold Wayne was already out of baseball but had left Pittsburgh as a hero. Hal W.'s dramatic, eighth-inning three-run homer in the seventh game of the 1960 World Series erased a Yankee lead and set the stage for Bill Mazeroski's ninth-inning, walk-off home run that gave the series to the Pirates.

Once, after a game in 1965, Hal R. emerged from the Pirate clubhouse to be met by an elderly lady who grabbed his arm. A dedicated fan from out of state, she talked compulsively about how the Hal Smith home run in the World Series against the Yankees had been one of the happiest moments of her life. She had driven 1,500 miles, she told the wrong Hal Smith, to see him and get his autograph. For a long moment, Hal R. stared into the lady's beseeching eyes. Then he smiled, thanked her for the praise and signed "Hal Smith" on her program, knowing that Hal W. would have approved. After all, the other Hal's signature had appeared under Hal R.'s photograph on a Topps baseball card. The two Hals also had appeared together on a baseball card in the Topps series and it became a treasured collectors' item. Hal, who was great at picking off base runners, was asked if he'd ever been picked off himself. "Once," he answered. "Picked off third by Hal Smith." It happened in an exhibition game. After their playing days, the two Hals and their wives became close friends. The two couples were breakfasting together in a west Texas golf resort when they heard the news about the plane crash that killed their former teammate, Roberto Clemente.

An auspicious trade made by Kansas City that winter dealt a promising, but injury-prone rightfielder, Roger Maris, to the Yankees. In return for Maris, the Athletics got Don Larsen, Hank Bauer, and Marvelous Marv Throneberry. Two years later, Maris hit the 61 home runs that broke Ruth's single-season home run record. In 1967, Maris was traded to the St. Louis Cardinals and played in two more World Series. He retired after the '68 season and a grateful Gussie Busch handed Maris an Anheuser-Busch beer distributorship in Tampa, Florida. Maris died in 1984. When Mark McGwire broke Roger's home run record in 1998, Maris' son was on hand at Busch Stadium to congratulate the Cardinal first baseman on his tremendous feat.

Eventually, Throneberry returned to New York as part of Casey Stengel's 1962 expansion team, the New York Mets. That year, the Mets lost 120 games. Watching one comedy of errors, Stengel said, "Don't anybody around here know how to play this game?" Throneberry tripled in a game but was called out for missing first base. Stengel went out to argue. "Jeez, Casey," the umpire said, "he missed second, too!"

14

1960

One major newspaper gave the Cardinals an outside chance to win the pennant in 1960. Most sportswriters thought the team had improved its offense and might progress to the first division of the National League. Such sanguine opinions followed the addition of Daryl Spencer and Carl Sawatski, two veterans who might supply some hitting, an ingredient missing in the 1959 Cardinal lineup. Pundits had pointed out that the Cards ranked sixth in team home runs in 1959. When spring training rolled around in 1960, Hal couldn't recall that the coaches had asked the players to practice swinging harder. They may have and, if so, it only caused the 1960 Cardinals more problems with hitting. The '60 club actually *lacked* offense.

The Cardinals got off to another shaky start under Hemus, losing 14 of the first 17 games of the season. His lineup in May usually had Bill White in center and Sawatski behind the plate, with Musial, Flood, Cunningham, and Hal on the bench. But on May 15, Hemus had all of them in the lineup for the second game of a Sunday doubleheader at Wrigley Field. They probably wished they had played in the opener because Don Cardwell hurled his best game ever against them in the failing light. In going nine innings, Cardwell struck out four while no-hitting the Cards. Cub Classics occasionally rebroadcasts this game on WGN during rain delays. Modern viewers get a chance to see Musial strike out swinging and he even looks good doing it! Cards' fans might have a particular interest in watching Hal set up behind the plate. Hal's stance and movements are strikingly similar to those of a modern-day catcher like Ivan Rodriguez. The two are about the same size. Hal sets up on the balls of his feet to receive a pitch. It's different from the old back-on-the-haunch crouch common in the 70's and 80's. Catchers like the Cards' Ted Simmons and Tony Pena used it.

Over the years, a number of baseball men were quoted in newspapers about Hal's skill behind the plate. *The Sporting News* wrote that, in the opinion of "Redbird officials," Hal was "unmatched as a catcher in the National League." With savvy behind the plate and the confidence of his pitchers, he "boasts a strong and accurate throwing arm." The article mentioned that Hal was at the top of the league in fielding percentage. Cardinal brass weren't the only ones who recognized the ability of Hal. Carolyn, his wife, once remarked that, "he was a good little catcher!" Gene Mauch was a bit more specific. "Hal Smith," Mauch said, "has the finest arm of any catcher in the league. Del Crandall doesn't even come close to him."[50] Cunningham remembered that Hal and Crandall were the best catchers in the National League at the time.

Despite what some called a "cold bat," Hal continued his clutch hitting for the Cardinals and ranked fourth on the team with a .357 average with runners in scoring position. In Philadelphia, on June 26, 1960, Bob Gibson started the game but gave up three runs early and Hemus jerked him. In the fifth, Hal doubled to drive in the Cards' first run. Hemus brought in Ernie Broglio, the Cards' No. 1 starter. That was an unusual move and Hal could see that little Sol really wanted to win this one. Broglio walked the first batter he faced, speedy Tony Taylor. Taylor tried to steal second. Hal threw him out and the play seemed to be a turning point. In the top of the ninth with two on, Hal hit one out of the park. Broglio held the Phillies in their half and the Cards won this game, 4-3, with Hal driving in all four Cardinal runs. It ranks among his best games. Hal liked it, too and began writing a new song to celebrate his feats against the Phils. The title was catchy—"I hit a Dilly in Philly, Millie"—but Hal never finished this promising tune.

Hal was playing more and the Cardinals were climbing in the standings. They were hot and the fans were turning out. Gussie Busch would later call 1960 his most exciting season. Hemus now had a productive lineup. He was starting Flood in center, with Musial in left, White at first, Cunningham in right, and Hal catching every day. In the right place at the right time, Flood and Hal were making a big difference. Bing Devine told sportswriters that when Hal was reinstalled as the regular catcher after being platooned with Sawatski, the Cardinals began to win. The only nagging concern about the play of Smith and Flood was their weak batting averages. Perhaps the 13 home runs the year before had depleted Hal. He was puzzled about it and had no explanation for the 42-point drop in his average from .270 to .228. Every other year, it seemed, he hit for a much lower average than the previous year.

Hemus still made odd managerial moves. He banned card games on the planes and once sent Grammas up to pinch-hit for Walt Moryn, who already had two strikes on him. In one of his better ideas, Hemus settled on a four-man pitching rotation for the stretch run. He scheduled rookie Ray Sadecki and veterans Jackson, Broglio, and Curt Simmons. Gibson pitched in relief and could be the fifth starter. Bullpen ace Lindy McDaniel rivaled the Pirates' great relief pitcher, Elroy Face, in saves and in games-won. Mizell now pitched for the Pirates after being traded on May 28 for Julian Javier. Face, Bob Friend, and Vern Law were leading the Pirates to the pennant and now they had Mizell's help. The Pirates had filled another gap with the trade for the other Hal Smith at the No. 2 catcher position. Hal Wayne Smith was showing off his power and veteran's confidence. Manager Danny Murtaugh liked him and so did the Pirate fans.

On July 2, the Cards climbed above .500 with Gibson's 7-1 victory over Warren Spahn and the second-place Milwaukee Braves before 21,000 in County Stadium. Hal drove in Musial to give Gibson a 1-0 lead that he never relinquished. Hal had another hit in the game and another RBI. When he came up in the seventh inning with a man in scoring position, Spahn intentionally walked him. Hal threw out his counterpart, Crandall, trying to steal second. Gibson went nine innings, blanking Aaron and Mathews, who struck out three times, and fanned a total of seven. Hal went two for two, driving in Musial and White. He threw out a runner, got "pitched around" by Spahn, and called all of Gibson's pitches. Incidentally, how many Hall-of-Famers are mentioned in this paragraph? (The answer is five, although Crandall and White almost made it in.) Most importantly to Hal, the Cardinals beat a contender and were back in the pennant race.

On August 17th, a warm Wednesday, the Cards squared off against the Giants at Busch Stadium before 15,000 fans. Rarely did a game in 1960 go past three hours. This one covered three hours and 24 minutes in a 6-5 San Francisco win. Hal caught Sadecki, the splendid young lefthander who had cracked the four-man starting rotation by this time.

The game had some memorable moments. Sadecki threw a really wild pitch over Hal's head that went all the way to the retaining wall. The runner on first broke for second as the ball bounced back to Hal, who turned and threw hard to try to get him. He put too much on it. The ball flew past Javier and the runner motored on to third. A sportswriter in the press box remarked that in twenty years of reporting he hadn't seen a play scored like this one. There was a wild pitch, a stolen base, and an error on the catcher. The fifth inning got a little better for Hal. For the first out, he tracked down a high pop foul off the bat of Willie Mays that disappeared above the light towers before it came down and into Hal's Spaulding mitt by the visitor's dugout. When Don Blasingame, now a Giant, tried to bunt his way on, Hal threw him out at first. Hal nailed Orlando Cedepa trying to steal second to retire the side.

Although the Cardinals lost this particular game, seven who played that night formed the nucleus of the Cardinals' World Series championship team of 1964. Javier was at second, White was at first base and Boyer, Flood and Sadecki all started. Tim McCarver pinch-hit and Gibson was a pinch-runner. But for the heart condition that shortened Hal's career, he would have been a part of that team roster in '64, too.

Sadecki was a gifted athlete from San Francisco. When he or Gibson pitched, Hal would be the receiver. With Hal's help as a battery mate, Sadecki won nine games in his rookie season. Four years later in 1964, he was one of the Cardinal aces and won 20 games with a 3.68 ERA. It was his best season by far in the majors. But the best pitcher for the Cards in 1960 was Broglio. In what he considered his best game in the majors, Broglio went 12 innings on August 11, 1960 at Forbes Field, striking out nine and giving up two runs. Musial hit a two-run homer in the top of the twelfth. Broglio, with Hal behind the plate, got the final Pirate out with the tying run in scoring position. His opposing pitcher, Bob Friend, also went the full twelve innings.

The next night, Ken Boyer hit a home run with two on, staking Gibson to a three-run lead. Hal got a base hit that drove in Boyer for an insurance run. Four runs were plenty for "Gibby," who went the nine innings for his third victory (and last of the year, as it turned out). The win pulled the charging Cards to within three games of the Bucs. In this stretch, Musial played and hit like he did in the '41 and '46 seasons. Musial said that his old high school buddies in Donora, Pennsylvania, quit speaking to him as he tried to derail the pennant express of the Pirates. The Cards' pitching was good and Boyer was playing well, too. Hal was chipping in with base hits and RBI's against the front-running Pirates.

Hemus decided to use the kangaroo court money—collected from players who had missed signals during a game—to finance a picnic for players and families at Tilles Park on August 22, an off-day. The picnic featured hot dogs and a horseshoe pitching tournament. In the finals, with plenty of good-natured razzing going on, Hal and Broglio went on a ringer binge to claim the horseshoe championship, 21-9, over Bill White and his partner, Bob Nieman. The recreational outing for the team seemed to relax the players before they started a make-or-break series with the Pirates on Friday, August 26th. Cardinal fans turned out in droves, filling Busch Stadium with lusty cheers as the Cards took the field for the opener. The battery was Broglio and Smith, the horseshoe champs. Hal drove in the first run for the Cards and got another hit later. He received two intentional walks from Bob Friend. Musial broke up the duel with a two-run homer in the seventh, thrilling the fans as the Cards won, 3-1, and Broglio got his sixteenth win of the season. On Saturday night, Hemus started Gibson. Hal was two for three and reached on a walk. For good measure, he threw out Dick Groat. It seemed that every time Gibson was on the mound, Hal's hitting and defense was just a little sharper. On Saturday, 30,000 St. Louis fans again were treated to a magnificent walk-off homer by Musial. He hit it off Pirate reliever Face as the Cards won, 5-4. On Sunday, the Pirates were on the wrong side of a 5-4 score as the Cards completed the sweep. Hal caught every pitch from Broglio, Gibson, Simmons, and Lindy McDaniel. He went five for ten in the series. Against the Pirates in August, Musial had homered in the ninth twice and again in the 12th inning. His homers had beaten Friend twice and the Hall of Fame reliever Face once.

Seeing his old roomie, Mizell, over in the Pirate dugout may have helped inspire Hal. Hal's new roommate, Lindy McDaniel, picked up his 21st save of the year to go with his ten victories. Pittsburgh gladly left town since the Cards were now breathing down their necks. St. Louis was just four games out with a month to play and had the momentum. The Cards packed their gear and headed for the airport. That night, they landed at O'Hare and took the bus to Milwaukee. On Monday, Larry Jackson faced the Braves. Hal got one hit, but it was Joe Cunningham's day as he doubled twice and scored two runs. Grammas scored an unearned run for the Cardinals after being advanced to second by Crandall's rare passed ball. With a three-run lead in the bottom of the ninth, Jackson needed to get Crandall, Mathews, and Aaron. And he did, one, two, three. Jackson's nine-inning gem brought the winning streak to four and put the Cards alone in second place.

Still, it was going to be Pittsburgh's year. Bob Friend had said, "We'd better win it this year. Our fans love us so much they'll kill us if we don't." Calmed by his constant tobacco cud, Bucs' manager Danny Murtaugh watched his team rally all year and survive late challenges from Milwaukee and St. Louis. Murtaugh observed that this "team always had shown resiliency. I can't spell it, but I know what it means."

The Cards finished in third, good enough to satisfy most fans as the number of glowing Letters to the Editor revealed. The season had made Gussie Busch happy, too, and he was quoted as saying he could hardly "wait for next year." He attended all of the Cardinals' home games. One day, he went down on the field as the Cards were taking batting practice before a game with the Giants. Gussie had spotted Mays and went over to speak to him. "Willie," Gussie Busch asked, "how can we get a player as remotely talented as you are?" "You already have one," Mays pointed out. "Curt Flood!"[51]

Hemus didn't think that at all. In fact, he did not think Flood would ever be a good major-league player and told him so. Years later, Hemus wrote a letter of apology to Flood, saying that he had terribly misjudged Flood's abilities. Flood denied his first impulse, which was to tear up the letter. He kept it and reprinted it in his autobiography.

This new respect from Hemus had come much too late to impress Flood. Keane, a Cards' coach, had told Flood that his day would come. Harry Walker worked with him incessantly to improve his hitting stroke. Still, Flood was not the starting centerfielder in the 1960 season. In fact, Hemus had convinced general manager Bing Devine at the winter meetings to get someone for centerfield, which he thought was a weak spot in the lineup. Devine sent feelers to the Milwaukee club for Bill Bruton, but he was soon traded to a team in the American League. Devine settled on signing outfielder Don Landrum for $20,000. Landrum, Devine assured reporters, could be another Richie Ashburn.

Devine watched with interest as the Yankees made some changes. Co-owners Del Webb and Dan Topping decided that the "fall guys" for losing the 1960 World Series were General Manager George Weiss and Manager Casey Stengel. They had decided that Stengel was too old to manage. The Yankees released a statement to the press that Stengel had retired. Stengel told reporters a different story. "I didn't retire," Casey said. "I was fired." He didn't say a thing about how many pennants (10) and World Series titles (7) the Yankees had won during his twelve years at the helm. The newsmen filled in the rest and left the impression that the Yankee front office was a bit ungrateful toward "the Old Perfessor."

At baseball's winter meeting, Devine floated a trade offer to new Yankee manager, Ralph Houk. Would the Yankees trade Whitey Ford, Elston Howard, and power pitcher Ryne Duran to the Cards for Hal, Larry Jackson, and Ron Kline? Very quickly, Buzzie Bavasi of the Dodgers learned of this conversation and made his own offer to Houk for the Yankee trio. The Dodgers would give up Johnny Podres, Duke Snider, and Gil Hodges.[52] No such deal was ever made and the Yankees asserted that they had no intention of trading away New York City native and Yankee icon Ford. Such rumors were only good for sportswriters and their readers and stoked the fires of the Hot Stove League.

Hal would be staying with the Cards and signed a 1961 contract which put him at $23,500, the highest salary he would command as a player. After all, good catchers were hard to come by, according to Dodger general manager Bavasi, who lamented, "there are 180 million people in the United States and there aren't more than a half-a-dozen real good catchers among them!" Hal was one of the half-dozen. The Dodgers had one of them, too in John Roseboro. When Casey Stengel resurfaced in 1962 with the New York Metropolitans, his judgment was even harsher. Looking around at the Met talent pool in 1964, he lamented that there are "two hundred million Americans, and there ain't two good catchers among them!" He may have been correct. By that time, Hal and Crandall were part-time players, Berra was managing, Campanella was confined to a wheelchair, and Johnny Bench was in the minors. Tim McCarver, who had been trained in part by Hal, was surely on Stengel's short-list at the time. Red Schoendienst summarized young McCarver, his World Series catcher, as having some great tools, that the Cardinals had done well in preparing him for the big leagues, and that "it certainly helped that he could watch Hal Smith there for awhile because Smith wouldn't do anything to get his team beat."[53]

During the winter months, sportswriters were focusing on player trades, but there was a bigger story on the horizon. After the American League finally granted two new franchises, expansion talk was in the air for the National League.

During the 1960 season, reporters had a hard time getting Gussie Busch to speak his mind on the possibilities of expanding the number of National League teams. Since 1876, there had been eight teams in the National League. Since 1917, each team had played a 154-game schedule, with 22 games against each opponent—11 on the road and 11 at home. Symmetry is wonderful! Ruth had hit his 60 home runs in 1927 with that arrangement. At a press conference, reporters asked Busch about adding new teams, but he turned the question around by asking them what *they* thought expansion would do to the league. Bob Broeg, the influential sports editor of the *St. Louis Post Dispatch*, warned against it at the conference and in his columns. Broeg thought that a ten-team league was too much too soon. If you want to expand, he told them, start with nine. Above all, he said, the 154-game schedule must not be tampered with or records would be distorted. Later, in 1961, the 162-game schedule became a factor in Roger Maris' pursuit of Babe Ruth's single-season home run record. The commissioner of baseball ruled that Maris' 61 homers must go into the record book with an asterisk. Regardless of such cautionary views, baseball owners had to consider Branch Rickey's bid for a third major league—the Continental—and Congress now favored breaking up the NL's eight-city monopoly. American League owners voted *secretly* to allow the Washington Senator franchise to move to Minneapolis-St. Paul. A part of that deal approved a replacement team for the nation's capital and a new team, the California Angels, would be joining the American League. Thus, plans for a ten-team American League were finalized in 1960 and the new schedule would start the next year. By 1962, the National League had ten teams, too.

One of the American League expansion franchise owners was a former telegraph operator from Oklahoma who had dreamed of a career as a baseball player. Instead, he made a fortune as a singing cowboy in the movies. As J. G. Taylor Spink wrote, "with or without his horse, Champion, you knew him as Gene Autry." It was sheer Americana. At first, the Dodgers' Walter O'Malley resisted Autry's bid for an American League team in *their* city of Los Angeles. O'Malley later had a change of heart and the Dodgers showed their graciousness. O'Malley sent around a memo advising all Dodger executives to help ease the Angels into the major leagues.

A comparable, seismic shift for baseball occurred in December of 1960 at the owners' winter meeting when the Kansas City Athletics were sold to a man named Charles O. Finley. At the time, no one could have forecast the impact that this newcomer would have on the national pastime. There was a glimpse of it, however, right after the sale of the team. Finley issued an odd statement that the Athletics would no longer make player transactions with the New York Yankees. He mentioned that the A's would wear white baseball shoes.

Baseball executives that winter were disturbed about events in Cuba and fearful that the revolutionary government of Fidel Castro might affect baseball in the Caribbean. How right they were! At the same time, another meeting was taking place in Washington, D. C., that involved our country's Electoral College. The first of these elector meetings in 1788 had certified George Washington's election to the presidency. This one, in 1960, certified the election of John Fitzgerald Kennedy, the youngest man ever to hold the office of U.S. President. In his inaugural address, Kennedy insisted that within ten years, we Americans would land a man on the moon. The young president was considered to be wise in baseball matters, too.

15

His Heart

Hal was glad to report to spring training two weeks early in 1961. He told Carolyn that he would feel more prepared for the regular season if he could get in some extra training time. Hal's hitting down the stretch of the past season had been timely and far better than earlier in the year. Yet, his batting average was .43 points off and he wanted to reverse the slide. He felt confident he could do this.

After a lackluster spring in Florida, the Cardinals headed to St. Louis with some unanswered questions. Hemus had not found a solid starter for centerfield and had resigned himself to letting Flood play there on opening day. Sportswriters who followed the Cards thought the success of the team hinged on whether Flood and Smith could have "rebound" years. If Hal hit for a better average and pitchers stayed healthy, then a hot pennant chase lay ahead for the '61 Cards. Some of the Cardinal magic was back, too. Red Schoendienst rejoined the club, although Julian Javier now was the regular second baseman. Red got his old Cardinal uniform number back, too. Hal had been wearing Red's No. 2 but graciously offered it to give it back. The clubhouse manager issued Hal the uniform with No. 9. Enos Slaughter had worn that number. Hal joked that if "they decide to bring him back, too, I'll just quit!" The remark brought some chuckles in the clubhouse, but it was strangely prophetic of Hal's year.

Just before leaving St. Petersburg for the trip north, Jackson suffered a broken jaw. Coming off an 18-13 year and slated as the Cards' opening day pitcher, Jackson had been on the mound when Gil Hodges' bat splintered. A piece of it hit Jackson, knocking him out of action for two months. Hemus picked his big right-hander, Broglio, to open the Cardinal season in Milwaukee. Hal was behind the plate for his fourth opening day start. The Braves sent their perennial ace, Spahn, to the mound in his sixth opening-day start in a row. Thirty-three thousand fans packed County Stadium to see the match-up and Spahn lived up to his billing as one of the game's premier pitchers. He allowed the Cards six hits and two runs in ten innings, but it wasn't quite enough to win. The Cards came from behind to take it, 2-1. Down 1-0 to the Braves after Ed Mathews' fourth inning homer, Musial tripled in the seventh with two outs but was stranded when Daryl Spencer lined out. In the eighth, Spahn got Cunningham on a ground-out, then Hal tripled over the head of Brave centerfielder "Thumper" DeMerit. Flood, who didn't start in centerfield after all, went in to pinch-run. Flood scored on Bob Nieman's pinch-hit single to tie the game. In the top of the tenth, Spencer hit a solo shot and Lindy McDaniel got the Braves out in order. For the first time as Cardinal manager, Hemus got the season started with a win and for the first time, Warren Spahn lost a season opener. McDaniel, who entered the game in the ninth, picked up a relief win. The major-league lifetime leader in relief wins is Hoyt Wilhelm with 124. Second on the list is Lindy McDaniel with 119. Goose Gossage, Rollie Fingers, and Sparky Lyle follow those two on this elite list of pitchers. Hal caught a lot of McDaniel's relief wins.

The next day, the Cards were back at .500 after losing to the Braves in 11 innings. Hal was two for five, but Aaron went on a tear with a double and a triple. McDaniel walked in the Braves' winning run on a border-line pitch. Plate umpire Shag Crawford didn't see it that way, but Hal didn't say anything to him. "I never got into an argument with an ump because I didn't know what to say to him," Hal noted. "After they make a call, they're not gonna' change it. So, what do you say to him?" Crawford may have been nursing hard feelings toward Hemus, who had jumped on him about a balk call against Bob Miller in spring training. Hemus had told Miller to throw to first without taking a step because the opposing pitcher had done the same thing and gotten away with it. Miller didn't get away with it and Hemus fumed. The players said that lil' Sol didn't win many arguments. Unlike Hal, he was never at a loss for words.

For the third game of the season, the Cards were back at Busch Stadium against the Reds and their manager, Fred Hutchinson. They got a good look at the team that would win the National League championship in 1961. Hal was one for three in the game. The Reds were led by Frank Robinson and Vada Pinson, a good one-two punch at the top of the lineup. They had Ed Bailey catching and good pitching strength with big right-hander Joey Jay and left-hander Jim O'Toole. The Reds were solid up the middle with Don Blasingame at second and Eddie Kasko at short. Jim Brosnan, Hemus' old nemesis, came out of the bullpen to pick up the save. He would have a good year in 1961, going 10-4 with 16 saves, and appeared three times in the World Series against the Yankees.

Saturday's game was called after six innings with the Cards up, 4-0. Only about 4,000 fans sat through the rain delays on this cold afternoon. When the game was called, Hutchinson came out of the dugout with eyes as big as saucers and began fuming at the plate umpire, Dusty Boggess. Hutch told Boggess he should have called the game in the second inning when it was really raining hard and he was going to protest the game. Broglio got the win and the Cards took the Reds on Sunday, too. They scored first when Cunningham tripled and came in on Hal's sacrifice fly. Showing the Cardinal pitching strength, Ray Sadecki went nine innings and allowed two earned runs.

Hal continued to catch every day but went into a hitting slump in May. He was playing good defense and helping to hold down the opponent's running game. Because of Hal's throwing ability, runners knew they needed to get bigger leads off first if they wanted to steal. This led to more pickoffs by Cardinal pitchers. Hemus started Flood in centerfield through May. Flood responded by raising his average to .280.

On Sunday May 25, 2008, a national television show presented events that had happened in history on this date. It included a flashback feature of a game between the Cards and the Dodgers in St. Louis on May 25, 1961, involving a classic pitching match-up—Sandy Koufax vs. Bob Gibson. The two future Hall of Fame pitchers dueled for nine innings and the Dodgers won it, 1-0. The only score came on a home run by Tommy Davis in the seventh. John Roseboro caught Koufax and Hal caught Gibson. A teammate asked Hal what pitch he had called for when Davis homered. "The wrong one," Hal replied.

On May 31st, the Cardinals lost in the bottom of the ninth to the Giants in Candlestick Park. Hal singled and scored and Flood was one for four. Hemus must have been disappointed because he benched Flood for the month of June, starting him only two times and using him mostly as a pinch- runner.

Hal went on a hitting streak, going five for 13. After going hitless in L.A. on Memorial Day, he started the longest hitting streak of his major-league career. It reached eight games on June 7 against the Cubs. His average climbed from below .200 to .248. Hal was "seeing the ball well," as the players like to say. Hal sat out most of the second game of a late double-header on June 6. He came in to catch in the ninth inning but didn't bat.

Before the game, Hal visited with his old Hamilton, Ontario, manager, Vedie Himsl, one of the four Chicago Cub coaches who rotated as manager in the 1961 season, a whimsical experiment it seems. Himsl was 10-21, Harry Craft was 7-9, El Tappe was 42-54, and Lou Klein was 5-6. Klein, with the fewest games as manager, was the closest to .500.

The Cubs finished this "year of the coaches" with a 64-90 record, ahead of only Gene Mauch's Phillies. The Phillies wound up eighth, despite the fact that Mauch was one of the game's best sign stealers. In the next three years, however, the Mauch-men started a steady climb to league contender. They stayed one slot below the Cardinals in those years. In a final irony, the Phillies collapsed and the Cardinals won the NL pennant in 1964. Maybe the Cardinals changed their signals in the end. Alvin Dark, Hal remembered, actually was the best sign stealer in baseball and managed the Giants to a third-place finish. The next year, 1962, he would have them in the World Series.

On Wednesday, June 7, Hal was at the ballpark early even though he didn't get too much sleep the night before. He parked his car in the small lot and signed a few autographs for fans, who came early to meet the players as they arrived. Hal had ridden to the park with Cunningham and didn't expect Carolyn to attend the game since it was a school night for his kids. Jackson, who had recovered from his jaw injury, was pitching for the Cards with Hal behind the plate. Hal knew Jackson's pitches and habits well and he reminded the big pitcher that his fondness for throwing the change-up when a fastball was called was not necessary.

As the game got underway, Musial launched a double off the right field-screen. It was a patented drive from the beautifully balanced, unmistakable swing of Stan the Man and few who saw it ever forgot it. Now in his 20th year in the majors, Musial went four for four with four RBI's and two homers that soared beyond the pavilion roof in right. Jackson worked seven innings and McDaniel racked up his third save. Hal was one for three and scored from first on Jackson's surprising triple in the second inning. As Hal started putting on his gear, a stabbing sensation around his heart froze him momentarily. Well, he thought, pitchers are not going to hit too many triples anyway with me on base. The win pulled the fifth-place Cards to within one game of .500. Flood did not play. A guy named Carl Warwick was in center.

The next day, a Thursday, the Cards had a day off. Hal went to Busch Stadium to see the trainer. Even before the previous night's romp around the bases, he had experienced a "kind of pain in my chest. It felt like if I could burp, it'd go away. But it kept lingering. The trainer sent me to see our club doctor. He examined me and couldn't find anything wrong. They wanted us to be on the safe side, so he set up an appointment with the heart guy." That afternoon, the heart specialist at Jewish Hospital gave Hal an examination that included an electro-cardiogram test, the first one he'd had. The doctor took a second reading that night and told Hal he could go home, but to come back in the morning. "Well, that gave me a heart attack, when he said that!

"But the next morning, I came back and they put me in the hospital. On about the second day, the pain went away, especially after they gave me some nitroglycerin stuff. I was in the hospital for twelve days and they ran all kinds of tests. At that time, the doctor came to the room and said, 'Is there anything else you can do?' I said, I can't think of anything else. He told me that I would have to quit. I don't think they would have stopped me today. I don't think they would have stopped me completely."

Hal was diagnosed as having an angina condition. As Hal explained it, "when your heart pumps, the veins open and they close. Well, mine would close and wouldn't come open enough. That's what caused the pain. So the doctor suggested that I stop playing. I told him, 'wait a minute. I know what the problem is: I've got an eight-game hitting streak going and I'm not used to anything like that and it overloaded the circuits.'"

Hal's doctor told Bing Devine the news, and the general manager came to see Hal. "Don't worry about a job," Devine told Hal, "We'll have a job for you somewhere."[54]

16

Instructor-Manager

The job, as it turned out, was perfect for Hal. After a short recovery period, he finished the 1961 season working in the Cardinals' minor-league programs where he instructed young catchers. According to veteran umpire and former catcher Charley Berry, Hal could "get the ball away quicker than any catcher I've seen since Gabby Hartnett."[55] Now, he could teach his defensive techniques to upcoming catchers like Tim McCarver. "Tim didn't have the strongest arm in the league," Hal recalled. "We worked on him releasing the ball a little bit quicker. He learned to shift his feet and get rid of the ball and, I think, he did get better. McCarver and I roomed together once at spring training. Sonny Randall came down to teach us how to run. Now, McCarver could run, I mean, he could really go for a catcher. So he and I roomed together that spring with Randall and when I sleep, I grind my teeth. We got up on the first morning and McCarver ask Randall, 'Did you hear that frog in this room last night?'"

Hal helped bring along another great Cardinal catcher, Ted Simmons. "I worked with him some—with his hitting, you know ... That's a joke! He could hit!! But here's a guy who didn't take a little crow hop when he threw. He just stood and flat-footed it. What can you do to help that? We worked with Simmons on blocking balls. At spring training, we'd get all the catchers together and block balls one day. Another day we'd hit pop-ups. In that Florida sky, it's really tough to see them sometimes. They call it a high sky and when that ball goes up, and some of those coaches can hit them where they come down with icicles, it's just hard to get your bearings right where that thing is going to come down. If you can do it down there, you can do it anywhere. At Candlestick, Willie Mays hit a pop-up a mile high and it finally came down, just missing a cable and I caught it. Once, in spring training, I was showing all these young catchers the way the Cardinals did it. We had them put on their masks, squat down in position, and then put their head down. When a catcher heard the crack of the bat, he'd raise up and go after the ball. Well, to show them, I got down, put the mask on, and I heard the fungo guy, who was George Crowe, hit the ball and I went after it. I was looking up when that ball came down and hit me right here on the side of the nose. I don't know how it kept from breaking every bone in my face. Those guys cracked up, especially Crowe. After coming to, I said. 'and that's the wrong way!

McCarver and Simmons stood out because of their hitting. When McCarver first came up, he had a stance where it looked like he was peeping over his arm when he was at bat. But he could hit the ball to the left side of the infield and he could beat it out because he was fast. Later, he changed his stance and got more experience. He hit a few home runs, too. Simmons was just a good hitter, a switch hitter, the best! Both started out as catchers. McCarver caught Bob Gibson in his prime, so he knew how to call a game. He was good at that. Steve Carlton wanted McCarver to catch every one of his games. He was like his personal catcher, you know."[56] Hal knew Carlton, of course, from managing him at Rock Hill.

On May 8, 1962, manager Johnny Keane asked Hal to return to the Cardinals as a bullpen coach. Hal joined Red Schoendienst, Vern

Benson, hitting coach Harry Walker, and pitching coach Howie Pollet on Keane's staff. The Cards finished sixth in the ten-team league, six games over .500. But, they were building the best National League club of the decade. Along with Gibson, Sadecki, Flood, Boyer, White, and Javier, the Cardinals had a new regular catcher, Tim McCarver.

In 1964, Hal got his chance to manage in Rock Hill, South Carolina, a city of some 30,000 people, about half white and half African-American, thirty miles south of Charlotte, North Carolina. When Hal arrived to manage the Cardinals' Class D team, the Rock Hill Cardinals were just getting established in the Western Carolinas League. Two other South Carolina cities, Spartanburg and Greenville, and five small cities in North Carolina rounded out the eight-team league. The Cardinal organization selected Hal for this job, in part, because of his winsome personality and because he was a good instructor and a solid baseball fundamentalist. All of these qualities came to the fore in the year of his managerial debut.

The Cardinals were making their debut, too, in the first year of a franchise with Rock Hill, which had been an independent team. Battles during the civil rights actions of 1961 had shaken Rock Hill, where police arrested nine students from Friendship Junior College because of a lunch-counter sit-in at the McCrory five-and-dime store and a white antagonist punched and dragged John Lewis from a freedom bus. Lewis later became a U.S. Congressman from Georgia. On a visit to Rock Hill in 2002, citizens gave him the key to their city. Today, motorists who enter Rock Hill are greeted by a sign that bears the city's motto, "No Room for Racism."

So, the Cardinals sent Hal to Rock Hill, but they gave him a little help, too. They assigned a lefty named Steve Carlton, who was in his second year of professional ball. Rock Hill had a good year under Hal's leadership. The franchise led the Western Carolinas League in attendance and finished second in the standings to the Salisbury Dodgers. Hal's team was one-half game back at the end, but earned a spot in the league's two-team play off. The Dodgers won it, two games to one.

Carlton was 10-1 with an ERA of 1.04 at Rock Hill. The Cardinal organization moved him to Class AA Tulsa before the year was out. Hal chuckled when he recalled Carlton's departure from his club. "That's when I became a dummy. I couldn't manage near as well."

Actually, he showed good managerial skills. In the first game of the season, Hal was puzzled when his young outfielder, Gary Stone, got in the batters' box on the left side. Hal said, "he was one of the catchers. In spring training every time he came to bat he hit right-handed. So, in this first game big Stone came to bat with the bases loaded and he went up there left-handed. I called time, and said, 'What are you doing?'" He said, 'Well, this guy's a right-hand pitcher and I wanted to hit left-handed.' I said, 'You ever hit left-handed before?' He said, 'No.' So, I had to turn him around." Hal didn't recall the outcome, but Rock Hill went on to post a 76-51 record, pleasing Hal and his seven-year-old son Dennis Smith, the batboy.

One difficult job of managing that Hal experienced was making roster cuts. His roommate and dear friend, Lindy McDaniel, had watched Von, his younger brother, struggle to remain in organized baseball. After his sensational debut year of 1957, Von lost his edge as a pitcher and could never rise to the big league level again. He spent nine seasons in the minors, mostly as an outfielder. Von, a bright, sensitive person, has been compared to Rick Ankiel, the Cardinal outfielder who had shown great promise as a pitcher. There was a third McDaniel brother, too. As Hal told the story, "Kerry Don McDaniel was the youngest and apparently was the best athlete of the three. But he just never could make it. I don't think he had the same desire [as Lindy or Von]. I was the one who had to release him when I managed at Rock Hill. That was the toughest thing in the world to do, you know, and I even wrote Lindy a letter explaining to him."[57] Hal shot straight with Lindy. His baseball friends knew that, for all the goodwill

Hal generated in a locker room, he answered truthfully and spoke from his heart. After the season, Harry Walker invited Hal to become part of his coaching staff at Pittsburgh. Hal accepted the job and never managed a professional baseball team again.

17

A Return to the Big Leagues

"In 1965," Hall recalled, "I went to Pittsburgh as a coach for Harry Walker. That's when I got to be on the active list again as a player. As a coach, you'd throw batting practice for hours. That is why I think my heart condition was not as serious as they feared." Hal had a chance to catch Pirate ace Bob Veale and another tricky knuckleballer, Wilbur Wood. Hal only got to the plate four times—three of them against the Cardinals—and is still looking for his first hit with the Pirates. That game at Forbes Field, on July 1, 1965, had to be a classic for one-line jokes. Too bad the catchers that day weren't wearing microphones. Hal was behind the plate catching Bob Veale, and Bob Uecker, a future announcer and comedian, was catching for the Cardinals. Neither of the catchers got a hit, but Uecker got plunked by Veale. Uecker threw out two runners but the Cards didn't test Hal's arm. After a four-year absence as a player, he was happy to be back on the field. The renewal of his association with Harry Walker and getting to watch all those great Pirate players every day was quite a thrill, too! Plus, the Cardinals were fresh off the 1964 World Series championship. Curt Flood, greatly appreciated now by the Cardinals and in the middle of his three Gold Glove seasons, batted fourth. Hal's ex-teammates loaded the Cardinal roster.

Throwing pre-game batting practice to the 1965 Pirates had its risks, as Hal and fellow coaches Johnny Pesky and Alex Grammas discovered. Roberto Clemente and Willie Stargell could hit the ball so hard you couldn't see it. Once, on the last pitch of batting practice before a game, Clemente smashed a line-drive off Gino Cimoli, his good friend. The ball caught Cimoli just below the heart, sending him down in a heap. He was out of the line-up for three days with a black-and-blue chest.

Hal liked watching Clemente. "Ah, he was an exciting player, you know. Willie Mays, I thought was the greatest. He put on a show every time he played, but Clemente could do things, too, that were just outstanding. In Forbes Field, the bullpen was set back in, recessed, and you had to look over the fans to see home plate. One day, we were playing the Cardinals and Lou Brock was on third base and some guy hits a high foul down there. Clemente ran over behind the bullpen, caught it, turned counter-clockwise, and threw right over the heads of the fans and got Brock at the plate after he tagged up trying to score! Clemente could throw the ball from centerfield 415 feet to home plate in the air and pretty much on a line."[58]

Hal enjoyed talking with Clemente. Like Hal, Roberto had a gregarious streak and a light-hearted outlook. Hal had friendships with Grammas, a former teammate, and Pesky, the first base coach. Hal remembered that, as a youngster, he had listened to the radio broadcast in 1946 when Enos Slaughter beat Pesky's infamous throw home in the seventh game. On one occasion, Hal cautiously brought up the subject with his fellow coach. "Pesky told me that, after that game, he wanted to try to keep anybody from noticing who he was. He went to this football game and he had his overcoat on and his collar turned up and his cap down and all this stuff. It was kinda' of a rainy, bad day and the quarterback was having trouble holding on to the ball and some guy down two or three rows in front of him said, 'Give the ball to Pesky, *he* can hold it!'"[59] The people in Boston remember and appreciate Johnny

Pesky. Even at the age of 80, he went to games at Fenway in his uniform. After his three years in Pittsburgh as first base coach, Pesky moved over to his beloved Red Sox, coaching from 1975-1983.

Grammas, who had a solid major-league playing career, coached third base for the Pirates during the Walker years and strengthened his friendship with Hal. The two had met years before at spring training in St. Petersburg. Grammas recalled that he and Hal were instant friends. According to Grammas, Hal was "the type person who you'd like to be around. He has a great sense of humor and is a caring individual." Grammas thought Hal was quite good at judging baseball talent and using his baseball knowledge to win a game.

Hal caught Don Cardwell in the Pirate bullpen. Cardwell had no-hit Hal and the Cardinals in 1959. Cardwell was the Pirates' No. 3 starter behind Veale and Vern Law. The Pirates finished third in the ten-team league behind the Dodgers and the Giants. Hal, of course, would do anything legitimate to help his team win. Still, he kept the Cardinals in mind and checked the stadium scoreboards to see how they were doing.

Harry Walker assigned himself uniform No. 3 and gave Hal No. 2. Bill Mazeroski wore No.9 for the Pirates. When playing St. Louis, Hal got to see his old Cardinal No. 2 on the back of Red Schoendienst. Musial retired from the game in 1963. Red was now managing the Cards after Keane switched to the Yankees following the 1964 World Series. In fact, later in the day when Walker had telephoned Hal offering him the opportunity to join his staff, Schoendienst, the new manager of the Cards, had Chief Bender call Hal offering him a coaching job on Red's staff. Hal, of course, kept his commitment to Walker, but years later Hal remembers his keen disappointment in not being able to join the Cardinals again.

After Pittsburgh, Hal was hired at Cincinnati by manager Dave Bristol, just as Johnny Bench and Pete Rose were beginning their major-league careers. "Bench was just a natural. Rose, he lived to talk about hitting and that's all he did, too. Rose wanted to come out and hit extra all the time. You know, he was a switch-hitter and he hit and hit and hit. He just was a different guy, a different person. He was a dedicated ball player, but he loved to get the attention of the press." Hal and Carolyn's daughter Sandra did young Johnny Bench's laundry and played tennis with the young star catcher.

While he was at Cincinnati in 1968, Hal got to see his old teammates—Gibson, McCarver, Flood, Javier, and Schoendienst, as well as Steve Carlton—who were on the way to their second pennant in as many years. Hal witnessed back-to-back no-hitters in 1969. One was by Reds' pitcher, Jim Maloney, against Houston. On the next day, Don Wilson of the Astros returned the favor by no-hitting the Reds.

The Braves moved to Atlanta after the 1965 season. It was the third move in the history of the franchise. Since dominating in the 1950's, the team had finished no higher than fifth place after the league expanded. Attendance had declined, too. The new owners wanted to relocate the Braves to a city with a wider television market. Atlanta, the hub city of the New South, beckoned. Led by their mascot, Chief Noc-A-Homa, the Braves pulled up stakes in Milwaukee. The Chief put his tipi on a landing just above the left-field bleachers in the new Atlanta Stadium as a new generation of southern-born men and women became dedicated Braves' fans. Atlanta competed for the Cardinals' huge fan base in the South, a process begun in 1962 with expansion and the Houston Colt .45's. In the 1990's, the Braves advertised themselves as America's Team thanks to exposure gained through owner Ted Turner's Superstation WTBS.

When the Braves set up shop in Georgia, Spahn and Crandall were gone, but the Braves had Mathews, Aaron, Joe Torre and manager, Bobby Bragan. Bragan, an Alabamian, had resisted the integration of major-league baseball. Beyond that failing, he had the ability to make people laugh out loud. Once, as reporters clustered in the dugout, Bragan gestured toward Torre. "Joe," Bragan said, "these guys ought to nickname you 'Chicken' so they could write stories about Chicken Catcher Torre!" Despite playful jabs at his players and making good copy for beat reporters, Bragan didn't last out the first year in Atlanta.

The National League expanded again in 1969 by adding the San Diego Padres, but owners feared that an 11-team pennant race might prove counter-productive at the gate. The solution to the revenue problem lay in halving the league. It meant that two races would be going on simultaneously with a playoff for the two division winners. In the first year of this configuration, Atlanta won the West and faced East division champion, the New York Mets, in the initial National League divisional playoff series. The Mets, managed by Gil Hodges, beat the favored Braves to gain a berth in the World Series, where the Miracle Mets put away the powerful Baltimore Orioles in five games.

The people of Milwaukee, including local car dealer Bud Selig, never got over the Braves' departure and clamored for a new team. The city and Selig got their wish in 1970 when the Seattle Pilots, an expansion team in 1969, relocated to Milwaukee. The Pilots' one season in the rainy northwest, however dismal for Seattle fans, yielded much raw material for Jim Bouton's book, *Ball Four*. Bouton broke new ground for baseball histories as he took readers inside the locker room. One of Bouton's main antagonists in the book, Pilots' pitching coach Ron Plaza, had roomed with Hal Smith in the Mexican Pacific League.

Despite having the Beer Barrel Man as its logo, the Brewers never had much fizz. Season after season, the team typically finished at the bottom of the standings and fired its manager. Selig, the owner, traded for Hank Aaron, who became a designated hitters for the Brewers and extended his career a few years as well as his home run record. At the end of the '75 season, Selig dismissed manager Del Crandall and hired Grammas. Grammas called Hal Smith.

Grammas managed the Brewers for the 1976 and 1977 seasons. Hal, who didn't mind the cold spring weather of Milwaukee, was glad to be on the coaching staff, back on the field, and in competitive situations. Grammas trusted Hal for his contributions to the club, like improving the Brewers' catchers and helping develop the game strategies. Grammas knew that honesty was one of Hal's traits and that he "knew the game as well or better than anyone and he was all baseball!"[60]

At County Stadium, bullpen pitchers often gathered around a fire built in a 55-gallon barrel and players were further cheered by polka music and suds-sloshing fans. Nevertheless, cold weather may have hampered the 1976 Brewers, who hit only .246 and finished in last place in the AL East in spite of having future Hall of Famer shortstop Robin Yount and first baseman George Scott, eight-time Gold Glover. In Boston's 1967 pennant-winning season, Scott's large and ferocious presence in the Red Sox line-up intimidated opponents. (His present-day counterpart would be Boston's David Ortiz). Before the opening of the 1967 World Series against the Cardinals, writers asked Scott what kind of ivory made up the showy, fanged necklace that he wore while on the field. "Second basemen's teeth," Scott growled.

Scott's teammate, Aaron, had hit more than a few rockets at second basemen himself (and at everybody else, for that matter) during his 23-year career. In 1976, his last year as a player, the 42-year-old Aaron batted only .229, but he did connect for ten homers—numbers 746 through 755. On July 20th, 1976, Hal was coaching first base in County Stadium as the Brewers faced California Angels' pitcher Dick Drago. Before Hal and 10,134 paying customers, Aaron launched the last homer of his career and his tenth of the season—a shot that sealed the Brewer's 6-2 victory. Aaron's last home run was back-to-back with George Scott's blast. Bobby Bonds looked up from his outfield position to see the drive land in the seats. Interestingly enough, the person who eventually broke Aaron's home run record, Barry Bonds, saw it, too. Bobby had brought his son along on this road trip so that they could celebrate Barry's 12th birthday together.

Though no one knew it at the time, that July 20th home run turned out to be the last one of Hammerin' Hank's illustrious career. With more than two months to go in the season, his 755 homers surpassed by 41 Babe Ruth's record of 714—once considered unassailable. When Aaron hit his 715th over Noc-A-Homa's tipi in Atlanta's County Stadium, the feat caught a huge amount of media attention. The attention, however, seemed to decrease as the season progressed and Aaron expanded the record. *The Sporting News* barely reported number 755 at the time. Aaron's No. 754, however, *was* a memorable event in Milwaukee and one that stuck in Hal's memory because it won the game in the 10th inning against the California Angels and continued a Brewers' winning streak. After the walk-off, the 29,000 or so fans on hand waited around for a bow from Hank and wouldn't leave the park until Aaron surfaced from the dugout and tipped his cap like a Shakespearean actor.[61]

Yet, Grammas could not get the Brewers into the first division. In the oft-repeated and cynical way of organized baseball, the axe had to fall. As Hal put it, "We were all fired." Hal had lived in an apartment in Milwaukee for these two seasons since buying a house and settling in Houston. Hal was happy to be reunited with his family but anxious about the future and wondered if another baseball opportunity might present itself. He and Carolyn hoped that whatever it was, it would come soon.

18

Cardinal Scout

Former Phillies' scout, Jack Pastore, once said, "the next best thing to being a major-league player is to be employed as a scout for a major-league team. You move around and do what you have to do, like Jonathan Livingston Seagull."[62] The only book written about baseball scouts is by Kevin Kerrane, who wrote that "scouts think of themselves as special perceivers and are also the forgotten men of baseball." Special perceiver must mean having the gift of prophecy. Statistics, however, show otherwise because scouts are prophetic only eight percent of the time. That is, about eight signees out of 100 will eventually make it to the big leagues. Of course, scouts don't necessarily think that all their players will go to the majors and some signees are meant to fill slots in a minor-league farm system. Each signee or draftee dreams of walking on to a major-league field as a starter and becoming a household name among baseball fans. Even astronauts have stated that playing professional baseball was their dream. On the other hand, Tim McCarver once told his broadcast partner, Joe Buck, that he had never heard any major-league player say he wanted to be an astronaut!

Kerrane likened baseball scouts to flashy characters from a Damon Runyon story, although Runyon didn't have to invent an early baseball scout named Sinister Dick Kinsella. Sinister Dick was not necessarily the role model for most modern scouts, although shades *and* the occasional shady move can be part of the package. Scouts gather in the stands right behind home plate at college, high school, and amateur games, armed with brief cases, charts and radar guns. They exude an easy familiarity with participants of the game in front of them. The straw hats, two-toned shoes, pleated slacks, and short-sleeved shirts with two fronts pockets from the Freddie Hawn era have given way to modern scouts wearing polo shirts, Nike running shoes, and wrap-around sun glasses, usually worn on top of the head.

Regardless of the attire or accoutrement, scouts have in common their great desire to find the "diamond in the rough." Branch Rickey started his historic baseball career as a baseball coach at the University of Minnesota and supplemented his income as a "bird dog" for the Cardinals. Later, he built a complex and much-copied farm system for St. Louis before moving to the Dodgers in 1942. As general manager for Brooklyn, Rickey sent chief scout Tom Greenwade in search of talented African-American players and he was able to find Jackie Robinson and Roy Campanella. Rickey could not keep Greenwade in his fold, however. The Yankees gained the services of this "special perceiver" and told him to search the country for another Lou Gehrig. One of his discoveries came eerily close to that mark. Hovering around high school fields in northeastern Oklahoma, Greenwade ran across a skinny, undersized 17-year-old. The young man, Mickey Mantle, was a left-handed batter, or so Greenwade thought. One day, Greenwade saw him bat from the right side against a southpaw. Mantle ripped a double into the gap. The scout realized that Mantle was a natural switch-hitter and a perfectly coordinated "baseball machine." He was quoted as saying, "now I know how Paul Kritchell felt when he first saw Lou Gehrig."[63] Tom Greenwade signed Mantle for a $1,400 bonus in 1949, the same year that Freddie Hawn signed Hal Smith.

In their business, scouts dream at unearthing this kind of talent. In the mid-fifties, organized baseball competed harder, maybe even ruthlessly, for what talent was out there. Bonuses reached $50,000 for Cardinal signees Von McDaniel in 1956 and $100,000 for Ray Sadecki three years later. Yet, some balked at such exaggerated spending. Branch Rickey, the steely-eyed bargainer, turned skittish after prominent failures of "bonus babies" and refused his scout permission to offer $10,000 for Sandy Koufax. So, instead of the Dodgers, Koufax signed with the Pirates. At about the same time and for the same reason, Puerto Rican star Roberto Clemente signed a Dodger contract. The scout who signed these Hall-of- Famers was Al Campanis, a Rickey protégé. Of course, Koufax wound up with Brooklyn and helped secure two World Series berths for the Los Angeles Dodgers. Clemente did the same for Pittsburgh, which won the world championship twice.

Hal had been a scout for a few years in the 1970's before his coaching stint in Milwaukee. He wanted to return to that field and, as he said, "I got lucky. The director of scouting for St. Louis had been the general manager at Rock Hill when I managed there. And so I called him, and he said, 'We just happen to have a place open.' He gave me the middle of the United States and then the following year, 1979, I was assigned to scout Texas."[64]

Mississippi and Louisiana were added to Texas for Hal to cover. For twenty years, Hal covered this enormous territory—it was expanded to include New Mexico—and plied his trade in the second best job that organized baseball has to offer. He set his own schedule, motivated by his desire to provide the Cardinals with the best scouting information they could get. They were pleased with his work.

Texas, of course, is dotted with high schools, junior colleges, and universities that have baseball programs. From Beaumont to El Paso, one must travel 810 highway miles. Hal drove from place to place and gained a thorough knowledge of Texas cities, small towns, blue roads, red roads, and dirt roads. His competitors flocked into Texas from all over the country, including the northern scouts who are called "snow birds." Ironically, Hal never got the chance to scout in Arkansas, since it was part of a different scouting region.

The Cardinals have twenty scouts out in the field in the United States and the Caribbean islands. Hal had an associate in Baton Rouge who helped him sort through all the Louisiana and Mississippi players. He had bird dogs, too. "A bird dog," he said, "is a guy that, if he recommends a player to you and you sign that guy and he makes it to Class AA, he gets maybe five hundred dollars. If he makes it all the way, he gets a thousand dollars. Now, these other part-time scouts, they get paid a regular salary, somewhere around $10,000 plus their expenses. But they only had to cover just a small area. I had a guy named Walker "Foots" Cress. He had been a pitcher for Cincinnati, a big, tall guy, who worked for me in Baton Rouge." Cress and Jimmy Smith, coach at LSU from 1966 to 1978 and the former Randall Victors American Legion teammate of Hal's, stayed in close contact.

After the institution of the player draft in 1965, changes in scouting followed. (Branch Rickey had argued that the owners had better get rid of the bonus system—and they did). Clubs sent out cross-checkers to verify a recommendation made by a scout in the field by comparing the prospect with somebody else's top guy. In this way, they formed an idea of the order in which they wanted to pursue the player in the major-league draft. The draft changed the way scouts operated. Now, they produced opinions and advice. Previously, in the bonus system, they had made decisions about players.

Hal did not usually carry a radar gun to judge a pitcher's velocity. "I never forgot what Freddie Hawn taught me, that you can tell when a guy has got a good fast ball if he throws it in the strike zone and they swing and miss it. If he can do that, he has a pretty good arm." A scout no longer pulled a contract out of his brief case. Now, scouts were more inclined to share information on prospects as they sat together through the endless innings on cold spring days or boiling hot July afternoons. They sifted through tens of thousands of throws, swings, running styles, and swaggering that filled the days of an active professional scout doing the work necessary to find the one in twelve who might be a candidate for the major-league draft.

Hal preferred to spend his time watching junior college and college teams because, as he said, "If you sign a high school player, he might get homesick, because I remember in my own case that I was! College, he's over that a little bit and he's had a couple years against better competition. High school kids fool scouts because the competition is not all that good." An Anheuser-Busch distributor in Lufkin, Texas, was so impressed after seeing a kid from a nearby, small town that he wrote Gussie Busch "that there's the best player that's ever been in this part of the country and you gotta' have somebody see him." Hal said, "Well, the kid was a left-handed pitcher. Carolyn and I drove up and sat in the car and watched that kid warm up and this kid couldn't even black your eye. He was pitching against little guys that didn't know how to hit in the first place. He was probably the best athlete in that part of the country, but you have to look at speed and he just didn't have it. We turned around and left."

While throwing hard was the essential quality, especially for pitchers, Hal reminded himself to notice the curve ball when judging the abilities of young players. "You have to look at the overall thing, the curve ball," Hal told me. "In fact, when I saw this kid that's pitching for the Cubs right now, he was in high school and had an excellent curve ball. And he got faster as he got older. The same thing happened to Steve Carlton, who played for me when I managed in Rock Hill. Carlton had a good curve ball his first year, but later on got to where he could throw faster, throw harder."

Hal liked scouting better than managing. He took satisfaction in watching his prospects as they climbed up the career ladder. "The majority of them don't make it. Then, when one of them does, it's really a thrill, like George Bjorkman, for instance. He was a catcher who played at Oral Roberts and I really liked him. I thought he was a pretty good receiver. He had a good arm, good hands, he could block balls really well, and he had some power. I was about the only one interested and so he got drafted and went up to Class AAA and then Houston traded for him." (Bjorkman, who played for the Golden Eagles in 1976-78, was inducted into the initial class of the Oral Roberts University Hall of Fame. He caught 29 games for the Astros in 1983).

Hal remembered another one of his prospects, Curt Ford. "I recommended him out of Jackson State and he made it all the way. He wasn't a big guy, but you could not throw a fastball by him, I don't care who it was. I saw Ford play maybe eight or ten times in Jackson, Baton Rouge, and Houston. After the Cardinals drafted him and signed him in 1981, I followed his progress in the minors through Johnson City and Little Rock, where he batted .324 in the Texas League. The Cardinals called him up at the end of the 1985 season and he got a hit off Lee Smith, the big relief guy for the Cubs, and nobody threw any harder than Lee Arthur Smith. Ford's clutch hit helped put us into the World Series against Minnesota.[65]

Roger Clemens went to San Jacinto Junior College from high school and was drafted but didn't sign. In junior college, he didn't throw near like he did at the University of Texas where he really blossomed."

Hal recalled being with his fellow scout, Red Gaskell, who was working for Cleveland. "Scouts called Red "the killer" because he didn't like anybody [as a player]. Gaskell did like this one pitcher, who was at Baylor studying to be a minister, and so he asked this guy, 'Uh, you'd think you'd be interested in playing professional baseball if you're drafted?' The Baylor man said, 'Yeah, but you know I'm just going to wait until the Lord tells me what to do.' And Red says, 'I'll tell you what, when He tells you, would you mind to call me and let me know?'"

Hal recommended Willie McGee to the Cardinals when the Yankees decided they needed the services of Bob Sykes, a Cardinal pitcher. They offered to exchange a minor-league player for him. The Yankees supplied the Cardinals with the names of three of their minor leaguers. Hal was assigned the task of evaluating these guys and he followed them around their leagues for three weeks, haunting Nashville where McGee played for the Sounds, a Yankee farm team. Don Mattingly played on the same team with McGee. Hal might have introduced a Nashville producer to one of his songs. Instead, he stuck with his baseball business and, at the end of the season, the St. Louis brass wanted to know his opinion. He told them to take Willie McGee and the Cardinals did. The next year, Whitey Herzog started McGee as a rookie. The Cards won the National League East and beat Atlanta in the playoffs. With the help of two home runs and stellar outfield play by McGee, they won the World Series against the Milwaukee Brewers.

19

Epilogue

Hal retired from the Cardinals' organization in 1997. Two years later, he and Carolyn sold their lake house in a Dallas suburb and moved to Fort Smith. Hal and Carolyn live near a golf course and he plays frequently enough to keep his handicap low. Their only pet is Dizzy, an African Gray parrot, obtained years ago in Florida. On occasion, Dizzy will launch into his favorite song, "Take Me Out to the Ballgame." Last year, Dizzy had to visit the veterinarian. When the parrot got out of the animal infirmary and came home, she had a new name—Miss Dizzy. She had been a female all along!

Dennis Smith and his wife, Brenda, followed Hal and Carolyn back to Arkansas from Atlanta, where Dennis had been in the music business. In western Arkansas and eastern Oklahoma, Dennis has an established music career, which includes performing and producing recordings for other musicians. Dennis grew up in a pure baseball family and absorbed the knowledge of the game. He had first-hand experience with some of the best players in the history of the game— Boyer, Law, Clemente, Bench, etc. When he was 13, Dennis was struck by a rare disease called Osgood-Slaughter that affects the growth and development of a person's knee joints. The disease prevented him from considering a career in baseball.

In Fort Smith, Hal is always available for public service. He plays in charity golf tournaments, speaks at civic club meetings, and volunteers time at his old favorite place, the Fort Smith Boys & Girls Club.

Hal received one of his state's highest honors as he entered the Arkansas Sports Hall of Fame. On a gala night, the inductees included one of Hal's former teammates, Carl Sawatski, who entered posthumously. Hal's other fellow inductees in 2005 were Bud Brooks, Scottie Pippen, Cortez Kennedy, J. P. Lovelady (also posthumously), Mickey O'Quinn, Maurice Carthon, Scott Hastings, Terri Conder-Johnson, and two world-class trap shooters, Doyne Williams and Nancy Williams. Hal's selection also followed that of his old teammate, Wally Moon. Yankee catcher Bill Dickey was among the Hall's initial set of inductees and former Cardinal Tom Pagnozzi entered with the class of 2007—bringing the total of major-league catchers inducted into Arkansas' Sports Hall of Fame to four.

While gathering material for this book, I drove to Hal's residence one day to conduct an interview. After I parked, one of Hal's neighbors, a young man, came rushing toward me. "Are you the guy who is writing the book on Hal?" he inquired. "Yes," I replied. He continued, "Be sure and let me talk with you before you finish. I want to tell you what a wonderful neighbor he is and how much my wife and my children think of him. I can give you numerous acts on his part that show his thoughtfulness and concern for people around him. He is the best neighbor any of us could ask for."

One of Hal's hobbies is wood-carving. He makes portraits out of wood, cutting the intricate figures with knives, gouging tools, and awls. Hal's pieces are artistically designed and show painstaking attention to detail. Several of them adorn the walls of his house. Hal showed me his shop and talked about some of his works in progress. One of them was a wood replica of Leonardo da Vinci's famed "Last

Supper" painting. One cold day when I arrived for an interview, a repairman's truck was parked in the Smith driveway. Inside, a young man in coveralls was working at the fireplace on the electronic setting for the gas logs. Carolyn explained that the storm had thrown off the computerized controls. As Hal and I talked for about an hour, the repairman experimented with the controls and finally the logs came on. Carolyn was happy, because the rosy warmth from the logs was something that her great-granddaughter loved and the little girl soon would be coming in from school.

As the repairman was leaving, Carolyn disappeared from the room. In a moment, she returned with Hal's portrait in wood of the Last Supper. Hal had just finished working on it. "You don't mind if he gets this, do you Hal?" Carolyn asked. Hal raised his eyebrows and shrugged his shoulders. "No. No, not at all," he replied. The young man, who had mentioned that his father was a minister, stood with the gift in his hand. He was obviously amazed and quite appreciative of the unexpected gift. I had again witnessed the spontaneous generosity of the Smith family.

On an August morning in the dry, hot summer of 2006, Hal stood meeting people in Barling on the occasion of the dedication of a new ball field for youngsters. It had been named Hal Smith Field in honor of Barling's most famous son. Several townspeople braved the heat to listen to speeches and watch as Hal stepped forward to receive a plaque. Hal said a few words of gratitude, told a self-effacing story, and then sat down at a folding table set up on the diamond to sign autographs. One lady and her grown son, both attired in St. Louis Cardinal regalia, had brought baseball cards, gloves, and baseballs to the autographing party. Hal signed and chatted with fans and well-wishers. Four hours later, every autograph request had been met. After a long lull, Hal looked at his watch and said softly, "would it be alright if I went home now?" The park director told Hal farewell and offered a few more congratulations. Hal left to help Carolyn pack for a trip that evening to Texas for a visit to see their great-grandchildren.

In 2001, Hal was inducted into the Fort Smith Boys & Girls Club
Hall of Fame, along with Jarrell Williams, Jim Harwood, Rick Tinder,
and Ira De Shazo. Both Jarrell and Hal were introduced by their
brothers. Darrell Williams, Jarrell's twin, had grown up in the Boys
Club and both had received football scholarships at the University of
Arkansas after their days as Fort Smith High School Grizzlies. Hal was
introduced by his younger brother, Tommy "Fishhook" Smith, whose
sense of humor set the stage for Hal to make his retorts and keep the
huge crowd rollicking. Hal demonstrated that he had neither lost his
sense of timing for comedy nor his knack for public speaking.

Tommy Smith played ten years in the minor leagues, making it to
Triple-A as a catcher. Tommy is several inches taller than Hal and,
during his prime, had the same rifle arm. His childhood nickname is
derived from his fondness for spending time on the banks of nearby
creeks and bayous, angling for small-mouth bass and blue gills. Tommy
achieved local fame as a gifted player on the Boys Club fields around
Fort Smith. One observer from those days swears that he saw Tommy
hit a ball out of Hunts Park that went over Old Greenwood Road, past
the Boy Scout offices and came to rest on an elevated railroad bed—
a distance of more than five hundred feet. Another sort of observer
hailed from the nearby town of Greenwood and later helped spread
Fishhook's fame across the Rockies into California. C. Grady
Robinson created a mythical short story about an awesome,
overpowering "Fishhook" as seen through the eyes and fears of a
twelve-year-old baseball player. The boy, who was about to bat against
a huge pitcher, was forced into an obvious life-or-death situation by
parental and peer pressures. Published as part of Robinson's book,
Where Have you Gone, Lance Alworth?, the author tailored the
suspenseful, yet grandly humorous tale for the banquet circuit.
Robinson was in great demand as a featured speaker and made the
rounds of baseball conventions and ceremonial dinners from Arkansas
to California. As Mark Twain once said, "all you need is one good

lecture." Fishhook certainly provided C. Grady Robinson with his material for that one good lecture. Tommy now lives near Fayetteville, Arkansas. He ran the official game clock at Razorback basketball games in Walton Arena for years, including Nolan Richardson's national championship season. Before one game, I walked down the aisle to the long scorer's table to see him. He stood up to greet me, a huge man in a striped official's shirt. He had that unmatched Smith family smile and twinkle in his eye. That's how I renewed my acquaintance with "Fishhook," who became an unforgettable character in a delightful short story, thanks to Robinson, who moved to Fayetteville from California in 2005. What an ironical meeting it will be when "Fishhook" and Robinson eventually cross paths, as surely they must, in a local supermarket!

Hal's three sisters—Virginia Wray, Nancy Weaver, and Becky Crawford—all live in Fort Smith. Herbert Smith, a catcher like Tommy and Hal, lives in Van Buren. Herbie had the opportunity to play baseball for the Kerwin's American Legion team coached by one of Hal's oldest and dearest friends from the Barling days, Lawrence "Squeaky" Smith. Carolyn's sister, Joy Wegrzyn and her husband, Emil, live in Tulsa. Brother Hobart, Jr. and his wife, Martha, live in Dallas, as do Hal and Carolyn's two daughters, Sharon and Sandra. Hal and Carolyn have six grandchildren and eight great-grandchildren. As he was in his playing days, Hal remains the dedicated family man. He fought the battles on the field that a professional athlete thrives on, competing against the very best in his sport. But, he found his comfort, solace, and inspiration at his hearth with Carolyn, his children, his close friends, and his extended family.

Hal Smith played seven years as a minor-leaguer in the Cardinal farm system and seven years in the major leagues—six with the Cardinals and one as a player-coach with the Pirates. He coached eight years with the Cardinals, Pirates, Reds, and Milwaukee Brewers. Hal managed one year in minor-league baseball and scouted for the

Cardinals for 23 years. These figures add up to a phenomenal, 39-year career in organized baseball, most of it with the St. Louis Cardinals. Even when he coached on other major-league staffs, it was because the managers had come to know and respect his abilities when they wore the Cardinal uniform together as teammates. Actually, Hal's 39 years with the Cards isn't quite the record. Red Schoendienst started earlier and still joins the club in spring training. As recently as the 2006 season, Red was hitting fungos to Cardinal infielders like Albert Pujols before ballgames. Hal's close friend and teammate, Joe Cunningham, works with the Cardinal organization in its successful "Say No to Drugs" program for kids. Stanley Frank Musial is an icon in St. Louis and represents the Cardinals almost with his every action.

From the time that Hal first heard the broadcast of the 1946 World Series, he has identified with the Cardinals and literally bled their colors. As much as any Arkansan could, he has symbolized the state's long love affair with the St. Louis Cardinals. In the sixty years between the 1946 World Series victory to the 2006 World Series victory, the dimensions of the baseball diamond have remained the same—ninety-foot base paths and a distance of 60 feet, six inches from the front of the pitching rubber to the back of home plate. The width of the plate is still 17 inches at its widest. The pitching rubber measures four inches by two feet. The batter's box is still three feet by four feet. There are still nine players in the field, three outs, three strikes, four balls, and nine innings. Yet, virtually everything else about the game has changed!

The impetus for much of that change came within the six years that Hal Smith was the starting catcher for the Cardinals. During those years, 1956-1961, a majority of fans began to arrive at the ballpark in privately-owned vehicles. The Giants and the Dodgers moved to the West Coast, which caused teams to switch from railroads to airlines for travel. Double-headers were transformed into day-night games or played only to make up rain-outs and were no longer a part of the regular schedule.

The Negro Leagues declined and then disappeared as the major leagues were integrated, a process just in its infancy when black Cardinal players and white Cardinal players were lodged in separate quarters at spring training. Hal was a teammate of the first African Americans to make the Cardinals' roster—Brooks Lawrence and Tom Alston. He played with the team's first African-American Hall of Famer and superstar, Bob Gibson, and caught Gibson's first victory as a major-league pitcher. Hal's career paralleled that of Curt Flood, a man who just wanted to go as far on the field as his ability would take him (and eventually that was quite far, indeed). Flood ended up as the player who contested and ultimately overturned the reserve clause— long sanctified in the law, courts, and by major-league baseball as essential for the "integrity of the game."

In Hal's day, major-league pensions depended on revenues derived from the mid-season All-Star game. The salary for an average first-year man in the majors ran about $500 a month. Because of Curt Flood's successful challenge to major-league baseball, today's players have the right to sell their services to the highest bidder. Now, owners often pay astronomical sums for players. The pension fund for players rivals that of the mighty Teamster's Union. Marvin Miller became the first lawyer to represent players in their struggle against the authority of the owners.

During Hal's first year in 1956, games were aired on radio. Only a few were televised and those were in black and white. One or two cameras struggled to catch the action but generally missed most of it and so did the audience. Rather than abandon its effort, the broadcast industry sought to attract viewers and advertisers by using more cameras of better quality. Technological advances came quickly and by 1961 color cameras captured the action for some games in big markets and for the World Series and All-Star games. As color television caught on, advertising revenues began to increase rapidly. This new wealth, shared by the networks and the major-league owners, increased stakes for major-league ownership to levels unimaginable in the mid-1950's. By 1965, Hal's last year to appear in a regular season major-league game, the New York Yankees had been purchased by CBS, one of the country's three broadcasting networks.

When the Dodgers moved to Los Angeles and left behind beloved Ebbets Field, they temporarily set up shop in the Los Angeles Coliseum. For their first three years under the southern California sun, they played on a football field while awaiting completion of a grand new home—Dodger Stadium. It was being built in Chavez Ravine, where an historic, but low-income Mexican-American neighborhood had been flattened to make room. The fabulous new stadium, easily accessible by freeways also under construction, had parking for 16,000 automobiles. Previously, ballparks were squeezed into the available space in downtown areas. The Dodgers' new stadium set an irreversible trend away from this kind of setting. Though Dodger Stadium was privately financed, the city helped Dodger management to acquire the property, get the rezoning approved and guaranteed loans to the organization. Los Angeles officials were confident that a major-league baseball franchise would attract middle-class people and thereby help stem the flight to suburbia. Ballparks soon became the centerpiece of urban renewal strategies as other cities followed suit. Architects designed stadiums exclusively for baseball and governments helped make the space available, even if derelict housing had to be bull-dozed. Baseball changed the urban landscapes of America. Smaller cities and villages across the country began to open baseball complexes with plenty of parking and lighted diamonds for players of every age.

Other, less dramatic changes occurred within Hal's six years as a St. Louis Cardinal. For years, each of the two major leagues had its own brand of baseballs made by separate companies. A common ball was adopted for the 1959 season. Umpires moved away from the formal attire of black coat and bow tie and dispensed with the balloon-type chest protector. Field dimensions changed, too. The LA

Coliseum showed that fences could be brought in or screens erected to tailor fields to the home team offenses. Uniform material shifted from heavy wool to lighter wools and synthetic materials. Batting helmets appeared. City directors revoked Sunday curfews and games could be completed, even if they extended beyond nightfall. Teams abandoned the roommate system as players wanted individual hotel rooms on road trips. In the 2006 season, one broadcaster heard that a bus transporting a team from the airport to the hotel had broken down. He speculated that players would use their cell phones to call for separate taxis. Rookies no longer carry bags of veteran players during the regular season. No rookie ever carried Hal's bags, anyway. After all, he was the master of rapport with rookie catchers and pitchers. He caught Bob Gibson, Ray Sadecki, Von McDaniel, Bob Blaylock, Ernie Broglio, and Bob Miller in their first or formative starts in the major leagues. In the pre-game ritual of how hitters would be handled, Hal calmed the nerves of these pitchers and gave them the confidence they needed. Rookie catchers Tim McCarver and Johnny Bench sought advice from Hal, the veteran. He was always approachable and spoke with authority on the subject of major-league catching. Ernie Broglio told me that Hal "always had a smile, was laid back, but oh so serious about catching." A baseball player is often reduced to a statistic, but the personality of the player and his chemistry with his peers can be immeasurably valuable to a team's success. Hal was among the players who were graceful off the field as well as between the chalk lines. It was typical of his teammates, too— men like Stan Musial, Red Schoendienst, Ken Boyer, Bob Gibson, Curt Flood, Tim McCarver, Wally Moon, Alex Grammas, Bill White, and George Crowe.

Hal Smith's major-league playing career came at a time when America and its national pastime turned a corner and faced a revolution in our society and in baseball. Neither would emerge from it "as we had known them." The revolution, led by technology, by individual will, and by the dreams of many, came without forecast or warning. Although acts of violence occurred aplenty during Hal's span as a major-league player and coach, 1956-1965, the revolution occurred peacefully enough, given what was at stake. Perhaps it was baseball that stabilized the country amid divisive and tumultuous struggles over Civil Rights, the Vietnam War, wars on poverty, and even urban design, all taking place with an ominous Cold War looming in the background.

Hal's years as a professional baseball player coincided with social and technological upheavals for America. The band—in this case, the game—played on, within and around these vast changes that were often ironic and may have seemed insidious to ordinary fans. Major-league baseball, traditionally locked into 14 cities in an area east of the Mississippi River and north of the Ohio River, had mushroomed into continental size. The game was not quite the same anymore. Neither was America. But, could it be that baseball and men like Hal Smith, "The Barling Darling," are America's glue—the indispensible bond for our national unity?

Appendix

Chart 1: Statistics

Hal Smith played in 570 major league games and batted 1,697 times. He had 437 major league hits, ninety-four for extra bases, including 23 lifetime home runs. His career batting average was .258. His career fielding average was .989.

Hal Smith and National League starting catchers, 1956-1961

Catcher	Teams	Career Batting Ave.	Career Fielding Ave.	Number of Years Played
Smokey Burgess	Reds, Pirates, Cubs, Phillies	.295	.989	18
Roy Campanella	Dodgers	.276	.988	10
Hal Smith	Cardinals, Pirates	.258	.989	6
Ed Bailey	Reds, Giants, Braves	.256	.986	14
Del Crandall	Braves, Giants, Pirates	.254	.989	16
Stan Lopata	Phillies, Braves	.254	.986	13
John Roseboro	Dodgers	.249	.989	14
Sammy Taylor	Cubs, Giants, Reds	.245	.986	6
Carl Sawatski	Cubs, Braves, Phillies, Cardinals,	.242	.988	11

Hal Smith and Cardinal catchers, 1945-2006

Catcher	Cardinal Years	Career Batting Ave.	Career Fielding Ave.	Number of Years Played
Ted Simmons	1968-80	.285	.986	21
Tim McCarver	1959-69, 1973	.271	.980	21
Bill Sarni	1951-1955	.263	.991	5
Yadier Molina	2004-2008	.262	.991	5
Hal Smith	1956-1961	.258	.989	6
Joe Garagiola	1946-1951	.257	.986	9
Tom Pagnozzi	1987-1998	.253	.992	12
Darrell Porter	1981-1985	.247	.982	17
Del Rice	1945-1955	.237	.987	17

Chart 2:

Hal Smith's Ten Best Games as a St. Louis Cardinal

1. **May 8, 1957, Polo Grounds, New York City.** Hal had a three-for-five day, including a home run and six RBI's, and led the Cards to a 13-8 victory over the Giants. Stan Musial drove in two more and Wally Moon three. Hal's base hit in the fourth off Giant ace Johnny Antonelli drove in the first two Cardinal runs and started their comeback from a 3-0 deficit. (p. 97).

2. **September 22, 1959, Busch Stadium, St. Louis.** Hal hit a grand slam off Sandy Koufax as the Cards defeated the defending National League champions Dodgers, 11-10, in the stretch run for the pennant. (p. 166).

3. **May 1, 1959, Forbes Field, Pittsburgh.** Hal went two for three, including a triple that scored Musial from first base. The Cards won, 7-6, despite a gargantuan home run by Dick Stuart off Cardinal reliever Jim Brosnan. (p. 152).

4. **June 26, 1960, Connie Mack Stadium, Philadelphia.** Cards won this game, 4-3, with Hal driving in all four Cardinal runs, the last with a dramatic ninth-inning homer run. (p. 177).

5. **July 2, 1960, Busch Stadium, St. Louis.** Hal's hit in the second off Warren Spahn drove in Musial to give Bob Gibson a 1-0 lead that he never relinquished. Gibson went nine innings, blanked Hank Aaron and Eddie Mathews, struck out seven. Mathews struck out three times. Hal went two for two, drove in Stan Musial and Bill White, threw out a runner, was pitched around by Warren Spahn, and called Gibson's pitches. (p. 179).

6. **April 11, 1961, County Stadium, Milwaukee.** Hal tripled against Braves' ace pitcher Warren Spahn. He caught Ernie Broglio and Lindy McDaniel in the ten-inning 2-1 opening day victory. (p. 188).

7. **May 9, 1959, Busch Stadium, St. Louis.** Hal hit two home runs and drove in five runs. His first home run in the fourth inning chased Cub starter Glen Hobbie. He hit another in the eighth inning to cap his one man wrecking crew day to lead the Cards to victory over their top rival. (p. 158).

8. **May 3, 1959, Forbes Field, Pittsburgh.** Hal's defensive work held the Pirates at bay in crucial moments in the game. He threw out two base runners, Roberto Clemente included, blocked the plate and tagged out Bill Virdon to keep the score tied at two in this classic, extra-inning pitcher's duel between Vern Law and Larry Jackson. (p. 153).

9. **July 30, 1959. Crosley Field, Cincinnati.** Hal caught Bob Gibson's first major league victory, a nine-inning, 1-0 win over the Reds. Hal's second hit of the day advanced the runner for Joe Cunningham to drive in the game's only run. (p. 162).

10. **June 21, 1957, Busch Stadium, St. Louis.** Hal caught Von McDaniel's first major league start, settling down his young pitcher and masterfully using his knowledge of Dodger batters to call effective pitches. The eighteen-year-old rookie, one year out of a western Oklahoma rural high school, shut out the defending World Champion Dodgers, 2-0, allowing two hits in going nine innings. (p. 101).

Chart 3:

Hal Smith's ten favorite opposing pitchers whom he faced 25 times or more.

1. **Sandy Koufax, Brooklyn/Los Angeles Dodgers.** Hal thought that Koufax tipped his pitches. Whether he did or not, Hal solved the Hall of Fame left-hander's deliveries, getting eleven hits in 31 at bats, six of them for extra bases. Hal's batting average with Koufax pitching against him was .355.

2. **Johnnie Antonelli, New York/San Francisco Giants.** Hal faced Antonelli 44 times and got 15 hits and had a .341 batting average against the long-time Giants' left-hander.

3. **Joe Nuxall, Cincinnati Reds.** Nuxall, who holds the record as the youngest player at 15 to ever appear in a major league game, did not match up well against Hal, who had twelve hits in his 28 at bats against the veteran left-hander for a .425 batting average.

4. **Curt Simmons, Philadelphia Phillies.** Hal, who later became a battery mate after Simmons was traded to the Cards in 1960, was eleven of 32 (.344) with five extra base hits off the left-handed Simmons.

5. **Bob Friend, Pittsburgh Pirates.** Hal had a Friend when he pitched and ripped the Pirates' ace for ten hits in 29 trips to the plate. Against this crafty right-hander, he had a batting average of .345.

6. **Moe Drabowsky, Chicago Cubs.** The right-handed Drabowsky was the Cub ace in 1957, his best year and the best year for Hal. Over five years, Hal faced Moe 27 times and got nine hits, three of them doubles, for a .333 batting average.

7. **Don Newcombe, Brooklyn Dodgers, Cincinnati Reds.** The huge, hard-throwing right-hander faced Hal thirty-four times and struck him out one time. Hal had ten hits for a .294 average against Newcombe.

8. **Glenn Hobbie, Chicago Cubs.** In the late 50's, Hobie became Chicago's best starter. In his 28 at-bats against him, Hal struck out three times and got eight hits for a .286 batting average.

9. **Harvey Haddix, Pittsburgh Pirates.** The soft-throwing lefty, nicknamed "The Kitten," once pitched no-hit ball for a ten-inning game that he lost. Haddix beat the Yankees twice in the 1960 World Series. Hal faced Haddix 52 times, banging out 14 hits for a .269 average.

10. **Warren Spahn, Milwaukee Braves.** Hal faced left-handed Warren Spahn 79 times at the plate, more times than he came up against any other major-league pitcher. Hal cracked 18 hits off the master, four of them for extra bases, and had a .247 batting average. But Spahn was careful with Hal, walking him seven times (against only three strike-outs) and intentionally passing him four more times.

Chart 4:

Hal Smith's six least-favorite opposing pitchers

1. **Don Drysdale, Brooklyn/Los Angeles Dodgers.** Hal once said that the toughest pitcher he faced in the majors was Drysdale. But, he said, sixty-one guys were tied for second toughest. The 6-5 Drysdale threw sidearm. At times, the ball looked like it came from third base. Drysdale was not afraid to throw close to the batter and made it difficult for any right-handed hitter. Hal had only two hits against Drysdale for a .125 average.

2. **Bob Buhl, Milwaukee Braves.** Hal faced right-handed Buhl, the third Milwaukee starter (after Spahn and Lew Burdette) 27 times and collected three hits, a .111 average.

3. **Elroy Face, Pittsburgh Pirates.** Face was one of the NL's top right-handed relief pitchers and allowed Hal exactly one hit in eleven at bats, a .091 average.

4. **Mike McCormick, New York/San Francisco Giants.** McCormick yielded seven hits to Hal in 38 at-bats, giving Hal a .184 batting average against this willowy Giants' lefty.

5. **Sam Jones, San Francisco Giants.** Hal caught Sam when he pitched for the Cardinals and knew the right-hander's pitches. Hal still couldn't solve Sam's big curve ball, who gave up just three hits to Hal in 16 at-bats for a .188 mark.

6. **Johnny Podres, Brooklyn/Los Angeles Dodgers.** Left-handed Podres, the most valuable player in the 1955 World Series, faced Hal 56 times, walking him three times and giving up 12 hits, a .222 average.

Chart 5:

Hal Smith's Major-League Home Runs
In annotations, Cardinal score is in bold

No. Date	Opposing Pitcher and Team	Ball Park	Inning	Men on	W/L
1. May 8, 1956	Bob Ross, Philadelphia Phillies	Sportsman's Park	6	1	W

9-1 final score. Hal's first big league homer.

2. May 9, 1956   Herm Wehmeier, Phillies   Sportsman's Park   5   0   W
3-0 final score; Phillies manager Mayo Smith started Wehmeier in this game at Fred Hutchinson's request because Frank Lane wanted to see him. Wehmeier gave up only seven hits in six innings and one run, Hal's second home run in two days.

3. June 27, 1956   Johnny Antonelli, New York Giants   Polo Grounds   2   0   W
6-0 final score; Hal's homer in the second inning followed Kenny Boyer's to give the Cards a 2-0 lead against the Giants' veteran lefthander.

4. July 2, 1956   Warren Hacker, Chicago Cubs   Wrigley Field   5   0   L
6-3 final score: Hal's homer in the fifth trimmed the Cub lead to 3-1. Manager Hutchinson was suspended for this game and the Cards were managed by Coach Johnny Hopp.

5. July 21, 1956   Ken Lehman, Brooklyn Dodgers   Sportsman's Park   8   0   W
13-6 final score; Hal added to the fire in the eighth when he joined Stan Musial and Hank Sauer in blasting shots out of Sportsman's Park. The Dodger losing pitcher was Roger Craig. Hal had three hits, including one of off Cardinal nemesis Clem Labine.

6. May 8, 1957   Joe Margoneri, New York Giants   Polo Grounds   7   1   W
13-4 final; 6-4 when Hal homered following Moon's triple off Margoneri, who had relieved.

7. June 11, 1957   Curt Simmons, Philadelphia Phillies   Connie Mack Stadium 2   0   W
6-4 final score; 1-0 when Hal led off the inning with a home run.

8. May 31, 1958   Mike McCormick, San Francisco   Busch Stadium   7   2   W
10-9 final score; Giants led 8-6 when Hal's three-run homer put them on top.

9. April 14, 1959   Johnny Podres, Los Angeles Dodgers   Memorial Coliseum   6   1   W
6-2 final score; Cards led 3-0 when Hal homered.

10. April 17, 1959   Stu Miller, San Francisco Giants   Seals Stadium   4   0   W
    4-1 final score; Cards led 2-0 when Hal homered.

11. May 5, 1959   Robin Roberts, Philadelphia Phillies   Connie Mack Stadium 4   1   L
    8-7 final score; Phillies led 2-1 when Hal homered in the fourth inning to give the Cards a 3-2 lead.

12. May 9, 1959   Glen Hobbie, Chicago Cubs   Busch Stadium   4   2   W
    11-1 final score; Cards led 1-0 in the fourth when Hal hit his first with two men aboard.

13. May 9, 1959   Joe Schaffernoth, Chicago Cubs   Busch Stadium   8   1 two home
    Hal homered again in the eighth inning, making the score 5-1. Joe Cunningham was run game on base
    each time.

14. May 29, 1959   Jack Sanford, San Francisco Giants   Seals Stadium   8   1   W
    4-2 final score. Hal homered in the eighth inning with the Cards up 2-0.

15. June 16, 1959   Curt Simmons, Philadelphia Phillies   Busch Stadium   7   0   W
    8-1 final score; Cards up 7-1 when Hal homered.

16. June 21, 1959   Harvey Haddix, Pittsburgh Pirates   Busch Stadium   4   1   W
    5-1 final score; Cards were up 1-0 in fourth inning when Musial doubled off the screen in right. Hal
    then homered.

17. June 27, 1959   Orlando Pena, Cincinnati Reds   Crosley Field   9   0   W
    5-0 final score; Hal led off the ninth with a home run to give Ernie Broglio his margin of victory.

18. July 10, 1959   Turk Farrell, Philadelphia Phillies   Connie Mack Stadium 6   0   W
.   9-7 final score; Phillies led 4-0 going into the sixth. The Cards erupted with Gene Oliver and Hal
    hitting back-to-back home runs in the inning.

19. Sept 5, 1959   Johnny Antonelli, San Francisco Giants   Seals Stadium   2   0   L
    3-2 final score; Hal homered in the second to tie the score at 1-1; Hal got both RBI's for the Cards,
    who had Mizell on the mound. Mays, McCovey, and Ed Bressoud hit solo home runs for the Giants.

20. Sept 20, 1959   Art Ceccarelli, Chicago Cubs   Busch Stadium   7   0   W
    11-4 final score; With the score 6-4 going into the bottom of the seventh, Musial and Hal homered to
    put the game out of reach.

21. Sept 22, 1959   Sandy Koufax, Los Angeles Dodgers   Busch Stadium   l   3   W
    11-10 final score; Hal came to bat with the bases loaded in the first and the Cards trailing 3-0. Hal's grand slam was one of only six allowed by the great left handed in his Hall of Fame career.

22. June 26, 1960   Chris Short, Philadelphia Phillies   Connie Mack Stadium 9   2   W
    4-3 final score; Hal's three-run homer in the ninth inning won the game for the Cards.

23. August 14, 1960 Vern Law, Pittsburgh Pirates   Forbes Field   4   l   L
    9-**4** final score; Hal hit a home run in the fourth with Daryl Spencer on to trim the Pirate lead to 4-2. It was as close as the Cards would come this day to the NL champs.

Hal R. Smith's home runs came against six of the seven National League teams he played against. Only against the Milwaukee Braves did he fail to hit a home run. Two of the pitchers on the list, Robin Roberts and Sandy Koufax, are in Baseball's Hall of Fame. Others such as Harvey Haddix, Curt Simmons, Johnny Antonelli, and Vern Law were staff aces of their time. Eighteen of his homers contributed to Cardinal victories, a phenomenal 78% production. He hit four homers in losing causes, but each of these games was dramatized by Hal's blasts and in only seven of the games was the margin of victory more than five runs.

Except for Wrigley Field, all of the major-league ballparks where Hal cleared the fences have been supplanted by newer stadiums.

For perspective, consider this irony. From 1965-1967, Hal was on Pittsburgh Pirate manager Harry Walker's coaching staff along with Alex Grammas, Johnny Pesky, and pitching coach Clyde King. Hal's 23 home runs in his seven years as a major-league player topped the staff in that category. Grammas had 12 home runs in ten years and Pesky had 17 in ten years. Walker, who spent most of his career as a hitting coach had the least of all——ten homers in his 11 years as a player.

Notes

1 St. Louis Post Dispatch, October, 1957.

2 David Halberstam, The Teammates: A Portrait of Friendship (New York: Hyperion, 2003), 64.

3 Interview with Hal Smith, July 27, 2005. Dr Pepper advised the public to drink its product three times a day (10 a.m., 2 p.m., and 4 p.m.).

4 Arkansas was one of the last states in the Union to leave predominant rural status and become more than 50% urban population, which it did in 1956.

5 The Doughboys had lost to Cincinnati in the final game of the 1947 national tournament, held in Los Angeles. Riley Johns, trainer for the Little Rock High School tiger athletic teams, was the trainer for the Doughboys as well.

6 Arkansas Democrat, August 17, 1948.

7 Fort Smith Southwest-Times Record, August 15, 1948.

8 Little Rock Arkansas Democrat, August 24, 1948.

9 There are many compelling stories of treatment of black major-league players during spring training in segregated Florida. Two of the best accounts are David Maraniss, Clemente: The Passion and Grace of Baseball's Last Hero (New York: Simon and Schuster, 2006), and Bob Gibson with Lonnie Wheeler, Stranger to the Game: The Autobiography of Bob Gibson (New York: Viking Penguin Books, 1994), 57-59.

10 DiMaggio, b. 1914, played 1936-1951, Yankees, lifetime BA .325, elected to Hall of Fame in 1955. Mays, b. 1931 played 1951-1973. Giants, Mets, lifetime BA .302, elected to Hall of Fame in 1979. Musial, b. 1920 played 1941-1963. Cardinals, lifetime BA .331, elected to Hall of Fame in 1969. Robinson, b. 1919 played 1947-1956. Dodgers, lifetime BA .311, elected to Hall of Fame in 1962. Williams, b. 1916 played 1939-1960. Red Sox, lifetime BA .344, elected to Hall of Fame in 1966.

11 St Petersburg Times, March 16, 1997. Joe Torre, Chasing the Dream: My Lifelong Journey to the World Series (New York: Bantam, 1998).

12 St Petersburg Times, March 16, 1997.

13 Rickey notes as quoted by Maraniss in Clemente, 61.

14 The Braves moved to Milwaukee from Boston after the 1952 season. The Milwaukee Braves finished second in the National League in 1953, third in 1954, second in '55, '56, and '59 and claimed the National League pennant in 1957 and 1958. The Braves won the World Series in 1957 defeating the Yankees four games to three (Hank Aaron hit three home runs in the series). In 1958, the results were just the reverse, the Yankees winning the seventh game for the world title. In the Braves' first season in Atlanta, 1966, Hank Aaron led the National League in home runs with 44.

15 Arthur Lee "Artie" Wilson born in 1920 in Alabama was 29 when he broke into organized baseball from the Negro Leagues by signing with San Diego who then traded him to Oakland during the 1949 season. His .348 batting average did not get him to the major leagues the next season, but in 1950 the New York Giants gave

him a try for 19 games. His .182 average didn't keep him up. Wilson went back to Oakland and spent the rest of his career in the minors, most of it in the Pacific Coast League where he was a career .300 hitter.

16 *The New York Times*, May 18, 1982, Obituary column.

17 See the recent interpretation by James Webb, *Born Fighting: How the Scots-Irish Shaped America* (New York: Broadway Books, 2004). Webb supplies evidence of an ethnic group common in the South that had independent, competitive, working-class values that resonated well on battlefields, in westward expansion, and in politics. Those values were often manifested on the baseball diamond, as well, as evinced by the play of Ty Cobb and Pete Rose.

18 *The Sporting News*, September 29, 1954, 50. Brooklyn called up Karl Spooner to join the major-league club for the last month of the 1954 season. He won his two starts, both complete games, giving up six walks and striking out 27. With the Dodgers in 1955, Spooner won eight and lost six in his fourteen starts. He was used out of the bullpen, too. He started one game in the World Series against the Yankees in 1955, his last as a major leaguer. See the whole remarkable Karl Spooner story in Peter Golenbock, *Bums: An Oral History of the Brooklyn Dodgers* (New York: G. P. Putnam's Sons, 1984), 376-81.

TIEFENAUER WINS PAIR IN FINALS

BOBBY TIEFENAUER'S two victories in the playoffs gave the Houston relief ace a 12-5 record for the season. After pitching the last four frames of an 11-inning, 4 to 3 decision over Fort Worth in the first game of the finals, Tiefenauer came back two nights later, September 16, and yielded just one run over seven and one-third innings to beat the Cats again, 3 to 2 in 17 innings. . . . In addition to his dozen victories, Tiefenauer protected the lead in 16 other games for the Buffs this year while making a total of 54 relief appearances. He failed on only five occasions. . . . Dick Rand, Houston catcher, has been nicknamed "Sandlock" after the knuckleball catching specialist, Mike Sandlock. Whenever Tiefenauer relieved in the playoffs, the Buffs also changed catchers, bringing in Rand to replace Hal Smith because of Dick's ability to handle The Knuck's fluttering knuckleball. . . . Fort Worth was deprived of the services of Outfielder Clint Weaver during the final two games of the play-

in second and another round-tripper by George Freese in third staked Pels to 4 to 1 lead against Leo Cristante. After off because of an injury. Weaver was hurt in the sixth inning, September 16, when he collided with Umpire Hal Smith after being retired at first base. . . . Karl Spooner's brilliant 17-inning performance while bowing to the Buffs, 3 to 2, September 16, completed a remarkable playoff record for the Fort Worth southpaw. In 34 innings, he yielded just five runs and 20 hits while fanning 32 and walking 16. Counting his three playoff decisions, Spooner had a 23-10 record for the Cats this year. . . . Bob Boyd was the victim of a prank by his Houston teammates just before the final game. Earlier in the week a big python had escaped from the Fort Worth zoo. Noting the story in the paper, Buff players purchased a toy viper at the dime store and put it in one of Boyd's baseball shoes. Boyd, who is deathly afraid of reptiles, almost bolted out of the clubhouse when he found the "snake" in his shoe.

---

19 Rip Repulski, Steve Bilko, and Ray Jablonski were dubbed the "Polish Falcons" by the St. Louis sportswriters in 1953.

20 *The Sporting News*, May 16, 1956, 5 quoting *Cincinnati Enquirer* sportswriter O. P. Caylor in his article that appeared on May 7, 1877.

21 *The Sporting News*, May 16, 1956, 5.

22 Jack Herman, "Hit and RBI Off Roberts Shows Class." *St. Louis Post Dispatch*, May 10, 1956.

23 Author interview with Red Schoendienst, February 5, 2009.

24 On May 27, 1956 Cub catcher Hobie Landrith dropped a third strike which led to the record four straight strike outs in one inning by Cub pitcher Jim Davis. Wally Moon led off the inning with a double and then stole third base. Davis, a knuckleballer, got Hal Smith and Jackie Brandt to chase his darting pitches. Then Lindy McDaniel struck out on a pitch that even escaped the catcher. McDaniel reached first as Moon scored. Shortstop Don Blasingame became the fourth strike-out victim then. The Cards won the game 11-9.

25 Jackie Robinson started at third base in all seven of the World Series games. The Yankees won the series four games to three, avenging their loss to the Dodgers in the previous year. In the 1956 series, Mickey Mantle hit three home runs, Enos Slaughter one, and Jackie Robinson one.

26 Mickey Mantle and Phil Pepe, *My Favorite Summer, 1956* (New York: Doubleday, 1991).

27 David Maraniss, *Clemente, The Passion and Grace of Baseball's Last Hero* (New York: Simon and Schuster, 2006), 48-49.

28 Author interview with Hal Smith, September 14, 2005.

29 Jim Bouton, *Ball Four Plus Ball Five* (New York: Stein and Day, 1981), 231. Charles A. Korr, *End of the Game As We Know It: Marvin Miller and the Coming of the Baseball Players Union* (Urbana: University of Illinois Press, 1998).

30 Solly Drake has a brother, Sammy Drake also born in Little Rock (1934), who played for Casey Stengel and the New York Mets in their first year, a team that won 40 and lost 120 games. In the last game of the season, Sammy Drake pinch-hit, singled, and then became the third out of a triple play, a fitting close to the Met's "amazing" year. Afterwards in trying to console his men, Casey told them "Fellas, don't feel bad about this season which has been simply amazin'. No one or two of you could have done this all by yourselves. This was a total team effort." This quotation is attributed to Richie Ashburn and is reprinted in Mike Shannon, *Tales from the Dugout* (Chicago: Contemporary Books, 1997), 202. Shannon has a different account regarding Bobby Bragan's suggested nickname for Joe Torre on page 28.

31 *The Sporting News*, October 9, 1957, 32.

32 Jack Herman, "Hillbilly Tunesmith in Catcher's Mask," *Baseball Digest*, July 1959, 75.

33 Ellis Kinder, born in Atkins, Arkansas, had his glory years with the Red Sox keeping them in contention during the storied season of 1949 by winning 23 games while losing only six. He came to the Cardinals in 1956 and stayed half the year appearing in 22 games in relief.

34 *The Sporting News*, August 3, 1960, 16.

35 Jan Larsen, "Stolen Victories," *The Baseball Research Journal #36*. (Lincoln: University of Nebraska Press, 2007), 116-119. Vic Power who had played in the Cuban League when Hal was there in 1956, is the only player to steal home twice in one major-league game, which occurred on August 14, 1958, in Detroit. Cardinal back up catcher Glenn Brummer stole home to win a game on August 22, 1982, during the Card's stretch run to the pennant that year. The last steal of home to win

a game was by Marquis Grissom on October 11, 1997, in the ALCS series and put Cleveland by the Orioles 2-1.

36 Ibid. July 10, 1957.

37 Bob Broeg, *Redbirds, A Century of Cardinals' Baseball* (St. Louis: River City Publishers, 1981), 154.

38 Paul Waner born in Harrah, Oklahoma, with a life-time batting average of .333 was inducted into the Baseball Hall of Fame in 1952. His younger brother Lloyd "Little Poison" Waner was inducted in 1967. Big Poison stood 5'8" tall and in his prim weighted 153 lbs. Little Poison was three years younger and about three pounds lighter. They were both outfielders and with the Pirates for most of their careers.

39 The 3,000-hit club's twenty-seven players do not include Ted Williams, Musial's contemporary and rival as the game's best hitter. The twenty-seven players and the year they reached that milestone follows: **Cap Anson** on 08/04/1894, **Honus Wagner** on 06/09/1914, **Nap Lajoie** on 09/27/1914, **Ty Cobb** on 08/19/1921, **Tris Speaker** on 05/17/1925, **Eddie Collins** on 06/03/1925, **Paul Waner** on 06/19/1942, **Stan Musial** on 05/13/1958, **Hank Aaron** on 05/17/1970, **Willie Mays** on 07/18/1970, **Roberto Clemente** on 09/30/1972, **Al Kaline** on 09/24/1974, **Pete Rose** on 05/05/1978, **Lou Brock** on 08/13/1979, **Carl Yastrzemski** on 09/12/1979, **Rod Carew** on 08/04/1985, **Robin Yount** on 09/09/1992, **George Brett** on 09/30/1992, **Dave Winfield** on 09/16/1993, **Eddie Murray** on 06/30/1995, **Paul Molitor** on 09/16/1996, **Tony Gwynn** on 08/06/1999, **Wade Boggs** on 08/07/1999, **Cal Ripken** on 04/15/2000, **Rickey Henderson** on 10/07/2001, **Rafael Palmeiro** on 07/15/2005, and **Craig Biggio** on 06/27/2007.

40 Herman, *Baseball Digest*, July 1959, 75.

41 For the whole story of the challenge of the player union to organized baseball, see Charles Korr, *The End of the Game as We Know It* (Urbana: University of Illinois Press, 2002).

42 Hermon, *Baseball Digest*, July 1959, 76.

43 Jim Weigand, "Rating the Catchers." SABR Research Library Pamphlet. Available at http://www.retrosheet.org/

44 Jim Brosnan, *The Long Season* (New York: Harper and Row, 1960), 62-65.

45 Alex Belth, *Stepping Up: The Story of Curt Flood and His Fight for Baseball Players' Rights* (New York: Persea Books, 2006), 58. See also accounts in Jim Brosnan, *The Long Season* (Chicago: Ivan Dee, 1960), 115-16; and in David Halberstam, *October, 1964* (New York: Villard Books, 1994), 109-110.

46 David Halberstam, *October, 1964*, 109. Alex Belth, *Stepping Up*, 57.

47 *The Sporting News*, August 5, 1959, 19.

48 Daryl Spencer normally hit 16 or 17 homers a year and stole one or two bases. He played one year for the Cards, becoming anything but a legend.

49 *The Sporting News*, November 11, 1959, 5.

50 *The Sporting News*, July 6, 1960, 18.

51 Belth, *Stepping Up*, 63.

52 *The Sporting News*, December 7, 1960, 27.

53 Author interview with Red Schoendienst, February 5, 2009.

54 Author interview with Hal Smith, August 31, 2005.

55 Hermon, *Baseball Digest*, July 1959, 76.

56 Author interview with Hal Smith, September 14, 2005.

57 Author interview with Hal Smith, August 24, 2005.

58 Author interview with Hal Smith, August 31, 2005.

59 Author interview with Hal Smith, December 9, 2005.

60 Interview with Alex Grammas, November 12, 2005. Transcription in possession of author.

61 Henry Aaron was paid $250,000 for the season, well above the other players including Robin Yount who made $65,000.

62 Kevin Kerrane, *Dollar Sign on the Muscle: The World of Baseball Scouting* (New York and Toronto: Beaufort Books, Inc., 1984), 2. The quotation is attributed to Joe Pastore of the Philadelphia Phillies.

63 Ibid., 16-17.

64 Author interview with Hal Smith, August 31, 2005.

65 Ibid.

Index